# TH
# HIDDEN POWER
# OF
# AIKIDO

MW00640229

"Sensei Perry's 6th-degree black belt, her founding, publishing, and editing of *Aikido Today Magazine,* and her 48 years as an Aikido student, dojo owner, and trusted sensei make her a rare combination of Eastern and Western, scholar and practitioner expert. Her work is simultaneously profound and personally applicable wisdom for all readers of living philosophy, martial arts, and other related disciplines."

JUDITH BLITZ, ADJUNCT PROFESSOR
OF NAROPA UNIVERSITY, AIKIDO 6TH DAN

"Susan Sensei encourages us to aspire to a deeper exploration of Aikido that will engage us at all levels of our lives. Using her knowledge of Aristotle's principles of virtue and O-Sensei's principles of Makoto, she makes the case for Aikido's ability to provide substance for anyone to live deeply and meaningfully."

MARY HEINY, AIKIDO 7TH DAN

"O-Sensei, the founder of Aikido, taught that we all must learn to live with the spirit of love and protection for all existence. I believe Susan Perry's words are inspiring, and I trust her book will help nurture this practice."

MOTOMICHI ANNO SENSEI, AIKIDO 8TH DAN AND
CONTRIBUTOR OF *JOURNEY TO THE HEART OF AIKIDO*

"Philosopher, historian, and nationally known Aikido instructor, Susan Perry gifts current Aikido practitioners with a deeper understanding of their art and provides aspiring students and the public insights into the potential of this martial art."

BARRY PORTNOY, PH.D., 4TH DAN

"In *The Hidden Power of Aikido*, Perry Sensei has distilled her years of deep unflinching curiosity for truth through the training, study, and teaching of Aikido. She offers a smoothly written and easily accessible book."

AIMEN AL-REFAI, 35 YEARS IN AIKIDO, 5TH-DEGREE BLACK BELT,
SENIOR INSTRUCTOR AT AIKIDO OF SANTA CRUZ

"Alongside being an author and the publisher of *Aikido Today Magazine*, Susan Perry simultaneously created and operated a major Aikido dojo. All of this, coupled with her formal training and teaching in philosophy, makes her a unique and special voice whose insights will reward the reader and help illuminate the path ahead."

DOUG DEARIE, TECHNOLOGIST, MUSICIAN,
ENTREPRENEUR, AIKIDO 4TH DAN

"The deep sincerity of Susan Perry Sensei's quest has enabled her to penetrate beneath the surface and enter the rich depths of this transcendent path. She has eloquently shared her discoveries in *The Hidden Power of Aikido*."

REV. LAWRENCE KOICHI BARRISH,
HEAD SHINTO PRIEST OF TSUBAKI GRAND SHRINE OF AMERICA

"Susan Perry has played an important and profound role in Aikido in America. It's enlightening to hear more of her stories as she looks back on her career in Aikido and offers her advice and guidance to those who have come after."

JACOB "BUDO JAKE" MCKEE, 3RD-DEGREE AIKIDO BLACK BELT

"Susan Perry shows us that Aikido, so much more than a martial art, provides a path for living as a good person. If you train in Aikido, read this book to deepen your understanding of Aikido. If you don't yet train, read this book to learn how Aikido provides that path, and then go looking for an Aikido dojo."

NANCY JANE MOORE, WRITER AND AIKIDO INSTRUCTOR

"Explores how Aikido offers not only a template for what it is to be a good human being but also a method to become one. Highly recommended for practitioners, both actual and armchair, of Aikido and other martial arts."

ROBERT KENT, FOUNDER OF THE PEACECAMP INITIATIVE

# THE
# HIDDEN POWER
# OF
# AIKIDO

## TRANSCENDING CONFLICT AND
## CULTIVATING INNER PEACE

**A Sacred Planet Book**

## SUSAN PERRY, Ph.D.

Park Street Press
Rochester, Vermont

Park Street Press
One Park Street
Rochester, Vermont 05767
www.ParkStPress.com

Park Street Press is a division of Inner Traditions International

Sacred Planet Books are curated by Richard Grossinger, Inner Traditions editorial board member and cofounder and former publisher of North Atlantic Books. The Sacred Planet collection, published under the umbrella of the Inner Traditions family of imprints, includes works on the themes of consciousness, cosmology, alternative medicine, dreams, climate, permaculture, alchemy, shamanic studies, oracles, astrology, crystals, hyperobjects, locutions, and subtle bodies.

Cataloging-in-Publication Data for this title is available from the Library of Congress

ISBN 978-1-64411-897-9 (print)
ISBN 978-1-64411-898-6 (ebook)

Printed and bound in the United States by Lake Book Manufacturing, LLC

The text stock is SFI certified. The Sustainable Forestry Initiative® program promotes sustainable forest management.

10 9 8 7 6 5 4 3 2 1

Text design and layout by Priscilla Harris Baker
This book was typeset in Garamond Premier Pro with Gill Sans, Legacy Sans, Minerva, and Optima used as display typefaces

To send correspondence to the author of this book, mail a first-class letter to the author c/o Inner Traditions • Bear & Company, One Park Street, Rochester, VT 05767, and we will forward the communication, or contact the author directly at **SusanPerry.info**.

Scan the QR code and save 25% at InnerTraditions.com. Browse over 2,000 titles on spirituality, the occult, ancient mysteries, new science, holistic health, and natural medicine.

*For my brother John—*
*who suggested I write this book*

*A journey of 1000 miles begins with a single step.*

LAO TZU

# Contents

# Foreword

## by John Stevens

*Aikido is hikari-no-michi (the Way of Light).*
MORIHEI UESHIBA

Susan and I have much in common. We were both born in the Midwest: Susan in Lincoln, Nebraska, and I in Chicago, Illinois. For some mysterious reason, we both became enamored of the art of Aikido, a discipline of body and mind that emerged in twentieth-century Japan. What was that mysterious reason? In Japan, there is the concept of *innen,* or "karmic affinity." *In* is karma, the seed that is believed to have been planted in some previous existence. Karma is what compelled a teenage boy in Chicago to develop an intense interest in Japan and Japanese culture. So intense, in fact, that he went to Japan, planning to stay for six months, and ended up living there for thirty-five years. Among many other things, he discovered Aikido, which was to become his lifelong passion. The way his life unfolded was his *en:* the affinities he had, the relationships he fostered with people and places, the seren-dipitous events, the ups and downs of his career.

*The Hidden Power of Aikido* is the story of Susan Perry's innen: her upbringing in Nebraska; her family background and its influence on her later years; her college days, more or less conventional; her trip to Heraklion in Crete, where she had a completely unexpected visit to a *taverna* and spent "a magical night of intense wonderment;" her eventful marriage to Ron Rubin, a college professor full of wit and wisdom, and a perfect companion for Susan; and then to the heart of her journey, her encounter with Aikido, which began primarily on a whim but then became the central focus of her multifaceted personal and professional life. Susan has been a student, a mother, a professor, an editor, a teacher of Aikido and yoga, a collector, and a late-blooming brush artist. Early on in the book Susan asks, "What is Aikido? A martial art? A religion?" She gives the answer: "A vision." She tells us about the founder of Aikido, Morihei Ueshiba. He was a social activist: as a young man in Tanabe he assisted Kumagusu Minakata in a successful protest against the government's Shrine Consolidation Policy, which threatened to destroy the local environment. In Hokkaido he was one of the pioneers to settle in the underdeveloped region, served on the village council, acted as an entrepreneur to promote the village economy, and saw to the construction of schools and sanitation systems. And in Ayabe he was deeply involved with one of the greatest revolutions in twentieth-century Japan, Omoto kyo. In 1925, Morihei had a new vision: "I realized that I and the universe are one. All at once, I understood the nature of creation; the way of a warrior is to manifest divine love, a spirit that embraces and nurtures all things." It was his mission to spread that message. This dramatic event marks the beginning of Aikido. Aikido eventually became a grand social movement with the aim of transforming human beings and building a peaceful world. Morihei had trained as a warrior in many martial arts. He transformed those lethal techniques into forms based on the principle of harmonization, which could be safely practiced by anyone. The techniques of Aikido are vehicles, stepping stones, and tricks that enable practitioners to progress on the Way of Harmony. Susan relates many instructive and sometimes humorous stories of how she walked along the path that Morihei opened for us, and then found her own Way within the context of her study of Western Philosophy—in particular Aristotle—coupled with her understanding of Eastern wisdom through the vehicle of Aikido. Her life is a synthesis of East and West; this book details the manner in which she learned to harmonize the two world-views over the years. Based on her interactions with her teachers, friends, students, and even the occasional jerk, Susan offers many insightful explanations of the physical, psychological, and spiritual dimensions of Aikido. She also waxes lyrical on Aikido and nature, particularly forests and mountains, emphasizing the cleansing of the spirit that a walk through the woods or a hike among the peaks can bring. Finally, she tackles the arcane, even mind-boggling, elements of Morihei's thought, primarily *misogi* and *kototama*. *Misogi* is "purification." As Susan notes, there is misogi of the body: ablution, washing away external grime with water, typically under a waterfall or in the ocean, and physical exercise to remove the "dust" in one's joints. There is misogi of the heart: separating oneself from malicious thoughts, removing all emotions of aggression and competition, and abstaining from hurtful and unkind speech. There is misogi of the environment: keeping your personal space clean and well-ordered and acting responsibly in regard to global pollution. And then there is misogi of the spirit: *chinkon kishin* (calm the spirit, return to the source) meditation.

*Kototama* is "word-spirit." It is a firm conviction in Asian cosmology (and now modern physics) that "all matter is vibration." Morihei had an idiosyncratic interpretation of kototama. Susan discusses her own experiments with kototama both on and off the mat and relates how important it is for Aikido practitioners to understand and apply its principles in various aspects of life. *The Hidden Power of Aikido* illumines *Indra's net*, "the cosmic web of interrelationships." Ultimately, everything is related to everything else; there are no coincidences, no random encounters, no meaningless activities, no empty thoughts or deeds. Everything intersects, shedding light on everything else.

JOHN STEVENS

JOHN STEVENS is chairman of the Classical Aikido Association and author of *Aikido: The Way of Harmony.*

# Foreword

## by John R. Perry, Ph.D.

If you had asked me a few years ago what Aikido and Aristotle had in common, I might have said, "My sister Susan knows a lot about both of them, and I know next to nothing about either of them." I have a Ph.D. in Philosophy, but it didn't involve much study of Aristotle. Susan also has a Ph.D. in Philosophy, but she wrote her dissertation on Aristotle. And along the way she took up Aikido, eventually earning a 6th degree black belt. Aikido is a discipline that, from a distance, seemed to me to involve a lot of exercise. Philosophy was done in a chair. Or I guess while walking if you are a peripatetic philosopher like Aristotle. Aikido is done on a mat, mostly while assuming uncomfortable-looking poses and executing strange movements—or so I thought.

Earlier on back in Nebraska, after earning a B.A. in Philosophy at the University of Nebraska, Susan went to Claremont Graduate School for her Ph.D. in Philosophy. I was ecstatic about this. My wife and I and our three kids lived in Santa Monica, not too far away. Ron Rubin was a brilliant professor and an expert on Descartes, on the faculty at Pitzer College, one of the Claremont Colleges. He became a good friend of mine and eventually, much to my surprise, a devotee of Aikido. I fantasized that he and Susan would meet and fall in love and get married.

By the time she finished her dissertation, in the late 1970s, it seemed that Aikido and Aristotle were battling for Sue's soul. She was an assistant professor of Philosophy at California State University, Fullerton and was giving a lot of talks on Aristotle. "She'll publish a couple of those lectures, maybe turn her dissertation into a monograph, and soon have tenure." Or so I thought.

By 1985 she was publishing a lot. But not about Aristotle. She had founded *Aikido Today Magazine* (*ATM*), of which she was to be editor-in-chief for twenty years. This publication gave all the Aikido dojos around the world a way of knowing about, and appreciating, other dojos, which was an important event in the history of Aikido. She wrote an editorial for each issue, and a lot of other articles. Around that time, she did meet Ron, fall in love, and got married without my lifting a finger. Bliss.

Susan finished her Ph.D. and began teaching at various state colleges in southern California. Ron finished his great book on Descartes.

She taught Aikido at a number of places, including Musubi Dojo in Claremont, which she founded with Ron. *Aikido Today Magazine* was published by Arete Press, which they founded together. *Arete* is Greek for virtue and excellence, an important word for Aristotle, so there was at least a hint of a connection.

Since Ron became a passionate devotee, I realized this philosophical fascination with Aikido couldn't just be another one of my sister's quirks. His favorite philosopher, Descartes, wasn't even a peripatetic philosopher. As far as I can tell, Descartes liked to sit in a chair in some secluded place and try to prove things, like that he existed, and that God existed. I couldn't imagine Descartes enjoying striking funny poses in a sweatsuit and throwing people around a mat any more than I could imagine Aristotle doing that. I must've been missing something that Ron and Sue saw.

If I drove out to Claremont, the three of us could sit around all afternoon talking Philosophy. But then our conversations began to take a turn. Instead of talking all afternoon about their favorites, Aristotle and Descartes, and my favorites, Hume and Frege, the conversation would turn to this thing I had barely ever heard of: Aikido.

They had learned Aikido and loved it. But they didn't just throw each other around on a mat. They learned all about the history of Aikido, got acquainted with the dojos in Southern California and the senseis that led them. When I went to visit for an afternoon, as often as not I would meet some sensei from a local dojo who had dropped in to chat about Aikido. Pretty soon Sue was talking about visiting Japan to find out more about their new passion. Which she did, coming home more enthusiastic than ever about Aikido, and full of stories about the founder, O-Sensei, and eager to earn more belts.

Susan didn't publish her dissertation or much else about Aristotle (there is still plenty of time). But as far as I could tell, her philosophical prowess kept growing. I became a great believer in Aikido—at a distance, without practicing it or reading much about it. But I have always wanted to understand what was going on in Sue's mind and Ron's, and in the many fascinating Aikido devotees I met over the years when they were in Claremont to visit Sue and Ron.

Now, thanks to this book, I can begin to understand it. We think of Aristotle as primarily the founder of logic, but he was also a "practical" philosopher, he thought not only about arguments for accepting statements, but reasons for performing action. Once we learn that Aikido was founded by O-Sensei, we think of him as an accomplished and charismatic Japanese martial artist, devoting his life to throwing people around on a mat and teaching others to do so. But O-Sensei saw the principles of Aikido as an activity, as a working out of one aspect of Aikido—which is a philosophy of life. Ethics and the good life were at the core of the visions of both Aristotle and O-Sensei. True principles of reason weren't just formal principles of logic for Aristotle but ultimately a means of practical activity, a guide to action. The principles of Aikido as a martial art were not just tricky maneuvers for O-Sensei but expressions of principles of interpersonal interaction, based on compassion, understanding, and values.

In developing these ideas, Sue tells us a lot about the history of Aikido, of its reception in America after our war with Japan, and the misunderstandings of Aikido and O-Sensei that were part of that. She tells fascinating stories of her trips to Japan, her visits to the important places in O-Sensei's life. She also tells some engaging stories about how Aikido has helped her give some jerks she has encountered what was coming to them—stories I enjoyed quite independently of their deeper philosophical significance, I must admit.

The need for *Aikido Today Magazine* as a way of keeping dojos around the world connected with each other lessened considerably with the rise of the internet. And in 2005, ATM's twenty-year run was celebrated on the eve of the publication of its 100th issue. Ron Rubin died in 2014, too early. Sue has continued teaching Aikido, as well as yoga, but she has also used her time to become an accomplished artist in the Shodo tradition of Japanese calligraphy, among other things. Before the pandemic, I regularly attended exhibitions of her work, where she also gave lessons in brushwork. But the pandemic gave her even more time, and she wrote this book. I'm very grateful and I think you will be too.

JOHN R. PERRY, PH.D.

JOHN R. PERRY, PH.D., is the Henry Waldgrave Stuart Professor of Philosophy Emeritus at Stanford University and Distinguished Professor of Philosophy Emeritus at the University of California, Riverside.

# Aikido, Lighting the Way

*Let your mind be as high as the highest mountain, as deep as the deepest ocean, and as vast as the open sky.*

MOTTO OF AIKO INSTITUTE

Aikido is a curious art. Within a year we had given up our smoking habit. My boyfriend was right: Aikido was a fun art to practice, and its study supported this tremendous change in our lives. But we continued together practicing the art for the next thirty-seven years! We became a power pack of creativity: We published an international nonpartisan magazine on Aikido for twenty years (one hundred issues), we opened one of this country's largest dojos, which enjoyed a thirty-five-year run, and I was asked to write a book on the Aikido founder, which included a paid trip to Japan! What was it about Aikido that inspired all this creativity? I dig deep to answer that question, for this book is not merely a reflection on the motivating factor of our curiously productive life in Aikido; it is about the transformation that changes your inner self and in so doing affects the world around you. I consider this phenomenon from many directions: the literary world from Aristotle, the *Kojiki,* and *King Lear* to the films of Kurosawa; the organic world of forests, trees, and clay fields as well as the elemental world of wind, water, and vibrations. I look back to see ahead and I find clarity for this "modern" art in the ancient and legendary worlds of Japan.

It may be true that the outside world and other people are to blame for our personal difficulties, but the enemy is not just outside of us. Often the barrier to solutions lies within us. Once we can see that we have the capacity to change, that we have options, a choice when we face a difficulty, we increase our capacity to solve problems, and as a result our confidence in ourselves and in the world soars. Nonviolence is not just some abstract concept; it is a way of dealing with the world. In this book I describe how I've learned from many real-world struggles and their solutions as well as from the "solutions" that failed. I share discoveries of how to deal with real-world encounters I've experienced with bullies, with overbearing humans, with doubt, and with a lack of confidence. These discoveries come from a deep study of the Warrior nature, and the application of ancient wisdom that surfaced along the way.

What is Aikido? Is it a religion? Is it a martial art? These are the two categories that have been offered so far. But we need to broaden our view: neither category fully explains this art. In this book the scholarly work on Aikido that has helped to clarify aspects of the founder's life enables us to build a more casual interpretation of Aikido's principles that applies to our everyday life. I am thrilled to introduce you to a phenomenal art that waits to embrace you with welcoming arms, not with the smothering arms of imprisonment but with the open arms of embracing change.

I feel impelled to inspire people to take a serious look at the art of Aikido with the hope that more people might try it out. Aikido has flourished with the influx of students who enjoy the joyful spiraling movements of training together on the mat. But I'm guessing there is a whole population of people who, although not so inspired by the physically active side of Aikido, would give it a try once they understand its incredible power for growth and transformation on a personal level as well as its beauty, which calms, relaxes, and restores a person weary from the onslaught of the problems in the outside world. In fact, I'm convinced that with this art we can solve many of these problems and unify toward a more peaceful existence.

SUSAN PERRY, PH.D.

# Acknowledgments

I have many Johns in my life, and I'd like to thank four of them here: my brother, John Perry, who has always created interesting projects for me (I suspect to keep me out of trouble); my son, John Schleis, whose watchful eye over his mother during the pandemic and this all-consuming project has kept my larders full and my other projects going; a co-director of Aiko Institute, John Schildmeyer, who was unselfish with his passion for photography when I needed some help; and my old friend John Stevens whose scholarly work on Aikido and the founder has provided a great stepping stone for further deliberation. But there are many others whose names are not John who have contributed as well.

Old Aikido friends from across the country unexpectedly showed up in the Zoom group I created for my Aikido students when our classes were shut down at the beginning of the pandemic—not the invasion it sounds like but a gradual change each week as local students dropped out and old friends from remote locations showed up until this most-welcome but unexpected group congealed amongst all the activity. This group is made up of high-ranking (mostly) retired Aikido teachers I've been happy to know from my travels when I was Editor of *Aikido Today Magazine.* I amused them by telling my many behind-the-scenes stories from my *ATM* days, and when they suggested I write them down, I found myself working on a writing project. When my brother suggested I write a monograph on Aikido that he thought I could publish more easily, the smaller project appealed to me as it seemed within reach. I must admit, however, that this book contracted and expanded several times before taking the shape you now hold in your hands. The Zoom group provided me with constant inspiration and support, and I doubt this project would have matured without it. Thanks to Doug Dearie who helped me with IT issues by actually reaching into my computer from the East Coast to find and set up an appropriate word-processing program and kept me on point by communicating on many deep issues we used to discuss on my annual visits to D.C. so many years ago. Also thanks to Nancy Moore, whose D.C. living room I camped in when taking a workshop in D.C. She is an author herself and she took to the trenches with me during this writing project, suggesting ways that I might tame the amorphous sea of ideas I had created with the focus of explaining Aikido off the mat. But Nancy is a lawyer too and she offered her lawyerly eye to review my book contract to ensure I hadn't missed anything. Barry Portnoy softly encouraged my voice to expand and advocated that I give much more attention to *maai*. Rick Triplett, the hyperbole king, generously gave his time to help me answer the publisher's marketing questionnaire, and he was always willing to look up details I needed even from my own magazine CD. Jude Blitz, who in her quiet wisdom showered me with blessings and deep insights about my prose; all of which lifted my spirit and made this book even better. I'm used to working alongside a brilliant someone I could talk to about ideas, but alas my beloved wolf dog Ame departed this earthly world during the writing of this book. It has been ten years since Ron died and I have been alone and unproductive for most of this time and so, I feel extremely blessed for this group of friends that appeared so unexpectedly. And I'm somewhat speechless that they so cheerfully banded together with me on this book adventure. I thank them for their tenacity and enthusiasm to read and reread the many versions of chapters I'd send along weekly over these past thirteen months. Our meetings are on-going, and I look forward to the next project.

I thank Sumi Foley who never entirely gives up on my ability to speak Japanese, for translating my letters to important Japanese teachers into polished Japanese. Also thanks to Jake McKee of Budo Videos for copy editing the initial draft of the introduction, which won me a publishing contract. It was heartwarming that Roger Levoy and Daniel Tran, my two *yudansha,* so willingly listened to my new chapters at our monthly instructors' meetings, and then responded so positively to my suggestions of how to bring the ideas into Aikido practice in their classes at Aiko Dojo.

I am grateful, too, for Richard Grossinger's help in securing a place for my book; we have known one another for a very long time as publishers in the field of Aikido, and it has been my pleasure to renew our friendship.

I thank Lisa P. Allen, my project editor, for her patient guidance and thoughtful suggestions as we made the final preparations of this manuscript for the typesetter.

I also have many Mary's in my life and I want to thank two of them here: my dear friend Mary Esquibel who once saved me with homemade scones when my brain and frayed fingers went on strike, and my long-time mentor, friend, and travel buddy, Mary Heiny, for piquing my interest in Japan by whisking me off on our first of many trips there after the death of my mother and also for taking me to the many places that followed me into this book.

Lastly, I thank the community of Aikido authors, teachers, and students from whom I've learned so much over the years. As someone who was constantly in touch with so many during my twenty-year editorship, there is not enough space here to enumerate them all—you know who you are! I am grateful to be able to contribute to the continual efforts to keep the lights on in the Aikido house.

# Introduction

Morihei Ueshiba,* a venerable Japanese man usually referred to as O-Sensei, whose vision of world peace gives us not only a philosophy by which to understand it but a practice through which to embody it, founded an art called *Aikido*. Because Aikido is a practical philosophy with a physical art embedded within, the two aspects—the physical and the hidden—constitute a unified whole. And it is this unified whole that is the focus of this book.

For nearly fifty years I have been a student of Aikido and, as a formally trained philosopher, I see this art not only as an answer for those seeking more meaning in life, but also as a way to bring balance to our everyday activities.

We typically do not recognize O-Sensei as a spiritual leader, but I think we should. Of course, Japan viewed him as a national treasure, and his hometown of Tanabe erected a memorial statue of him. So I hope this book contributes to a deeper understanding of and appreciation for what great strides we have all made as a direct result of studying Aikido. Perhaps with time his stature in the world for his contributions will be realized and honored by more than a small cadre of students and teachers.

As I will discuss in this book, to classify Aikido as a martial art, which has been done for its lifetime in the West, is to downplay Aikido's unique power as a transformative discipline, which it delivers to the

---

*I am putting the family names last, contrary to Japanese custom.

modern world. Aikido holds keys to unlock how inner and whole-self transformation occurs. I believe O-Sensei saw this as Aikido's central purpose. Many notable teachers of Aikido agree, as do his son and grandson. Kisshomaru Ueshiba, his son, writes,

> Ultimately, Master Ueshiba concluded that the true spirit of budo is not to be found in a competitive and combative atmosphere where brute strength dominates and victory at any cost is the paramount objective. He concluded that it is to be realized in the quest for perfection as a human being, both in mind and body, through cumulative training and practice with kindred spirits in the martial arts (Ueshiba 1984, 15).

Moriteru Ueshiba, O-Sensei's grandson, quotes O-Sensei in his preface to his father's book, *A Life in Aikido.* "The objective of Aikido is [to] polish one's mind and body and to produce an individual of high integrity." And, at the end of his preface, Moriteru Ueshiba adds, "It is my desire that with this publication, many more people may come to understand correctly the true core of Aikido." Moriteru Ueshiba leads the Aikido World Headquarter in Tokyo, Japan, which is regarded by many as the ultimate authority on Aikido.

Aikido is not easy to explain, and we must have patience with the founder and maintain an attitude of compassionate understanding for the many difficulties he faced in articulating what he was doing, as he was creating Aikido during the time he lived. To help us along the way, I have chosen to draw upon an ancient philosopher—some say he was the father of Western Philosophy—with whom we are familiar. I have found, then, that Aristotle may be helpful to this discussion if only because his way of thinking is more familiar to an everyday Westerner's thinking. That is, he speaks in a logical, ordered manner, distinct from O-Sensei's *Kojiki* allusions and non-sequitur reasoning. The major overlap in the thought of these two thinkers is the insistence of embodiment as a necessary condition of self-cultivation.

At the time I began Aikido I was writing my Ph.D. dissertation on Aristotle's theory of moral development. Aristotle was an ancient Greek philosopher responsible for much of how we see the world today: his formative writings from drama and poetry to biology have influenced those who've come after him. With the *Nicomachean Ethics*, he is said to have introduced a practical philosophy (rather than a theoretical one) with his considerations of how to live the good life. This seems to be an innovation of Aristotle's—presenting a practical rather than a theoretical philosophy—and, as I study the deeper aspects of Aikido, it has struck me that the Aikido founder has also presented a practical philosophy in his development of Aikido. The Aikido founder relied on stories from Japan's oldest book, the *Kojiki* (see page 81), to illustrate his thinking to Japanese youth who, whether they themselves were religious or not, knew the stories from their childhood. And so there are the makings of an argument that his use of the *Kojiki* was not religious, but illustrative of a philosophical system, a system I attempt to set out in this book for a deeper understanding of Aikido. I have given much thought to the systems of these two thinkers even though they lived on different continents and at quite different times, and I have found that they have important things in common.

Both Aristotle and O-Sensei are concerned with what constitutes the highest form of a human being. O-Sensei in lectures describes what he considers the highest form of a human being, and in so doing he discusses the good life. But his explanations include many sayings inscrutable to the common person as well as references to the fantastic stories of the *Kojiki*. And so understanding the deeper points of his presentation is left for only those who are already knowledgeable with the material.

For Aristotle, it was paramount that for a person to act virtuously, the act has to spring from a firm and fixed disposition. Just behaving virtuously is not enough; the propensity to act in a virtuous way needs to be embodied—that is, ultimately it has to come from one's body and soul. And, as you will see, for Morihei Ueshiba the embodiment of a compassionate but fierce nature is necessary for the realization of peace and harmony. So, not only do we have two thinkers who have much to say about the good life, but they both are practical philosophers in that they agree that embodiment is critical to the cultivation of the self.

Also, both thinkers aspire to lofty ends: for Aristotle it is happiness, and for Morihei Ueshiba it is world peace. But it is Morihei Ueshiba who—a few steps ahead of Aristotle—has offered a physical art to help embody deep principles. To me, there is a fundamental agreement between these two thinkers, an agreement that has helped me realize a deeper understanding of their practical philosophies. And so I have been inspired to write this book, a book about the practical philosophy of personal transformation.

It seems to me that this makes both thinkers relevant for people living today. Moreover, although happiness and world peace may seem like different ends, they are commensurate. That is, more virtuous, happy people in the world may be just what it takes to realize world peace. And so I believe we have something here that is not just relevant but critical for us today in our wayward evolving world.

Aikido is an art from the East that, when discovered in the 1950s and 60s by the West, seemed exotic and paradoxical, but alluring. At that time, we were a culture still stinging from the trauma of having faced Japan in a recent world war, and so we were measured in our attraction to and interest in the culture of Japan. We owe much to those curious and courageous individuals who willingly wandered into this enticingly different culture; some were military men stationed in Japan as a part of the occupying force, while others were artists, poets, and writers drawn to the aesthetics of this radically different world that was Japan.

Today there is a much better understanding of the cultural differences between Japan and the West and, as friends, we even have participated at times in preserving one another's culture. The Japanese youth have been fascinated by Elvis Presley and the cowboy culture of the Wild West, while those in the West have been equally fascinated by the samurai and martial arts practices. After the war, the United States helped

Japan develop a business model to bring about recovery from the devastation of the war. Western MIT professor Edward M. Deming lectured in the 1950s to Japanese businessmen and helped them produce the business model that resulted in, among other things, Toyota's successful economic boom of the 1980s! I remember when my philosophy colleagues at California State University, Fullerton actually put together a philosophy conference about Japan's innovative business model. So in a business model, the Japanese saw the functioning of the employees in toto, as a single energetic system, which was much more critical to success than viewing the system of employees as consisting of separate individuals. And so we were introduced to the dichotomy of East/West worldviews: while the East centers on the group as a unit of agency, the West looks to agency as a matter of individual performance. So with Prof Deming's help, Japan has profited from incorporating their home-grown philosophy into a new model of quality control for a business, while we in the West have surely benefited from understanding how Japan's worldview of group effort can make things move more smoothly. In terms of aesthetics and spiritual practice in the West, it was the Beat Generation who first noticed what Japan had to offer in terms of the aesthetics and spiritual practices like Zen.

Much was made of Eastern practices in the movies and television series of the West, such as a glimpse into a judo practice in the *James Bond* movies; the intriguing sidekick, Kato, to Inspector Clouseau in the beloved *Pink Panther* movies; and the adventures of Kwai Chang Caine in the *Kung Fu* television series. Schools (dojos) of judo, karate, and taekwondo immediately sprung up across the country, often taught by military men returning home after the war who were excited to engage in the practices they studied while living in Japan. These schools filled up with young kids who learned self-control and confidence through these Eastern martial arts.

The development of Aikido's physical side has given us many dojos and opportunities for practicing it in classes, workshops, and camps. This worldwide spread of Aikido has been a major effort on the part of

Kisshomaru Ueshiba, O-Sensei's son, and two generations of students. In the United States, many of us have participated in Aikido's growth as a serious but fun physical practice, open to everyone. It is because of this participation that Aikido enjoys the popularity it does today. Although replicating observable movements is much easier, we must not overlook the hidden side of Aikido that holds the promise of realizing the tremendous transformative power that can make us better people, and thereby contribute to O-Sensei's dream of a world of peace and respectful stewardship.

The physical practice of Aikido is flourishing; classes are now offered in dojos around the world. And, because every Aikido student becomes familiar with the Japanese names for techniques, it makes it possible to engage in practice in foreign countries, even if you cannot speak that country's language. This, in turn, makes it possible for students to travel and participate in an Aikido class sometimes far from home. I found it exhilarating to step into a foreign dojo and be welcomed to practice. Certain gestures of openness are universal, and one realizes communication on a rudimentary but meaningful level is possible wherever you go. If the instructor calls for a *shihonage* every Aikido student, foreign or not, will know what technique to do. Being able to so easily make foreign friends through practice, to see their schools, and to experience different teachers opens the world in new and pleasing ways. With a physical practice that is so joyful, and with the ability to practice anywhere, I began to feel Aikido's power to bring a transformative movement of peace to the world.

Aikido has been a rewarding study for me. I have learned at the feet of prominent teachers in seminars around the world. Also, I have had the privilege of hosting at my own school many of these teachers, which enabled me to participate in deep, late-night conversations, and to become good friends with some of them. These interviews and epiphanies I shared in my publication, *Aikido Today Magazine,* for twenty years, to help the worldwide Aikido community understand the rich messages from visiting teachers. Through this kind of outreach and personally expansive study, I began to see how Morihei Ueshiba's art of Aikido straddles the physical and the hidden.

My study has been intense, and it has led me to the edge of Aikido's deeper fields, where I could see the vast world that lay before me. And, although I do not think a student can embrace the secrets of this art without participating in its physical practice, stepping on the mat doesn't have to be the starting point for everyone. There is a hidden aspect to Aikido that is waiting to be understood and disseminated. I am indeed grateful to those who have gone before me, and for the scholarly works that have been written that can inform a dedicated student through ardent study.

Now the public seems ready for something that promises solutions for the overwhelming difficulties we are facing in our world today. In this book, I will help to present this hidden side of Aikido to readers, hoping that it will be the first step toward finding a rewarding practice of Aikido at a dojo near them. I share many personal stories—some uplifting, some not—to show how Aikido's lessons are expressed in an ordinary life.

Aikido's founder appeared before a broad audience. He lectured on and demonstrated Aikido to Japan's military brass, businessmen, martial arts teachers, religious leaders, royalty, and even dancers. And his words guide us in our search to find the depths of Aikido's physical practice. Some say Aikido is a modern martial art, yet a cursory look at books about Aikido show it coming out of and inextricably bound up with ancient traditions of Japan, and the samurai arts of Japan's more recent past. Aikido's uniform is largely based on samurai dress, which strangely enough comes from aristocratic women's exercise wear of that period. Those who focus on a Confucian rendering of Japanese culture refer to the seven virtues being represented by the pleats of the *hakama* (trousers) students wear in practice (although some say O-Sensei was not drawn to Confucian thought). Nevertheless, it is not uncommon to hear mid-level students reciting this view. And so, Aikido evolves. The lessons, from the open-hand techniques the samurai practiced (in case they were without a sword) to the postural and timing elements found in swordwork, join with the older staff arts to provide a rich tableau essential to Aikido's open-hand practice. But Aikido is much deeper than this too.

O-Sensei lectured and demonstrated and even brushed diagrams, wrote poems and characters but he did not produce anything like a textbook in his later years as would be expected of an accomplished philosopher. Not all thinkers are avid writers. For instance, Socrates, one of the West's earliest philosophers, was not a writer either. We know about him largely through Plato, one of his students, who is said to have written down Socrates's conversations with people as he engaged in his social life in Athens. These "transcriptions" of Socrates's conversations with politicians, poets, and the like constitute the corpus of the Socratic dialogues, philosophically meaty conversations that philosophy students study in most introductory classes at today's universities. There are other intellectual leaders in history who are known from the writings of their students and followers, and Morihei Ueshiba is one of them. Although he was a literate man whose personal library was vast, it was through his students' and followers' transcriptions that his thought has been made available. So, preservation of Morihei Ueshiba's lectures and sayings are regarded today as the major source of his thinking. I have been inspired by these sayings in studying his philosophy, and in composing this book.

It is one task to translate these passages and quite another to fully grasp their meaning. Morihei Ueshiba often speaks in riddles. And so these passages of Morihei Ueshiba's are often viewed as impenetrable without the help of an Aikido teacher to guide you. And, of course, in my searches for such teachers over the years, I was lucky enough to find a handful of scholarly teachers to guide me. But finding such a teacher is often difficult, and this will become even more difficult as many of us pass on. For those interested, then, I want to offer a picture of the deeper, hidden side of Aikido as a tool for self-transformation and as a preservation of Morihei Ueshiba's philosophy for generations to come.

At the head of most chapters, I have presented a translation of one of Morihei Ueshiba's statements relevant to the material in that chapter. These sayings may seem impenetrable to one who doesn't study Aikido, and maybe to some who do! But it's not the translator's fault, and it's not the founder's fault; it's just the inherent difficulty of articulating deep thought. As someone who has spent her life clarifying the words of deep thinkers, I can offer some help.

The physical is easier to see than the hidden. Thus, we presume we understand the whole of Aikido if we have read a fair number of Aikido books and practiced the techniques pictured within them. But there are too many books on Aikido techniques and too few on Morihei Ueshiba's philosophy of self-cultivation and his aspirations for how his art could help humankind. For long enough we have put on the back burner Morihei Ueshiba's sayings. And if we treat his revelations as relics, as the rarified utterances of a wonderful but old man, we will miss the advanced maturity of his transmissions.

Throughout the book, I use "O-Sensei" to refer to the founder of Aikido. I should say, however, that the proper Western form of this name is Morihei Ueshiba (family name last, although this is not the Japanese practice). But because of the respect with which most people address him, you will either see his name written elsewhere as *Ueshiba Sensei* where *sensei* is his teacher title, or, as I refer to him here, as *O-Sensei,* which means "great teacher," an honorific title reserved for the founder of Aikido.

In chapter 2, I write about the life of O-Sensei. I have chosen certain aspects of his life that I've found most interesting and remarkable. More than other aspects of his life, they have explained how he became the man he did—which in turn illuminates how his art grew in the direction that it did. As editor-in-chief of *Aikido Today Magazine* for twenty years, I was able to talk to and learn from many of O-Sensei's direct students. They helped me understand certain of O-Sensei's choices in life, and his views of life as well. But I must say that I am not a historian, and so, for someone interested in a fuller presentation of O-Sensei's life look at the biographies *Invincible Warrior* by John Stevens and *A Life in Aikido* by Kisshomaru Ueshiba.

I am saddened to find some dojo webpage accounts of O-Sensei as a World War II warmonger, and also as someone who was not interested in teaching Aikido to students from other countries. This is completely false. Also, the aging founder of Aikido transforming his art as he grows older does not appeal to a part of his previous membership; they cannot appreciate his direction and they prefer an older formative practice while discarding the rest of O-Sensei's innovation. Unfortunately they insist that this is the real Aikido and discount the rest. We should leave it to them to enjoy their practice, hoping that one day they may aspire to practice in the founder's later direction. But judging and pronouncing that the older aspect of the art is the only real part is to throw away O-Sensei's final arrival at an art that has the power to quell the world's discord, if only person by person. It is only with this latter development that world peace becomes relevant.

In a recent conversation with me, a friend expressed concern that the memory of O-Sensei may become distorted by such statements, especially as the older generation of students may not be around much longer to protest and correct it. It is clear that O-Sensei was a man of change and curiosity; indeed, change is the very nature of his art.

These are timely topics in a world where we yearn for more honorable and virtuous people as well as for a deeper understanding of how best to steward our future in a physical environment that is suffering due to our lack of prescience.

It is my hope that by presenting a simple version of this very deep and esoteric art, many readers will be inspired to consider an Aikido practice for enriching their lives. My students and friends have encouraged me to use my own personal stories to clarify and illustrate points about Aikido that might be difficult to explain. And so I hope with this book I have managed to give you, the reader, a lively glimpse into an amazing art. I would be very pleased if this book inspired some of you to enroll in an Aikido class, and for Aikido teachers everywhere to up their understanding and teaching of Aikido.

As my stories express, I have found and enjoyed the lessons of Aikido in all that I do. It has made for much joyful living, and it has made me a better person. My hope in presenting these personal stories is to encourage others to try a life with this valuable vision. For I am convinced that Aikido teaches what we need to make our lives safe, full, and peaceful. It teaches a way of meeting others, of being with others, and of assessing situations with other humans that head off problems and instill peaceful coexistence.

We need a vision for the human world, a vision where cooperation trumps divisiveness, trust replaces suspicion, where benevolence rises above greed and selfishness, where peace overshadows war, and where truth is honored above all. The need is so abundantly clear, yet it's difficult to see what change we could manifest to make things better. I want to offer a solution.

ONE

# Aikido
## *Embracing Change*

Aristotle, the ancient Greek philosopher, wrote on a great many topics, among them happiness and the good life. To him, happiness is the end of all ends as everyone strives to be happy. Of course, *happiness* can mean many things. In today's world it may be mindfulness or tranquility that defines the happy life. But clearly whether it's called happiness or tranquility, Aristotle is not talking about buying an expensive car, or the immediate gratification of eating ice cream. For Aristotle, happiness is about living the good life, which for him is a life lived virtuously. There is another thinker who sets an even higher bar to living the happy, tranquil life, by adding world peace to the list of important ends. I'm talking about Morihei Ueshiba, the founder of Aikido.

Ueshiba was a vibrant visionary; he was committed to world peace, and he honed an art based on ancient secrets that he believed could deliver it. In the last sixty-five years, Aikido—the art he founded—has quietly spread worldwide. It is teaching people of all ages how to enjoy and protect life through a calmer, healthier, more tranquil existence. It is reminding people to be in the moment, where they can truly experience the joy of life.

Many students come to Aikido class seeking an answer for the frustrations they're experiencing with a world that is not behaving in

*Fig. 1.1. Three kanji (linguistic elements in Eastern writing) make up the name Aikido. Ai means fitting, harmony; Ki means spirit or energy; and Do, which means Way. Thus, "the Way of harmonious energy."*

an agreeable manner. We all experience the ups and downs of life even when we're doing well; such is life's nature. Each of us manages to move through the highs and lows differently. For some, life's experiences are par for the course, and for others they are traumatic and disturbing. For those who have not found a smooth and elegant way of dealing with life's difficulties, Aikido can serve as an even keel for a life sailing through confused and troubled waters. Aikido is a wonderful guide for discovering joy and happiness—and, if enough people were to be guided in this way, I imagine world peace wouldn't be very far behind.

It is difficult to explain how a non-competitive practice of peace can be a martial art. Like other Japanese martial arts, Aikido does offer a physical practice that can be used for self-defense. But whether this training is Aikido's main thrust, or a useful byproduct, is an issue of some controversy, which I will take up in chapter 5. Still, most would agree that Aikido is an attractive antidote to the ever-growing epidemic of fear because it teaches us how to achieve and maintain a calm, balanced state of being from which we are better able to deal with difficulty. In fact, Aikido is often described as a moving meditation.

O-Sensei says, "Those who earnestly desire to make progress in Aikido must always keep these principles in mind: perceive the universe as it really is, root all your actions there, and open your own individual gate to the truth" (Ueshiba 2007).

Aikido is the practice of facing reality. Put another way, it is the practice of being present, of being "here and now," as we used to say in the counterculture of the 1960s. I remember my astonishment when my mother told me that she looked forward to special events like birthdays and vacations, and enjoyed thinking about them afterward, but as for the events themselves, they were not her favorite times. So my mother looked forward and looked back but neither of these count as being in the here and now. I understood her to mean that she didn't enjoy the here and now, but maybe it was that she hadn't been taught how to experience it. When she said this, I thought she was an anomaly, but I've since come to believe that she speaks for a great many people. Our world encourages this attitude. We see it all the time in commercials and ads addressing planning for special events—weddings, births, graduations, trips, even retirement—and the emphasis on the production and management of photos of these meaningful events. Folks who suggest enjoying the moment are often from the "alternative" side of things. In this spirit, practices like yoga and even Aikido encourage practitioners to be in the moment, to notice your breath, to take stock of the beauty all around you, to just be where you are at this very moment. This is the practice of being in the moment, it is relaxing, and it helps busy people develop a strong and coherent center of being. (I will talk more about this concept in chapter 4.)

But there's another reason to be here now, and it has to do with the ability to deal with life in a powerful and respectful manner. Life can be intimidating when it isn't going the way we expect. But when we expect something, we are thinking ahead and planning how things will unfold at a future moment in time. To stay in the moment is difficult; it means we accept the next moment as it is and when it comes without trying to control it. When we're afraid, we tend to turn away from what we're seeing, or to mentally reclassify it altogether so that we don't have to face a reality that seems disturbing to us. Aikido teaches skills to deal with the moment such as how to develop a calm, strong center. I like to think that Aikido is training to face reality.

Our desire to avoid conflict sometimes prevents us from seeing things clearly. It's much easier to choose to see something other than the way it truly is, choosing a more appealing view. But with a little practice we will find that reality is not so disturbing: whether standing calmly in front of another Aikido student as they deliver a punch, or seeing that someone is taking our right of way as we drive. If we see clearly, we can avoid trouble before it starts: you might choose to avoid the problem of walking into a gang of rowdy looking teenagers you see down the street, or you might decide to avoid being overly social upon seeing in your neighbor's smile the clear glint of an oncoming and needlessly troublesome conversation. It's important to be aware, and to stay calm. These are two hallmarks of Aikido training, and Aikido classes offer many ways to develop these skills. A third hallmark is Aikido's ability to transform the energy of hatred and violence to peace and joy. The possibilities for a transformed world through a cultivated populace are appealing.

So how does the transformation work? If we notice a pattern of bad behavior, that alone can help us prevent bad acts through imaginative pro-action on our part. Consider this simple example: seeing the gentle teasing of a group of schoolchildren at the end of a baseball game might urge one to find a way to interrupt this brewing energy of the kids lest it become focused on a particular child. Of course, the traditional methods of interrupting are giving a word to the coach, to the parents, to the teachers, or to the children. But these methods don't always work as well as they should. However, wandering into the group yourself with friendly conversation and a gift of cold drinks may just interrupt things enough to make the whole situation better. This example seems oversimplified, but it illustrates how interrupting a situation before it becomes overtly aggressive can transform it into something good—perhaps the return to the joy of postgame enthusiasm. Of course, not all situations are as straightforward and as easy to solve as the one in this example. But even so, if we open our minds to consider events in new ways, solutions are available. Aikido offers a person peaceful options of safekeeping in our often violent and frightening world.

The most celebrated stories of success in resolving conflict are those that do not involve violence. Aikido rounds out its strong, effective, non-violent action with its philosophical underpinnings of respect for all living things. This is not in keeping with the image of a "kick-ass" martial art, and to those who are attracted to arts of that kind, it will seem like a conundrum that Aikido is peace-seeking. However, every martial arts teacher I've had the pleasure of talking to agrees that avoiding needless conflict is important. Also, many students from other martial arts have been sent to me to learn centering by their teachers. My teacher used to say that Aikido teaches the base lessons that all martial arts use. By this I took him to mean that in Aikido classes we have practices for learning to center and ground, whereas in other arts, it's often assumed that students will pick this up along the way. Aikido ultimately attracts those people who do not act from hatred and anger, but who strive to do what's right when threatened; people who desire to learn how to respond appropriately from a quiet confidence and desire to be effective citizens in the world. Aikido is a big picture art, and Aikido training is a step-by-step process of cultivating that peace within ourselves by embodying it. Over the past forty-seven years, Aikido has provided me with much happiness and joy amid my perpetual struggle to learn and understand it.

And for a half century, children in the West as young as five or six years old have been learning Aikido through city recreation offerings, after-school programs, and classes in Aikido dojos. These children, as adults, may indeed be our hope for the future of our freedom and liberty by embodying these lessons of peace and respectful stewardship of a troubled world. There are many young people taking up the charge to work on the world and the humans in it. If they were asked whether they knew of Aikido, we might be surprised to find they had been students of the art as children.

Having lived in relatively peaceful times, we see the benefits to civilization when peace—rather than fighting, destruction, and mayhem—is our daily fare. When I was a girl, upon hearing the violence described in the evening news, I would argue with my father that conflict is not necessary! But as my Aikido teacher used to say, if lions lie down with lambs instead of eating them, then we would have problems of overpopulation of the lions and lambs and probably starvation too, because there wouldn't be enough food or space for them all. Of course, this was my teacher's way of illustrating that a certain amount of conflict is necessary for life. My father would agree.

There is another illustration of the need for conflict that I find more compelling: a seedling's root must push away the dirt to make its way to the nutrients below and its expansion above. Not only is this necessary to its survival, but it counts as a form of conflict on a seedling's scale: by pushing aside the earth both above and below to claim enough space to support its physical expansion, the sprout is displacing other forms of existence to claim property for its own well-being. How does this differ in principle from a classic act of conflict? I daresay the taking over of another's space has been the reason for many wars, even a very current one. The difference here is that by usurping another's property we're no longer talking about natural conflict; the line has been crossed to unwarranted aggression, which is beyond the basic conflict of nature.

So basic conflict of the sort we use in our own ambulation—pushing against the ground to propel us forward—is a conflict that is the natural production of life, like the sprout's pushing aside the dirt in order to grow. Conflict, then, is a normal part of life. As Laurie Anderson sings, "Every time we take a step we fall a little bit and catch ourselves." And, as the Delta Air Lines ad for the Olympics says, "You have to have gravity to create lift." Here the pressures against another living entity, the Earth, help us move about in space even though with each innocent step we may be putting an end to the life of many small living things like insects and seedlings. But it is not malicious. So, conflict seen in this way does seem unavoidable and necessary to life. It is aggression that is blameworthy and generates bad acts. Such aggressions are an over-escalation of basic conflict. And it is aggression, like an attack, that Aikido can transform. Such acts are an aberration of nature and cross the line of acceptable behavior.

Aikido comes from sword and staff arts. But it is worth noting that such lessons emphasize the importance of being in the moment: critical to good sword and staff work is the awareness of distancing, timing, and posture—subtle aspects of reality. In Aikido we train to see the energy of an attack as a gift, and so the stronger the attack the better the gift! In the Aikido perspective, the more energy we have to work with, the easier it is to unbalance the attacker. Far from overwhelming the attacker with one's own strength, we use the attacker's own power to off balance them, which interrupts their attack. And we do this while we conserve our own energy. The strategy of overwhelming an attacker with insurmountable strength is not practical as there will always be someone stronger, someone with more guns. This kind of contest of strength against strength is a losing battle. So Aikido practice will prepare us to fight if the fight is worthy of our time and effort.

To create peace from the aggression of an attack is a transformation worth learning. In fact, this is Aikido's true purpose: training students to use the attacker's lethal energy to bring about a peaceful conclusion. Based on the principle of loving kindness and protection of all living things, Aikido even teaches compassion so that we bring the least amount of harm even to the person who attacks us. Aikido is a path for creating peaceful living through responsible stewardship.

The self-defense training of the Shaolin monks was based on what they observed in animals during attacks and conflicts between the forest creatures living there. And so there are many kung fu forms: tiger, crane, praying mantis, leopard, boar, snake, and eagle, to name some of them. Clearly the movements of snake kung fu differ from the movements of the praying mantis. Like a bad science fiction scene, the physical bodies of these many creatures produce different natural movements. That is, how could a snake replicate the boxing type of movement of the praying mantis? The physical forms of the animals present the limitations of their movements. As humans we have a form that can imitate the movements of many animals and insects. Even our spine deep inside each of us enables the snakelike movements as does our tongue. At the very least, we can see that the snake's flexibility is a useful quality to seek.

On Saturday afternoons, my late husband and I often would watch Chinese martial arts movies together, and I found the movements associated with these different forms of kung fu fascinating, because they all emanated from the different forest creature's use of the natural movement of energy available to them. This opened my eyes as I had never thought about animals and insects in this way. Later I would come to understand a dog's or wolf's behavior and be able to read them when their hair, tail, ears, and head stood high in confident potential aggression. As animals ourselves, many of us have lost—or have never been trained in—the natural, organic realities of our body. Whether we override them or incorporate them in an appropriate response, recognizing them puts us ahead of the mark.

As a Nebraska girl, I was more familiar with the many forms wind could take as it raced across the Northern Plains. With the ongoing coverage of storms across the world, we have seen how awesome Mother Nature can be. Her spiraling powers make us fearful and sad at the destruction she has left behind as tornadoes and hurricanes destroy communities. The force that nature can generate is often unstoppable and yet, rather than respect her forces, too often we have chosen to try to control them. We are too ready to fight and assert our control. But opposing Mother Nature is not a fight we should choose to take up.

If we study how nature's forces work, we can use that awareness to help ourselves. Noting that a palm tree can survive a wind that would break a sturdy oak, or that palm trees and bamboo are what's left standing in the path of a hurricane while everything else is dashed, we can surmise that flexibility might be a strength to respect and study. We know that staying flexible is to stay youthful as, if not countered, stiffness will slow us down until all possibility of movement is gone. We

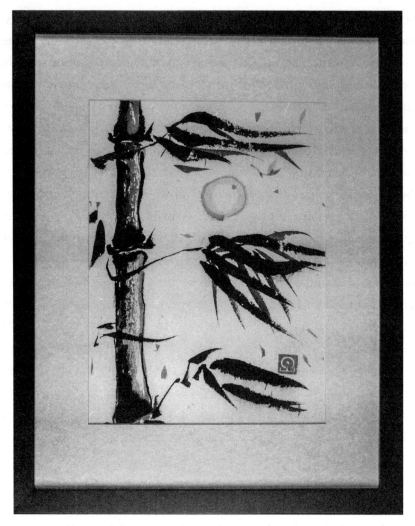

*Fig. 1.2. Bamboo blowing in the wind.*

can choose building materials with more flexibility, and, in general, use flexibility as a prime consideration in all that we create and do. Noticing that flexibility is essential to survival, with practice we can take the power out of rigid responses that might lead to a bad end. So, the power of the hurricane or tornado is not bad or evil in itself; it is just a force of nature.

In Aikido we study how to use those same spirals we see in hurricanes and tornadoes to generate our own power. That is, we learn to use the power of Mother Nature's forcefulness to our own advantage, to control violence, and to bring peace. Although we cannot stop the force of the spiraling winds of tornadoes, cyclones, and hurricanes, we can learn how to locate ourselves in a more protected geography when choosing where to live. Also, when building a house, we can insist on architecture that will withstand greater forces to keep ourselves safe, such as the Earthships in the deserts of the Southwest. We can learn the generative causes of such forces, and work to prevent winds from being fed by excessive heat and cold. In this way we work to align ourselves with the forces of Mother Nature as we are doing today with wind turbines and solar panels. Our existence will be more secure if we understand and act in accordance with the natural forces of which we are already, by nature, a part. The view that we are completely self-sufficient and separate from the workings of the natural world must finally be cast aside if we are to survive.

The study of the power of spirals is critical in understanding how air and water move. Even Bruce Lee, who was known for his incredible martial arts punches and kicks, says, "Empty your mind, be formless like water." And so even Bruce says that we must look to nature to cultivate ourselves.

The following story illustrates the benefits of working with nature in order to move forward. It is a story about my experience one quiet afternoon while I was enjoying a field of clay as a break from my studies. I write it now because it presents such a good illustration of blending energies.

### Yankee Hill Brickyard

*I was a serious student when I was taking university classes, and so I would venture out to parks to give myself a break. This was one of those times. As I teetered on the top of the wire fence surrounding the clay fields behind Yankee Hill Brickyard all I could see was a landscape of pink, purple, tan, and red ground. The colors of a Persian carpet were inviting and irresistible to me in my moment of being in the here and now. I thought I'd take a ride on a magic carpet of clay!*

*As I hopped off the fence, I was surprised that my feet began to slowly sink down into the cold dark red clay of the brickyard. Fear immediately rose up inside me with the thought that, like quicksand, the sinking would never stop, that I would not find ground. Would I be like Alice in the rabbit hole and discover a portal to a new reality? The clay was thick, and, although I was slowly sinking down, I finally began to feel that the clay had some resistance. Then all of a sudden, I could feel a bottom, a ground, under my feet. Relieved and less fearful I took a look around. Why were certain places purple and others pink? Was the clay field even walkable?*

*The virtual Persian carpet was enticing, but I decided I'd best make a plan or map for dealing with the clay field before me; the variations of color suggested differing states of existence. Gingerly taking a few more steps I found that where the clay was darker red, even purple, the surface beneath me was more receptive and so I began to sink down more quickly. The areas lighter in color were firmer and resistant. It made sense when I realized that the receptive dark clay held more moisture than the lighter-colored clay. More water in the clay meant it appeared darker red in color; less water in the clay resulted in a light pink or tan color. Gradations to this occurred everywhere, and sometimes the change in color was immediate where water had pooled in a crevice and soaked into the clay. In this way, I was able to color-code the field by noticing how my foot met the different colors. And, as I walked slowly, not only did the moisture of the clay underfoot affect my step, but my step would also leave its imprint on the clay as a mark of our meeting.*

*So our energies—the clay field's and mine—affected one another whenever there was contact. If the clay was wet, my foot would sink into it easily and the clay would keep my shoe as a souvenir; but where the clay was dry and flaky, my shoes could shield my dancing feet as I made arcs and swirls in the dusty pink and tan ground beneath me.*

*Even though the entire field was composed of the same substance—clay—it existed in very different energetic and receptive states given the amount of moisture it held. Respecting the nature of the clay and water I could walk around, investigate easily, and return to the joyful feelings of dancing on the colorful Persian carpet that initially called me over the fence. The glory of being in such a unique place amid all these amazing colors was boundless. And I learned something useful about meeting and joining something outside me. Years later I would see this experience as illustrating a basic and important concept in Aikido: receptivity and acceptance. There was so much variation in the field of colors and textures of the clay field, and I daresay that human interaction is not in principle so different.*

So, like the field of clay, there are cities filled with humans. And like the different patches of clay, there are differences between individual humans that we can discern. Just as it was critical to be aware of the differing consistencies in the clay, it is important to notice the differences among humans as well. Although we are all human and made of the same stuff, our natures differ from one another so that the receptivity of any one of us may be considerably different from another. Gina may be as receptive as a human gets, greeting everyone with a big smile and open arms that, like Mother Mary, almost energetically draws us into her embrace; while Katrina presents with a frostier demeanor, and maybe a sharp hard look with a fortress-like posture. Just as with the clay field, where the receptive states differ given the amount of moisture involved, so with Gina and Katrina the receptive states describe differing amounts of warmth. There is no good and bad here, this is not about value judgments. Rather it is about observing what-is by being in the here and now. In the clay field I managed to walk around without harm by producing a kind of mental map relating to the hues of red, purple, tan, and brown. Is a map for humans possible? Imagine how useful that would be in moving through life!

*Fig. 1.3. Demonstration of an Aikido throw.*

An Aikido school offers a kind of laboratory for the respectful and discerning observations of the natural movement of humans. As we go along, it will become clear that a large part of Aikido training has to do with this energetic relationship between humans. And schools of Aikido are the places where we learn, in people, how to differentiate agreeable from disagreeable, strong from weak, compassionate from dangerous. Of course, the first step to safe living is to learn how to tell which humans are safe and which are dangerous. This is doubtlessly a deep and multifaceted field of study, as there are those complex humans whose agreeable nature camouflages a danger lurking beneath, not to mention the mercurial nature of many people in general. But we can begin with the basics and go from there. In learning the techniques of Aikido, we often hear strange phrases like "blend with your partner's energy," "become one with your partner," "inhale your partner," and so on. These seemingly inscrutable instructions hold the key: learn how to absorb your partner's energy and you will learn how to read energy. In the clay field, an analysis of the meaning of the different colors let me know how receptive each spot of clay was. With humans, too, we can come to know what to expect as we meet another and, just like with the clay, we meet with a barrier or an invitation.

It is worthwhile, then, to create a kind of map of the human energies we're likely to meet. A seasoned student of Aikido may learn how to read another's energy in the moment before actual contact. Understanding what gives rise to our own fears and anger, we can begin to observe the same in others, and in this way come to understand the movements and signs of these energies in general. I notice that when I'm stressed whether it is due to fatigue or fear I hold my shoulders high and tight—maybe a way of containing myself when I'm not feeling in full control, or safe. I am not so unique, as I notice others behave similarly in this regard. So when facing someone, if I notice they are holding their shoulders high, I can with some probability make an assumption about their inner state of being. Noticing the predictable nature of Nature's behavior, from its shapes and forms, helps us when we look for some way to read animals. It's not too surprising that the founder of Aikido continually looked to Nature for guidance and inspiration.

Energy, which is necessary to live life, is not limited to a single body, but flows from the planets above throughout space, and affects all living bodies—animal, vegetable, and mineral. It would be wise of us to study winds, water systems, and the Earth below our feet to deepen our understanding of energy moving around us, as all these systems are interdependent. By first finding and understanding the energy in our own body, we can expand our energy awareness beyond our own body to the community of bodies, human and nonhuman. Finally, in this way we can understand what we have in common with others and with nature as a whole. We can come to understand how we are one with nature, which is another of the Aikido founder's maxims.

In conclusion, Aikido is an art of transformation. To study Aikido is to become a student of the nuance of conflict—not so much to execute a technique, but to examine timing and distancing as a consideration of the alternatives for response. Its practice offers an opportunity to identify the energies at work in excessive conflict and to choose the most appropriate response.

The fictional prize fighter, Rocky Balboa, spends a lot of time training to keep his body strong and healthy. Implicit in Aikido is this same kind of lesson: how to live well. And so what Aikido has to offer is not just sword-training or a self-defense technique, but a way of being that will keep us safe, healthy, and ready to act when the need arises. To learn an art like Aikido is to transform our poorer life habits into ways that will sustain us as a vibrant and healthy human with the awareness of a human's place in nature and our human nature. And this transformation rests upon creating and using the powers of natural attraction in all that we do. It is this transformation that is the subject of this book.

Many have remarked that we must all pull together to continue life on Earth. It seems incredibly odd that given the opportunities we've had, it has taken all this time to realize that it is this perspective that will bring us peace of mind and a life of joy . . . and possibly world peace.

# TWO

# O-Sensei
## *Unifying Two Opposing Worlds*

Morihei Ueshiba (1883–1969), to whom students respectfully refer as O-Sensei, was one of the world's most celebrated martial artists. His gift was to marry effective martial arts technique with a deep spirituality. A renowned teacher, he had the presence of mind to present a big picture philosophy with a means to embody it—a true practical philosophy.

*Fig. 2.1. Founder of Aikido, Morihei Ueshiba. (Courtesy of John Stevens)*

Aristotle, another practical philosopher, saw a person's choice of action as a confluence of mind and body. What O-Sensei and Aristotle have in common is a refusal to neatly separate mind events from body events; both thinkers see them as inextricably woven together into the organic whole.

A master of many martial arts, O-Sensei brought out of *budo* (the martial path) a deep philosophical element that, when combined with the physical practice of Aikido, uniquely guides us to experience greater joy. His son writes,

> As he stood by helplessly watching the tough hoods of the village beat up his father because of political differences, young Ueshiba vowed that he would never give up trying to become strong no matter what the cost in suffering and time. He would one day be able to handle them. One day they would flee in fear. He would have power (Ueshiba 1978, 3).

From the time he was a young boy, O-Sensei wanted to be a strong man. But he was not naturally strong; in fact, he was sickly as a young boy. He was drawn to studying spirituality at the temple near his home. Concerned that his son was not an active, healthy boy, his father hired martial artists to come to the home to teach his son martial arts. His father hoped that this would help inspire his son to be healthier, and to become more active.

Probably as a result of his desire to be strong, O-Sensei as a young man tried to enlist in the Russo-Japanese war. He was rejected upon application because he was a half-inch too short. He immediately became obsessed with correcting this deficiency by hanging from the rafters in the family home as well as from the trees in the yard outside. This seemed to work as he finally was accepted into the army. He did have a military talent as is shown by his survival without injury. There were also stories of his leadership abilities in the war, and even legendary stories of his unusual talent for dodging bullets. However, it seems the experience left him with a distaste for war; it is said he did not like to see death and suffering.

Then it is not surprising that years later, the prospect of another war—World War II—would cause him to retreat: He retired from his teaching duties at his Tokyo dojo as well as from his post teaching combat arts to the military officers in Tokyo. He left the city altogether for his farm near the small town of Iwama, sixty-two miles north of Tokyo. His retirement from his teaching posts in Tokyo indicated his position with regard to Japan's impending attack on the United States: he did not support it. O-Sensei actively tried to prevent this war with his student Shigeo Tanahashi, a staff officer in the Imperial Military Headquarters. In 1938, they made a plan that Tanahashi, as war planner, took to Japan's cabinet members, including Prime Minister Prince Konoe, advisors to the emperor, and the emperor's brother Prince Chichibu, which these men approved. O-Sensei's involvement in this plan was kept secret to protect his life. Shigeo Tanahashi's son, Kazuaki Tanahashi, writes, "In Prewar Japan any civilian or soldier who openly mentioned another nation's military supremacy or voiced intention of preventing war would be arrested, tortured, and perhaps killed" (Tanahashi 1995). It's interesting that this plan of theirs did win the support of several well-known wealthy Japanese as well as Harry Chandler, publisher of the *Los Angeles Times*. But in the end, "the military leaders of Japan, who saw any effort for peace as a sign of weakness, decided to crush all peace negotiations" (Tanahashi 1995).

Between these two wars O-Sensei's thinking had developed in meaningful ways. Just after the Russo-Japanese war, in his hometown of Tanabe, O-Sensei met the brilliant environmentalist Kumagusu Minakata who was involved in Japan's nature conservation movement. The government declared a shrine consolidation movement that would decrease the number of shrines and allow the government to claim the forested land on which they were located. Kumagusu Minakata was against this for several reasons.

To Minakata, local shrines, surrounded by sacred trees, were the symbol of genuine Japanese nature worship. He knew that Wakayama prefectural officials were hand-in-glove with developers (the kind of cozy tie up that exists throughout Japan to this day), and that trees formerly protected by local shrines would be felled in a wholesale manner. He pointed out that this would decrease the bird population for lack of nest sites—and so lead to an increase in the insect population. Farmers would then resort to using insecticides, which in turn would get into the water and harm the livelihood of both freshwater and inshore fishermen. . . . Minakata created a mandala to demonstrate the interconnectedness of all natural phenomena. . . . He stands as a global pioneer in the ecology movement. His philosophy and actions can teach us a great deal today (Pulvers 2008).

Minakata lived in Tanabe with his wife and children, and he was by all accounts very visibly social. In his home laboratory, Minakata studied slime mold. He made several original scientific discoveries in the field of mycology (the study of fungi), and he is famous for his work on mycetozoa. He looked at the ecological relationship between nature and humans through biology, as well as through folklore, ethnology, and religion. He was already well traveled and well versed in Western experiences. Minakata had developed intellectual relationships with people of all ethnicities everywhere he went. He was even held in high regard by Emperor Hirohito, Japan's Emperor Showa. By 1904 he had settled with his family in O-Sensei's hometown of Tanabe.

O-Sensei heard loud and clear Minakata's call to action to help save the shrines and forests from destruction. O-Sensei became active in this protest; he was able to contribute to Minakata's environmental efforts. I imagine working to save some shrines from the government's shrine consolidation project was a great hands-on way to cultivate O-Sensei's ecological awareness; he already had a deep experiential relationship with those very mountains and shrines.

But Minakata, who was sixteen years senior to O-Sensei, influenced O-Sensei to be active in another program. He encouraged O-Sensei to lead a group of eighty-five people in a Hokkaido land claim the government was offering in order to develop the far reaches of northern Japan. This was a big ask. It would take real fortitude to move eighty-five people from Tanabe to Hokkaido (720 miles) and then to build a community in the cold and empty land of northern Japan. But again O-Sensei rose to the task and he, with a community of people, moved to Hokkaido. Maybe Minakata's influence on O-Sensei had some part in developing O-Sensei's interest in issues of world peace, if only in widening O-Sensei's vision of community-building.

While living in Hokkaido, O-Sensei braved the hardships of community-building and faced the storms of survival in the unforgiving climate of Japan's most northern island. It was in this rugged and harsh environment that O-Sensei met a samurai's son—Sokaku Takeda—who had learned from his father hand arts, sword arts, and spear arts, and who was an itinerant teacher offering classes in what he called *daito ryu aiki jujutsu,* "the art that the samurai used for ground fighting."

Perhaps because O-Sensei had already had experience with some martial arts study, he became interested in what Sokaku Takeda had to offer. We can imagine that the opportunity for martial arts training must've seemed to him like a bright light in the bleak and desolate Hokkaido landscape. O-Sensei was accepted as a student; in fact, it is said that Sokaku Takeda favored him. O-Sensei studied earnestly for a good period of time while he lived in Hokkaido. This martial arts study ultimately gave O-Sensei a solid form to his martial arts interests and practice; more importantly, it would figure in important ways to the physical foundation of Aikido, an art that he had yet to create.

When O-Sensei received word that his father was on his deathbed in Tanabe, he was eager to travel home to be by his father's side. But another experience delayed his arrival in Tanabe. O-Sensei heard that there was a healer in the small town of Ayabe that had spiritual powers that might help his father. O-Sensei, who had studied spiritual traditions in his youth, was enthusiastic to meet this person, Onisaburo Deguchi. O-Sensei eagerly and immediately made the detour to Ayabe. This detour did not save his father, but it was an extremely important life-changing meeting for O-Sensei. Also, it was to give new breath to Aikido, which was then in its infancy.

First, it is useful to give a little background on Onisaburo Deguchi, as the story of both Onisaburo Deguchi and Nao Deguchi, is quite fascinating in its own right. Onisaburo, as a young man, came across Nao Deguchi, a devout mother of three who had fallen on hard times and was selling rags in the streets of a small Japanese town near Ayabe. But Onisaburo noticed that, although she was illiterate, he saw her writing in Japanese hiragana (Japan's syllabary language). Upon reading what she was writing, he believed she was being used as a medium by a spirit of the northeast, Ushi tora no Konjin. From Nao's brushed writings, Onisaburo began to prepare a text from this transmission that became the basis of Omoto kyo, a sect of the nature religion Shinto.

Word traveled and many people followed these two groundbreakers, including O-Sensei, who was invited to take up residence on the Omoto kyo grounds. He moved his family to Ayabe as a result. Onisaburo was someone who would have a profound effect on O-Sensei's personal development and on the art of Aikido. It was Onisaburo who encouraged O-Sensei to make his art "round"—by this, Onisaburo may have meant to include compassion as a pillar of the art, and in physical terms to explore the power of circles and spirals apart from the straight lines and angularity of other martial arts forms.

Certainly Onisaburo saw some leadership skills in young O-Sensei, presumably his reason for asking O-Sensei to open a dojo on the Omoto kyo grounds to teach community members his martial art, then called daito ryu aiki jujutsu. And so, O-Sensei opened his first dojo on the grounds of Omoto kyo in Ayabe. O-Sensei was influenced by the Omoto kyo tradition of bringing people together in peaceful living. Moreover, it is worth appreciating that Onisaburo Deguchi's Omoto kyo was based strongly on creating world peace for all people; even today Omoto kyo is strongly driven to bring people of all walks of life, as well as people born of all countries, together through its many programs. O-Sensei was trained in this open and accepting attitude towards human beings around the world.

At this time in Japan there were many such movements of unification, but Omoto kyo led the way as an extremely popular movement with hundreds of thousands of followers. It became so popular that the Japanese government became concerned. It is not surprising to find a government up in arms about a popular movement that begins to amass a tremendous following. Omoto kyo was not grabbing political power, but there was a report of some of its followers violating the strict Japanese standards of respect pertaining to the government. It was enough to concern and alarm the government, and they razed the Omoto kyo grounds and imprisoned the leaders as a lesson in humility. I was familiar with this story from the history books on Aikido, and so when, on my first trip to Japan, I saw in the train station hallway an impressive poster depicting the rebuilt cedar buildings, in Ayabe, declaring the Omoto kyo grounds an architectural treasure, I was surprised—then shocked—when I learned it was a government poster.

Just before the razing of the Omoto kyo grounds, Deguchi told O-Sensei to leave Ayabe to escape imprisonment. And wanting O-Sensei to succeed in developing his art, Onisaburo set his far-flung Omoto kyo community into helping O-Sensei, which they did in many ways. For instance, they arranged through small demonstrations for Omoto kyo members living in the many remote villages throughout Japan to help grow O-Sensei's recognition. One of these remote villages was Shingu, not too far from O-Sensei's hometown of Tanabe. The Kumano Juku Dojo in Shingu has functioned throughout the years as a strong training center for Aikido. Making the most of this start, O-Sensei eventually was able to open the headquarters for his art in Tokyo. With daito ryu aiki jujutsu as his physical base, and Omoto kyo's inclusive philosophy beginning to influence his teachings, O-Sensei was on his way to developing a deep and meaningful art that is so unique we are still trying to plumb its depths today.

It is clear that Aikido is an art of spiritual transmission. By this I do not mean to suggest that what O-Sensei transmitted to his students was a religion, but he did think it was natural to ask someone who wanted

to learn a martial art to discover a deep reverence for life, a compassionate outlook, and a spirit of loving protection for all creation. For many,
this presents a conundrum at the heart of Aikido: how can Aikido be
both a ferocious martial art, and promote love and compassion for all
living things? But clearly O-Sensei did not see a contradiction.

Not long before O-Sensei's teaching emerged, the samurai were
fighting to the death. For them, their sword skills and Daito Ryu ground
techniques were of the most serious nature, a matter of life or death, a
matter of survival. They didn't view their arts as competitive or as a
sport. Doubtless this attitude of seriousness was passed on to O-Sensei
by his teacher Sokaku Takeda. Even today most traditional teachers do
not view Aikido as competitive: There are no tournaments or contests.
However, public demonstrations, very popular today, were not given
at this early stage in O-Sensei's development of the art. Samurai did
not publicly demonstrate their skills as they wanted their adversaries
to remain ignorant of their fighting skills. And similarly, O-Sensei did
not think of his art as a game, but as a deadly serious art. While it was
one thing to give a demonstration for a select group of Omoto kyo followers and their friends, a public demonstration is different. It would
be years before O-Sensei would give demonstrations open to the public.
He knew that if his art were treated in a disrespectful manner, it could
be dangerous.

Years later, a student did die from an overzealous college class practice in Japan that turned competitive. When O-Sensei heard the news,
he was outraged and saddened that his art should be so misunderstood.
And even though O-Sensei really had nothing to do with the class or
the teacher whom he had never met—much less trained—because they
were training in an art he created, he felt responsible for the tragedy.

Prior to World War II, in order to study with O-Sensei, a person
would have to have black belts from other martial arts along with letters
of recommendation from noteworthy teachers just to be accepted as a
student. Knowing more than one martial art might make a person more
dangerous in a certain respect. I remember when I enrolled in Aikido

classes I was, for this very reason, reluctant to pair up with a black belt student. But I soon found the danger resided in beginners who didn't know what they were doing. Black belt students are experienced and most of the time display tremendous control over what they're doing; they can be most helpful and compassionate to a beginner student. Doubtless it is this cultivation that O-Sensei wanted in a student seeking his instruction so that O-Sensei could dispense with the laborious initial lessons and dive deeper into his art. It would enable him to teach in a more meaningful way.

Today anyone can walk into an Aikido dojo and sign up for classes. In fact, today you will see posters across the country announcing open classes for beginners; new students are enthusiastically welcomed to sign up and join. But this is a post–World War II reality. That is, it wasn't until after the war that O-Sensei eased up on the formality of application standards. I will say more about this in chapter 5.

After the many fire raids of World War II, the Tokyo dojo Kobukan, which remained standing through them, closed for a time as it took in neighbors whose houses had been damaged. His farm in Iwama gave O-Sensei land on which he could grow food, and he enjoyed taking up working the land as he had done in Hokkaido. O-Sensei retired to his farm in Iwama as a part of his protest of the war. O-Sensei brought to the Tokyo dojo the food from his Iwama farm to feed the neighbors as well as his family there. Of course, at this time, classes were not offered; neighbors were living there, and food was scarce. I was told a party consisted of four to five people sitting on the mat with a dish of three grains of rice to share!

The Ueshiba family began to take in young men roaming the streets who were finding their sustenance in old sweet potatoes they found cast aside and run over on the street as garbage. The days of requiring letters of recommendation for potential students were over. O-Sensei was saving a generation of young men from starvation and an unsheltered life, and in this way his *uchi deshi* (coterie of live-in students) grew. Because the Ueshiba family housed and fed them and even gave them a little spending money, they were at the disposal of O-Sensei. If he traveled somewhere, a student would go along to handle the bags and tickets, and make sure his needs were met. If he needed help farming, they were there. An intense man, he is said to have awakened students in the middle of the night to go with him for mountain training. This is intense training, but in those postwar days the students did not have the many distractions that young people do today. Now, I'm told, young, wealthy Japanese boys would not give up the distractions of parties, fast cars, and girlfriends to travel with an old man, help with harvesting potatoes, or practice sword arts on a cold, dark mountain at inconvenient times.

With the occupation of the Allied Forces after World War II, a ban on all martial arts curtailed activities at O-Sensei's Kobukan Dojo. In interviews with some of the old-timers at Hombu Dojo, it was said that because of the perceived bad influence of State Shinto on Emperor Hirohito, anything related to Shinto after the war was frowned upon by the Allied Occupation Forces.

In 1942 O-Sensei retired to Iwama and in that same year he named his art *Aikido*. He left the Tokyo school in the hands of his son, Kisshomaru Ueshiba. It is not surprising that wartime events take many forms and I find differing accounts given for the same event. Suffice it to say that eventually after the war "permission was granted by the Occupational Forces and the Japanese Ministry of Education to organize an Aiki Foundation to promote Aikido as 'A martial way dedicated to the fostering of international peace and justice,' and . . . the Tokyo dojo officially reopened" (Stevens 1997).

In this way Aikido classes could meet under the approval of General MacArthur of the Allied occupation, and Kisshomaru Doshu (*Doshu* designates the next Aikido leader) would be the Director of the Kobukan Dojo. O-Sensei's son, an educated economist, was reluctantly succeeding his father in providing for a new educational model and overseeing the growth of Aikido. We should be, as O-Sensei was, very grateful for Kisshomaru Doshu's insights and personal sacrifices for the sake of protecting and developing Aikido.

Family succession was the proper way in Japan for an art like Aikido to be handed down. Kisshomaru Doshu had not planned on a career in Aikido; he was educated for a professional life in finance. Kisshomaru Doshu had two older brothers that he never knew as they died that first year when his parents moved to Ayabe. He did have a sister, but it was not fitting for a female to be a successor and, although it looked like her husband, a kendo master, might have a future as O-Sensei's successor, their marriage ended in an early divorce. It fell to Kisshomaru Ueshiba to succeed his father.

So postwar we find classes meeting, and life in Tokyo beginning to survive and build back under a foreign occupation. Classes could meet, but because the dojo was registered as an educational institute, classes would be open to the public; that is, anyone could walk in and join. This was a far cry from the educated students O-Sensei was used to teaching.

O-Sensei was inspired to community building work and ecology movements by Minakata. Onisaburo Deguchi further inspired O-Sensei toward a more compassionate goal of unifying the world. Here O-Sensei, who once required letters of recommendation and previous black belt rank from potential students before admission to his dojo, found himself having to open the doors of the dojo to anyone who walked in off the street. O-Sensei went to extremes to support Kobukan's neighborhood by housing them in the dojo and also by growing and hauling sweet potatoes from Iwama to Tokyo. As his art grew in popularity, he had to embrace many changes to accommodate the times.

# THREE

# Beginner's Mind
## *Discovering the Enemy Within*

At the end of the 1970s, two rebellious, skeptical, and critical Western philosophers walked into a community Aikido class in Claremont, California. To embrace an art that promises world peace would have been out of character for us and extremely difficult to imagine. My late husband, Professor Ronald G. Rubin, who could sit on his ponytail at that time, was a handsome, free-thinking, spirited young man with a charismatic laugh and quick mind. We lived together for a couple of years before starting our marriage. We shared a wonderful relationship together for thirty-eight years before his death.

When I was only a year or so into my graduate studies, we considered taking an Aikido class together to help us stop smoking. For the past year we had run together, smoking as we walked to and from the college running track three blocks away from my house. In the darkness, we would carefully store our shared pack of filterless Camels and Zippo lighter on the curbside for our après-run smoke. We ran in the quiet dark of night with a watchful owl as a sentry safeguarding our route; he would fly from lamppost to lamppost as we followed him around the track. Five miles was our limit, but not because we lacked muscular strength; it was our wind that ran out. It was 1976, during the smoggiest decade in Los Angeles history, and knowingly we were

*Fig. 3.1. Ronald G. Rubin and Susan Perry in 1991 at Mount Baldy Zen Center.*

smoking in the smoky air. What were we thinking!? Our own idiocy compelled us to stop smoking right away.

For those who have an entrenched habit, stopping cold turkey with no plan can be sure failure. We decided to stop on New Year's Eve, which was only two weeks away, so, although we were quitting cold turkey, we took some time to agree on a plan. To get ourselves through the day, we discovered easy remedies to distract us from the physical habits of smoking a cigarette. We found that to satisfy our need to put something in our mouth at certain times of the day, an everyday object like a toothbrush or a straw seemed to work fine. To satisfy the need for that divine feeling of the smoker's first inhalation, I would grab a handful of whole cloves on my way out so I could pop one in my mouth when the need arose. A simple bite down would release that explosion in my mouth: a good imitation of that full inhalation a smoker treasures.

But Ron rightly added that we must do something entirely different to break up our established smoking patterns. Smoking functions as a keel to a life sailing through many activities as a smoke would mark the transition from one activity to another: a smoke with our morning coffee, a smoke as we began to write, a smoke after writing the chapter, a smoke after dinner, after a nightcap, at the end of the day, before bed, when we arose in the morning. Smoking would hold the day together while we negotiated the currents keeping ourselves afloat. In this way, smoking embedded itself in our lives, it kept us sane; without it we felt lost. This is no doubt why it's so difficult to quit.

So Ron suggested we take Aikido. And there just happened to be a city class beginning in the new year, which made perfect timing, as we could begin something new and challenging right away. Ron had seen some footage on television of the late George Leonard demonstrating Aikido; he said it looked interesting. When he told me Aikido was a Japanese martial art, I was unenthused: At that point in my life, I had no interest in Japan or martial arts. But he encouraged me; he said he thought I'd like it, and he pressed me to try it out with him—and so I did.

My preconceptions about martial arts were sophomoric; I thought it was exercise for guys who liked to fight and compete. I grew up on a Nebraska lake in Lincoln, the capital city of Nebraska. I was a very active young girl, and my family was athletic. I loved to swim, and my big brother taught me how to water ski when I was six. I sailed and fished with my father, and in the winter when the lake froze over, I ice-skated. My mother taught me how to care for and ride a horse. But I hadn't developed an attraction to competitive sports. The encouragement for competitive sports came largely from my father and my big brother, but I was not really competition material: the sting on my legs from their fast tennis balls did not motivate me to press on in order to win. My heart was not in winning a game.

The Aikido class met close by in an old fire station that the city had acquired for recreation classes. I felt I had walked through a portal into another world even though its trappings were that of a simple gym. When I saw one person moving in circles and somehow producing lift into a huge, soaring, expansive round forward roll across the Aikido mat, I wanted to do that. The movements were beautiful. It was as if that student took flight. Ron was right about Aikido and me. We signed up for classes that night.

We moved the gym equipment each class in order to open the matted floor for Aikido practice. Years later I would remember the nondescript aesthetic, when I fashioned my own dojo, when I wanted my dojo to reflect the beauty of this Eastern art. But I fondly remember the feeling of that first class when we stepped into unknown territory, when we stepped into change.

## The Way through Resistance

When Ron and I stepped onto the Aikido mat for the first time, our main reason to be there was to find some distraction from a long smoking habit, and to create a new pattern to our daily life. There were plenty of distractions: Our muscles reluctantly accepted new states of repose as we learned how to stretch them out. I was surprised to find that I had tight hamstrings from sitting too much when a simple forward bend made me feel like my legs had grown overnight. And we practiced *seiza,* (sitting on our heels) which is a natural position for an enormous number of the world's population, but my Western legs didn't accommodate this position right away. I remember Ron would take an egg timer to his college office so that during his break between classes he could practice sitting seiza. I remember at one point he thought it was impossible and said that he must be anatomically different from the rest of the world. It took him a long time to stretch out his quadriceps so that he could actually sit on his heels. He took it nice and slow, increasing the minutes every day until he finally did it.

But probably the most challenging practice was learning how to harmonize with our partner. Aikido has no competitions or tournaments, and so we don't block or go against our partner's movement.

It's easy enough to appreciate this idea, and although it sounds conceptually attractive to "harmonize with your partner," to do it was more challenging. The good thing is that although I didn't care for competition, I love a good challenge! But you can imagine how frustrating it was for the instructor to deal with two philosophers who wanted to know what "harmonize" meant in this context. I knew to learn this Eastern art I would have to be open to some new ways of looking at things. And I found there is a phrase for this open state of mind: beginner's mind.

To have beginner's mind is to be receptive. As we grow older and become knowledgeable about the world, sometimes our minds become full, and we may be protective of its often hard-won contents. When we have an opportunity to learn something new, many of us are so full of ourselves there is no room for something new to come in. Beginner's mind makes room for new information by putting all our precious mental cargo in a closet for safekeeping. In this way we empty our minds to be open to new experiences. This is to have beginner's mind. It is much like a child's mind, with the natural curiosity and capacity to learn and the space to soak up new lessons.

As an Aikido teacher years later, I would tell students to leave their mental baggage on the shoe bench where they leave their shoes when they come into the dojo. I would ask that they leave their worldly concerns about what to have for dinner, the argument with their daughter they just had, and political issues of the day on the shoe bench for safekeeping. Like their shoes, they could pick up and take with them all their worldly concerns on the way out. By this simple instruction, they were introduced to beginner's mind. I wanted them empty and receptive to the amazing things they were to encounter in class.

In part it is because of this open state of being that being a beginner is so worthwhile. As a beginner we can shed all responsibility for leadership, and just enjoy the exciting ride of learning something new. Learning something new doesn't mean we accept these new ideas; as a beginner we are trying them out, they are something new, so we need to see what they are. Like a new recipe, we may try it, but we may decide after the meal not to revisit that recipe again. Probably more objectionable to most people is the specter of looking idiotic. This is truly unfortunate, for we will miss many amazing things in life if our pride gets in the way. We struggle to fill ourselves with good ideas and practical theories about how the world works, so it is difficult to let that go for a while and to consider possible new ways of doing things. It may be scary, but this is how change works. Besides it does a person good to shock the system every so often. So why not embrace it and enjoy the ride?

To suspend judgment in this open state we need guides and protectors to show us the way, and to keep us safe in the process. In the West we call them teachers, and in the East, they are called sensei (literally, "those who've gone before"). In our beginners' class there were a couple of advanced students who assisted the teacher; they seemed eager to help a new student learn. Once I thought about it, advanced students are necessary to the smoothness of the class; otherwise, a room full of beginners pairing up with one another is like the blind leading the blind. Imagine a room full of beginners telling one another what to do. Doubtless it would lead right away to power struggles and mayhem. Advanced students were helpful, and they were always around as a regular feature of Aikido classes. If we were too embarrassed to ask the sensei a question like how to properly leave the mat to use the toilet, an advanced student was ready to help. Because Aikido is not competitive, these advanced students, who would never meet us in a competition, had no secrets to hold back. In fact, just the contrary: The more proficient we became, the better partners we would make in our own practice. So, advanced students have every reason to do what it takes to make beginners better at Aikido; it's almost a selfish motivation except that it's not.

Beginner's mind usually does not involve judgment, for if we begin judging something we know nothing about, our ability to learn narrows. However, I would often take beginner's mind too far believing that, by sheer willpower alone, I could somehow manage to do things beyond my abilities. My big brother taught me to aim high, and he would set for me harrowing experiences that he thought I could manage; he had great confidence in me when I was doubtful, and usually he was right. And so now in this Aikido class I was ready to explore, to try things I might otherwise not choose to experience. It wasn't always successful: a bruise here, a pulled muscle there; I figured it was the price for pushing myself too far too fast. Because of Aikido's noncompetitive nature, a serious injury is rare. This is really a credit to the teacher. For a teacher must keep the practice safe; a good teacher is a guide and protector. A lot of thought goes into how to keep students safe in Aikido class, not to mention the close observation necessary from the teachers to address frustrations before they become class problems. So even though Ron and I were rebels at heart, we quickly realized it was reasonable to follow the directions of the instructor and assistants. After all, we knew that if they got too tired of our continual questioning, they had other means of persuasion.

Ron and I were unaware of how significant studying Aikido would be for our own development individually and for our relationship as well. All of the changes we experienced at the hands of Aikido made us better people and brought to us an enjoyment of life that we had not experienced before. In the process of this study our relationship deepened in wonderful ways. We did succeed in kicking the smoking habit, or maybe we replaced an unhealthy addiction with a better one. This art held our interest for the next thirty-seven years as we created together a successful dojo and, through our publishing company, produced Aikido books, Aikido Expo events, DVDs, and one hundred issues of a bi-monthly non-partisan, international magazine. Through our own dojo, Musubi Dojo, we created many events: workshops, seminars, field trips, and camps. I met many leaders in Aikido in the United States, Canada, and Europe, as well as in Japan, and at our dojo we hosted many of them for events that were open to all Aikido students. Aikido classes began as an innocent start to what would become an enormous change in our lives. An inner transformation produces waves, and our waves were big and covered a great distance.

It turns out that Aikido training is a great way to moderate anger, which was good because Ron and I discovered we had anger issues. Looking back I can see now that we both had internally repressed quite a lot of rage. Doubtless that had something to do with a smoking habit to begin with. Smoking is a great suppressant and, for an angry person, a puff on a cigarette at the right time can prevent antisocial words from seeing the light of day leaving only a wisp of smoke to reveal (to perceptive observers) the angst boiling inside. I, myself, had a habit of smoking several packs of filterless Camel cigarettes a day (or rolling my own Genuine Bull Duram smoking tobacco ciggies). Ron was not far behind me. I met Ron when my brother funded a trip for me as my undergraduate graduation gift. This trip was to determine where I was going to locate myself for graduate school; I had my eye on a couple of graduate schools out West. One had actually promised me an assistantship if I was to go there.

My first encounter with Ron was on this scouting trip as I was considering Claremont Graduate School; he was a professor at Pitzer College—one of the Claremont Colleges. We ended up sitting next to each other at a philosopher's lunch. Right away we noticed the brown stain on each other's middle fingers. We both knew what that brown stain meant: we smoked filterless cigarettes too far down. I remember the moment so well! When we both looked at the stains on the other's finger, and then looked up to check whose finger it was, our eyes met—clearly soulmates from the start—and I knew which school to choose right then.

We had both suffered abuses of one form or another in our early lives. Ron grew up in a home with an unbalanced and intrusive mother who was overwhelming and accusatory most of the time. His father was a wonderful man but quiet to a fault. For a sensitive and studious young fellow like Ron, I can imagine that such a domestic scene was stifling. He fled to Amherst College where he began his impressive academic career. I had experienced my own bumps and scrapes in an early marriage with a man who only knew unacceptable forms of communication. I, too, found university studies a direction to a better life.

Help with deeper issues surreptitiously crept in as our curiosity in Aikido and things Eastern developed. The help, of course, was in the guise of Aikido, which offers an incredible platform from which to work out one's anger often, as in our case, without realizing it. But an angry body is a tight body, and energy does not move easily through a tight body. So right away, and without knowing it, learning how to relax ourselves was a self-correction for our anger. And since relaxation is key to Aikido, we would work on this aspect of ourselves in every class.

It is one thing to intellectually understand that bodily resistance makes the flow of energy more difficult, it's quite another to rid yourself of that resistance. It's amazing how much resistance can reside in a body, but in an intimate art like Aikido it reveals itself when you feel touch and movement from the outside. This is subtle: resisting someone's grab can mean several things—running away, pulling your arm away—but it might just be a tensing of the musculature in order to close off access to unwanted incoming sensations. I had thought of myself as a friendly and open individual, but when I began practicing Aikido, I realized that I was open up to a certain point. When a large, strong man grabbed my wrist, for instance, I was surprised to find myself tightening slightly, and holding my breath, which would send my shoulders into my ears. Clearing out old fears and unuseful habits is a good practice, and I found the close proximity to another human, which Aikido affords, helpful to me. I realized how easy and common it is to move through life with little connection to human touch outside of close relationships.

In those initial three years of Aikido training I enjoyed working out with my fellow students, but there were precious few other women in class. The men were wonderful, and they were all very big and strong. I would tie my long hair into two braids to keep my hair out of my face during class. Some of the fellows in my class thought it was fun during multiple attack practice (one of my favorite practices because it is so dynamic) to grab onto my braids as they moved by me. For me it was quite painful to be moving and then suddenly have someone pulling my hair. My hair was long and soft, but I found if I spun around very fast my braids would become, in effect, long whips standing out horizontally from my head, which made getting a hold of my braids—and of me—very difficult. They also produced the whip-like "cut" when they hit someone close by. This became my personalized clearing movement: I called them my razor braids. I would later become efficient at throwing someone with a long soft rope. I believe they are related. Also, it brought home to me the difficulty circular movement posed for someone trying to grab onto you. Spinning around does not give openings unless you lose your balance.

However, once these fellows did get ahold of me, it seemed impossible for me to move freely, and even harder for me to move them. Although this was frustrating for me in the beginning, it was to prove very beneficial over time, I learned how to move under a strong "vice grip" grab. As a small woman, my center was beneath theirs, which worked in my favor. And it took some practice to learn which angles of connection could help me the most. I had to do it exactly right or I could not budge them a bit. It occurred to me how lucky I was to have partners like this. Despite sporting some small bruising to my wrists as a reminder that I should not try to use force, this practice helped me to become quite skilled at moving a large person under extreme duress (and without bruising myself). And I wondered how these fellows—who were all big and strong—would come by such useful feedback in their own training. I wasn't able to hold them like they held me. Would they have to find someone bigger and stronger? And without such honest feedback, how would they ever find those special angles, how would they learn not to muscle through it? At any rate, these big strong classmates helped me considerably while they thought they were just having fun.

I remember on the drive to my first interview as a graduate student looking for a part-time teaching job at a nearby college, I had the great idea of loosening up on the way by doing some breathing exercises as I drove down the freeway. I wanted to interview with a calm and powerful center like the center I sometimes felt in Aikido class. I had come from the dentist and the numbness in my face was taking longer to wear off than I had predicted. I entered the faculty office and met the several professors who were to interview me that day. They greeted me with a cup of hot coffee. I was pleased and sat down to take a sip as I normally would, forgetting momentarily that my face was still numb from the dentist. As a result the coffee dribbled down my face and onto my blouse, and then in my hasty attempt to set the hot cup back down, I spilled it all over the table. I discovered that day that breathing exercises when you are already in a car and nervous about an interview will result in hyperventilation. Then not taking the numbness of my face into account, I sipped the coffee normally, a big mistake. I had lost focus. My apologetic smile must've looked strange with one half of my face numb; I didn't get that job.

When you make mistakes like this, it makes you feel ridiculous. Here you are studying an art that is supposed to expand your global awareness and you fail miserably at seeing a small point. I began to question my rank. This stayed with me for a while and during that time I watched many samurai movies, Westerns, *The Pink Panther, Kung Fu,* even boxing matches with my husband. We would analyze the moves. In quiet times I'd try the moves out alone just to see how to move through them. I would practice spins on a walk down the street, kicks outside the dojo while waiting for Ron, *jo nage* (throwing with the staff) with my wolf dog Sparky on the mat after class. Then at some point, I knew I had messed up, but what mattered was what followed. How do you take a moment that reflects badly on yourself and move with it? Do you let it take control over you? Do you let it defeat you? I remember in the many martial arts movies in which the hero usually gets beat badly in an initial scene just to be healed by some pretty village girl, or wise old healer. He's lost a fight. He's near death. But little by little he begins to get stronger until we see him practicing again to make himself stronger for the next fight! Such a story was meaningful to me in my many "losses" even though I may not have been bested in a physical fight. The lesson remains.

In training I might miss the timing or screw up a technique, but I did know it was the purpose of training to look at where you are and get better. After all, it wasn't about the technique or the speed. It didn't matter how mean a person could be. I don't build a strong center to make myself strong against others, I build a strong center so that I can invite everyone in without losing balance. And I don't practice 1000 sword cuts to make my arms strong, I practice 1000 sword cuts to release holdings in my body. The person who comes with the singular goal of making their body strong just cultivates aggression, and that is the losing side. Aggression is ugly partly because it is a posture that cuts a person off from the energy around them, from other people, from love. I had blundered in getting a job; that's a little different from a mistake on the training mat. But I have come to see that what happens on the training mat is important. When we improve ourselves with training, it reflects throughout our life, not just in Aikido class. I was learning things, but clearly, I needed more training! I had been too cavalier with my job interview: I had practiced breathwork in the wrong place and I had scheduled myself too tightly. This was impractical and it came from the thought that I could do it all: too much ego! Unfortunate that I didn't get a job offer, perhaps . . . but my mistake identified where I needed work to make myself better.

As you might expect, there is a full spectrum of teaching methods used in the many dojos around the world. And, you may have to visit more than one dojo to find the right teacher. Some Aikido dojos teach forms without much acknowledgement of anything else; others may spend too much time talking and not enough training. So, if you don't see them addressing what you are excited to learn—whether it's self-defense, harmonizing, or how to develop tremendous inner strength— keep looking, and you may find the right one. An old adage is, "It is better to spend two years searching for the right teacher than it is to spend two years training with the wrong one." And yet I've heard a senior teacher say about a wonderful Aikido student who was training under a notoriously bad teacher: "It's funny that even though she had a crappy teacher, it was enough to allow her to practice and shine. She will be fine." As a gardener I thought of the incredible plants that sometimes flourish in spite of neglect.

Many are the practices that enable us to slow our system, quiet our nerves, and clarify our vision. And as one learns how to slow and relax, one creates time and space. An unwatched pot of water boils quickly, but watch the pot and you will have more time to luxuriate in. We choose what plane of existence on which to live. We all witness the fast-paced world where layer upon layer of responsibilities can begin to smother a person. How much we engage in a way of living is up to us; but there are other ways to perceive the world. Aikido helps us to see our options.

## Deception

If you see an Aikido demonstration, one thing you notice right away is the falls. Most people do not view falling as joyful, but, with practice, it can provide a liberating feeling to take to the air and toss oneself upside down through space and time. Sometimes it seems I've entered an alternate world, a fold in reality where the fall seems timeless, and still I come back again. Falls enable my partner to practice a throw all the way through. That is, my partner can finish the throw as it would happen on the street given that they are partnered up with someone who is sufficiently skilled at coming out of the movement safely. And, although there's no talking during practice, communication of another sort does take place.

Aikido uses the notions of "giving" and "receiving" to describe the interchange between the *nage* (person attacked) and the *uke* (attacker). As an uke I attack by delivering a certain form of energy to my partner—they receive that energy and return it in the technique or throw. My falling ability allows me to receive this technique or throw. This going back and forth in giving and receiving is a kind of dialogue.

When we generate power through a spiral movement, that energy has to go somewhere and so, at upper levels, skilled partners can put that energy into the throw. And, as a throw is composed mostly of the attacker's energy, the attacker can present some parameters in the attack. Remember, in Aikido you learn how to use the attacker's energy to off-balance them and then, because the movement is spiraling, you return that energy to them in a throw or take down. Students who are attacking quickly learn that by moderating the amount of energy they commit to an attack, they are moderating the energy that will return to throw them. So, without talking, a student who has a sore shoulder may choose to be kind to themselves that day and attack with a slow but deliberate attack, thus signaling to a receptive partner that they are not up to a grandiose fall.

These falls might sound fake, and working with a beginner, it's true, the falls may be deliberate. After all, there is much to learn about how to move safely, which is a primary focus in the Aikido dojo. I can't stress this enough: If we take care of our partners and keep them safe, then we can work out with them again the next day and the day after that. But if we abuse the privilege of training practice by not following instructions or lashing out in anger, we risk losing a partner, albeit temporarily, to an injury. In most dojos, injuries rarely happen because students are primed to be careful and are taught how to move. In movement, energy can be controlled and distributed evenly throughout the body. It is when we don't move that we face the most danger.

I recall seeing a complete failure of this at a popular Aikido camp years ago. I had come onto the mat a little late that day. I noticed the EMT ambulance taking someone away on a stretcher. As I entered the mat room and bowed myself into class everyone was already partnered up . . . that is, except for one fellow standing and looking for a partner. I bowed into him. He said, "Are you sure you want to work out with me?" I asked him what he was talking about, and he said, "The student those EMTs just put into the ambulance was my last training partner!" I found out later that this fellow was a recent black belt, and the practice was to deliver a sincere punch to the face. Well, he did: He delivered a very fast and powerful punch to his partner's face and smashed his nose to the point that surgery was necessary. The problem was that his partner was a rank beginner who didn't move off line and got hit. This black belt fellow seemed very remorseful and embarrassed about having caused such an injury; he was not skilled enough to assess the situation properly, and someone got hurt. It happens, but not very often.

But getting back to whether falls are fake or not: in a regular Aikido workout among black belts who are skilled at moving, you won't find them taking falls for one another if their partner fails to take their center. They are skilled enough that they fall when their balance is taken, and not otherwise. Aikido's falls, however, are often rolls, so that the fall is likely to be a projection into a spiral that can return the attacker to their feet again at the end. Yes, it looks fake, and sometimes it might be, but among dedicated black belts it is not.

In fact, every so often someone might take my center so well and seamlessly that I am launched into an awesome flight where I discover the folds of reality. This kind of throw is joyful and that feeling brings students back to the dojo again and again because they want to experience joy: it is the lure of the here and now. But this feeling comes at other times in one's practice as well. It might be an entry with a partner, or it might be the result of a solo practice with a wooden sword or staff. It is of another world, and I never know when I will experience it. But I continue to train and be ready for that experience when it arises again.

During that first or second year of training, I had finished my graduate coursework and had begun writing my Ph.D. dissertation. At this time, I had been offered a two-year post as Ombudsman of the Claremont Colleges as a graduate student there. However no one told me the job included practicing Aikido! Attacks come in many forms, and they can be hidden in conversation. For example, family and friends may try to change our minds about something, or attempt to manipulate us. Often, they may (lovingly) employ personal attacks in their presentation. The same can be said for relationships in the workplace as the following story illustrates:

### The Dean

As Ombudsman of the Claremont Colleges, I had a duty to find a solution to a problem when college grievance procedures (the Claremont Colleges were made up of six separate colleges each with their own grievance proceedure), the regular lines of complaint, didn't work. But I was also to help with off-campus consumer complaints, and landlord-tenant issues when they arose. I was hired to provide help in all these areas for the students, staff, and faculty of the six colleges that make up the Claremont Colleges—each with their own grievance procedures!

One day I was to help an undergraduate talk to the Dean of Students at the college where she was a freshman. It seemed like a simple task: she was not satisfied with her conversation with the dean of students, and his office was not making any appointments for her to follow up; she needed some backup. After I scheduled the meeting for her, it was time to show up. The dean's office was pretentious, as was the dean. He was a large man, and his face revealed displeasure at our appearance in his office, but he managed to force a strained smile. My presence seemed to make him uncomfortable, and so I took a seat off to the side of the student so that she could speak for herself. It was clear that the dean was not interested in hearing what this student had to say. So I made a short and clear statement to the effect that we were here to resolve the issue according to the student bylaws as found in the current college handbook on page such and such. And as I began to ask him to please hear the college student's explanation, the dean turned to face me, his beady eyes narrowing to little pressed slits in his fleshy, feisty face. He fixed me in his visual field, and I felt a chill go down my spine. This seemed very creepy. Then, as if propelled by an inner explosion, he suddenly lifted off the chair to full figure. Standing bolt upright and facing me, he huffed and puffed and waved his fist at me a few times before he pounded his desk and yelled at me. I couldn't believe my innocent officious statement could produce such a violent response. But basically, I just wanted to flee, my solution of choice to brewing trouble. I was beginning to doubt myself, and looked for the door, when I remembered something I had learned in Aikido class the evening before: there is no real power behind a feigned attack. Looking back at the dean, I asked myself: Was this a real attack? Might it be feigned? This question sent me immediately to my center, and I calmed myself. I needed to consider the circumstances. I looked at the dean again and considered the drama he was bringing, and I noticed the cowering student in her chair. It did seem frivolous and empty. Would he really punch, slap, or otherwise hit me? Attacks take energy to produce; they don't just happen. He had enough energy to stand up and pound his fists and yell, and yet it would have to escalate quite a bit more if he were to cross the room to do me physical harm—which, of course, was his threat. He probably got his way many times at this campus of young, inexperienced women. Moreover, I observed that we were in his college campus office with his secretary visibly present at her desk in an adjoining room with an open door, not to mention the college student who was sitting in front of him. The picture windows surrounding his office gave a decent view of the stunningly green campus outside, but nothing prevented students from seeing in if they chose to look. Surely some dean beating up women inside his office would draw some attention! Would tomorrow's campus paper carry the headlines "Dean is arrested for beating a female graduate student in his office"? I didn't think so. The whole thing suddenly seemed ridiculous and absurd. It was so clearly a fake-out that I couldn't suppress a smile. So what was I afraid of? I looked up at the dean who was still standing and still yelling. He now seemed like a cartoon.

Aristotle defines fear as the perception of imminent danger coupled with a feeling of pain. But I no longer felt the pain and discomfort that earlier was motivating me to flee. More and more I could see that the dean was posturing. I exhaled, my shoulders dropped, and, quite by surprise, my spine moved me into a standing *position. I relaxed a bit more, and then smiled a nice and confident smile at the dean and waited for him to finish. I was so surprised at my calmness I laughed at myself. I could tell it was over. As I calmly stood there, I could feel the ground firmly under my feet, time slowed, and I moved toward the dean. He stopped yelling and creating a fuss. I could feel the secretary's presence in the doorway behind me, and I thought I saw the dean's jaw loosen and drop. He had nowhere to go unless he was going to escalate to violence. The wind suddenly came out of him, and he plopped down on his big leather chair in a kind of deflated huff. I reminded him of why we were there, and asked if he couldn't help resolving the simple matter before us. I could tell he was grateful he had an off-ramp, and he took it: he resolved the matter in her favor right then.*

*Relief rose up in me. What power that simple observation brought to me. Simply discerning a feigned attack gave me immediate calm and power to resolve the issue in favor of the student. And that this Aikido lesson was so useful, off the training mat, in a campus meeting, astounded me. I've never forgotten this experience or this lesson. I was able to act appropriately for everyone's benefit, and it all turned on my seeing that the dean's threat was empty. If I hadn't taken that Aikido class that brought to me the idea of a feigned attack or empty threat, I probably would not have handled this situation so well, and perhaps would have even failed to help the college student. Being able to see through to the truth of the matter is critical; it helped me do my job well.*

Learning how to tell a feigned attack from a real one is a lesson that helps in so many aspects of a person's life as we'll see in the stories that follow. As one learns how to distinguish a feigned from an honest attack, one begins to learn how to recognize falsity from honesty in a person, an invaluable skill.

Excited that Aikido was so helpful to me as an ombudsman, I started looking for more Aikido lessons that could help me; I began to see everything in terms of Aikido. I was lucky that Ron was involved as I had someone to talk to about Aikido, and we talked about Aikido all the time. We would work on staying balanced and centered by sneaking up on one another with a surprise "attack." When I was standing washing dishes and lost in thought, Ron would slip in behind me to try to off-balance me with a gentle tug on my shoulder. When I found him deep in thought I'd surprise him by a grab around his waist from behind. We would try to creep up on one another from behind to press our knee into the other's, a popular off-balancing ploy. Kato and Inspector Clouseau became a thing with us, and we enjoyed watching them in the popular *Pink Panther* series as well as fooling around in our own quasi-martial arts play. We learned to be aware of our surroundings this way.

On the mat in Aikido class we train to take a person's center (this is the topic of the next chapter), to off-balance our partner through timing and distancing: move too far away and you invite another attack, move too near and you get hit. As I've said, in order to take someone else's center, you must have your own. So you're learning both things simultaneously—keeping your own center and taking someone else's center—which offers a couple of perspectives. Lessons on posture, balance, and centering teach you how to focus your strength and power. Lessons on breathing give you the calm to properly assess a situation, and the space to access natural movement. I was a serious student and worked hard to master these things. But these kinds of lessons take time to learn as one already has habits of breathing and moving that may be less than ideal and may need some adjustment, and that change takes time. So first one has to realize the habits that are counterproductive and then one can work to make things better. At first, it's a checklist to remember; but over time we learn the feelings and sensations to the proper movements. Once we find our center, we must operate from there at all times. It makes things better: we have more balance, more power, and more calmness; movements are more unified and take less energy. But it takes time and repetition to embody the sensations and feelings of having your center, and to move from there as a natural response. At least for me it took a lot of time not to initially lose my center when someone grabbed my wrist, but it does eventually happen with a lot of practice.

Once a person can move in a balanced and centered way, then it is easier for other aspects of the practice to come into view. This will create a deeper training experience. Aikido technique is about taking the attacker's center. So once we have developed a stronger center of our own, we can begin learning how to take our partner's center. Taking our partner's center is to receive them as a part of our center, so balance and stability are key. This is what is often called harmonizing, or "becoming one with your partner." Although it's not difficult, it can be a life's study, how deep with meaning the practices can become. Even on a superficial level, learning how to center, to harmonize, and to become one with your partner takes quite a lot of practice. This is, perhaps, the central lesson of Aikido. As I will discuss later, it is this practice that can transform conflict into harmony. So, in taking my partner's center, I offer my own center as the balance to the whole system so that my body *and* my partner's body are moving around one center: mine.

# FOUR

# Centering

## *Finding My Warrior Nature*

In our Aikido class, attacks were the basic exchange. That is, in order to work on my response to physical conflict, a partner in class would present me with an attack in the form of a punch, strike, or grab. There are three dimensions of attacks (with or without a weapon): up and down (overhead strike, uppercut, kick to the groin), in and out (punches), and circular (strikes or roundhouse kicks). Each dimension of attack is distinct: you don't enter to the side with a round strike to the temple, for example. So developing a center helps one to calm down so you can detect what kind of attack is coming. Developing a strong center keeps you stable so you don't flee out the door when presented with an attack—so that you can stay focused and learn how to move out of the way of an attack. Centering practice is invaluable to avoid getting hit or knocked to the ground.

Aikido draws students from other martial arts who want to supplement their training by developing a strong center. In fact, Jigoro Kano, the founder of judo, impressed with what he saw O-Sensei teaching, sent two senior students to study with him: Minoru Mochizuki and Kenji Tomiki. Given enough time most athletes, dancers, and martial artists who develop mastery of their art will have to find their center, but focused training on developing your center has been a recognized and respected trademark for Aikido. So you can hope to discover it over your life, or you can learn how to develop it from talented teachers. My teacher used to say that Aikido training supports all martial arts by its commitment to this fundamental training of the center for the focus needed to enhance power. Often a martial arts student would show up at our dojo who was sent by his martial arts teacher precisely to learn these things. I was impressed with that teacher's insight.

Centering is a basic lesson in Aikido class that students practice to perfection. Dropping the source of movement and strength to my hip area is not so difficult for a woman as women have a lot going on in that area every month. But for men who have spent time developing their upper body it could pose quite a challenge. Centering is creating a whole-body balance that maintains my line of posture and provides a point of stability as I move. It is called *center* because it is located in the central part of a body: there is a horizontal line that passes through my body about two inches below my belly button. This point is probably my center of mass as well. As an Aikido teacher I found da Vinci's *Vitruvian Man* drawing helpful if only because it clearly displays the center of body mass located well below the shoulders and closer to the hips. Having taught yoga I was familiar with the vertical line of energy that travels along your spine from head to stern, often called the *sushuma*. In Japanese martial arts, this central point—where the vertical and horizontal lines connect—is called the *hara*, an important physical as well as spiritual concept.

The Japanese view hara as a spiritual center that connects us to the earth below and to the heavens above. In O-Sensei's view of the world, humans are standing on the Floating Bridge of Heaven (*Ame no ukihashi*), the bridge that connects heaven to earth. Humans then stand between heaven and earth between openness and density. We are an integration of the lofty, ineffable mind and the dense, material body. We have a front and back as well as an up and down (not to mention an inner and outer), and all of these organic aspects come into play when moving from your center. It can get quite confusing to move if you're thinking of all these parts of the self as separate. But it all comes together at the center, at your hara. So if you move from there everything moves together, as one piece. Simple, but not easy.

The hara is the place of our vital source of energy. Our center is viewed as the repository of ki energy, which is supplied in part through our connection with the earth. Ki energy, is the source of power for life as well as for movement in Aikido. Whether we are offering a strike to our partner or performing a technique, the energy of our movement should be moving from our hara and expanding outward (this is often called extension). And so as we learn how to move in this way, our movements become more stable and free as our whole body moves as one.

Finding your center in a static position helps in finding your balance; standing on one leg is advanced practice. Even more advanced practice is moving from the center. If we're moving from our center, it becomes a much more safe and comfortable way to avoid attacks. Being centered, then, makes our movements solid, smooth, and efficient. And this is big. Once the fear of getting hit is gone, we can more easily focus on other aspects of attacks: speed, direction, and whether the attack is real or feigned.

Centered movement is powerful because the whole body is moving around a single focal point, and so we can move quickly if need be. But if someone is trying to push us, this focal point is also what makes us centered, strong, and immovable—like Fudomyo on the rock (who we'll learn more about in chapter 9). When my son was little, he had an uncanny talent for being immovable, especially in front of a toy or candy counter. And in my first years of Aikido study, our teacher would test us on *fudo shin/fudo tai* (immovable mind/immovable body). Learning how to be immovable makes responding to an attack much easier—you may not need to do much more than turn out of the way.

Centering presumes both grounding and balance but focuses on our access to powerful energy. Aikido's energy is all about the center as the source. All of these terms apply equally well to one's energetic or emotional state; a calm, reasonable person is a centered person.

In my own experience, I have trained powerlifters who were terrifically strong so long as they stood in one place, but had no center to help them keep their strength while moving; I've trained small children whom I see return again later in their life to the Aikido mat as stiffer and taller adults who must relearn how to do the Aikido rolls that once were so easy for them because their body has changed so much; and I've been amused that in teaching how to turn with balance and center to a class of elders in Pitzer College' s Elderhostel Summer program, I ended up working more on getting them to slow down.

O-Sensei seems to use alternate means of strength in his demonstrations. The four-to-five students he would call up to push against his sword as he held it out horizontally could not make it budge. That isn't done by muscular strength. Seeing footage of his demonstrations presents a mystery as this is very difficult to do, and I have not seen anyone else do it. Certainly footage like this challenges our imagination as it suggests we must change our focus and reliance on muscular strength to something else—maybe our center!

Learning the Aikido rolls—how to make them smoother and practicing different entries into the fall—is an investment in my protection from injury, as a roll is a way of exiting from an applied technique. In fact, one sign of progression from a beginner-level student to a more advanced student is being able to give fully to the technique so that the roll becomes a natural response to a throw as I describe below. This, of course, signals a complete trust in my partner but also a trust in myself. A trust in my training and aptitude for falling. A confidence in my ability that chases away the fear of falling.

At this point in a student's study they must surely have been told about another important Eastern concept: ki energy. For in order to extend ourselves there is an energetic component that the East uses to explain how we are more than a lump of flesh and bones standing on the mat waiting for an attack. *Ki* means energy and, with some training, a person can learn how to direct this energy. It can be extremely focused as in the breaking of a board; it can be expansive as you create

*Fig. 4.1. The kanji for ki.*\**

a welcoming field that can draw in your partner to your center; and it can be the healing energy you use to break up a knotted muscle tissue or the teasing children on the playground. The practice is to view our center as the source of this ki energy and to learn how to extend it throughout our body and out our fingertips and the bottoms of our feet. *Aiki* shouts (*ki ai*) are piercing shouts that are enhanced by the use of ki energy. There is also a study of kototama, sacred sounds, which uses ki energy as well. I will talk more about kototama in chapter 11.

Going back to the harmonizing and off-balancing of our partner then we can physically off-balance them, or we can distract them. Distraction is a big deterrent, and I remember several classes where we would push this to its limits by making funny faces, piercing shouts, or even by offering a kiss. Such ploys are strangely powerful and effective. There is more power to distractions if they are unexpected behaviors; that is, the more out of the box and disarming they are, the better they work given the right timing. At the dinner table when I was a little girl, and wasn't eating my dinner fast enough, my brother sitting next to me would suddenly

---

\*More than a word, a kanji signifies a categorical meaning often through an ideogram or story presented in that kanji's etymology. So, for instance, ki (気) is made up of the kanji for rice, which originally consisted of six strokes (as in my brushwork and unlike the *x* in this modern version). The strokes above the rice kanji signify the vapor ascending from rice cooking. Such is the staple for the East and the source for their energy!

exclaim and point off in the distance as if I would miss something really amazing if I didn't look to where he was pointing right then. But he was using the age-old distracting ploy to sneak something off my plate!

Being centered became an everyday practice for me; I struggled to bring my awareness to my center during everything I did: walking to school, gardening, washing dishes, cooking, writing, and especially conversing with others. I learned that attacking from your center is what makes an attack honest, and that attacking without your center opens yourself to injury; if your body is not integrated, undue stress is put on those parts held together by fascia and soft tissue. But I knew I still had a lot to learn. So when I wasn't centered, for instance, I would catch my toe on the huge iron book press that lived in our dining room, or I would wander off while something was cooking or otherwise get distracted as I stood by the stove and get splattered by hot oil. Or when using knives in the kitchen to prepare veggies, I would often cut myself if my attention wandered. I would even cut myself when handwashing a glass by using too much pressure.

Once, while visiting a prominent sensei, I was helping with a dinner prep when I was handed a knife and told to cut a butternut squash into cubes. Not familiar with cutting butternut squash, I didn't know you must first soften the skin so it would yield to a knife's blade. Instead I did my best, but the knife slipped off the hard waxy surface and I cut my thumb instead. Embarrassed at my lack of skill, I quietly tried to stem the bleeding until it was clear that I needed a few stitches. So instead of a nice dinner that night I was driven to an emergency medical center and stitched up. Besides learning about how to deal with butternut squash, I learned about knives. In fact, before I flew home, I bought a very sharp knife to take with me so I could learn how to use a knife in the kitchen. Dull knives are a hazard, but sharp ones will do your bidding easily—so long as you stay focused on what you're doing. Focus is, of course, integral to being centered. I've never cut myself since. With the advantages of being centered I moved through activities in my life fluidly, with confidence and gusto.

Far from the formal techniques of philosophical reasoning and logic, Ron and I learned new ways of communicating with people, different ways of resolving conflict, ways to persuade another not by pointing out a logical fallacy, but by a gentle physical touch that seemed to invisibly alter another's attitude to an easy acceptance of a new idea. We discovered how change could be affected even in silence with body shapes (mudras) over a distance as when someone waves from a distance for help. One can use the voice or sound to affect a situation, as in calling out sharply when a child is about to put their hand in a flame. There were so many well-developed studies of these things, and we enjoyed discovering the theories behind them. But they all seemed to demonstrate to me the power of Aikido and ki energy.

Ron and I experimented with Tibetan bells and the vibrations they produced. I took up a study of kototama (sacred sounds), and when we retreated to a mountain cabin one weekend, I found that wild donkeys particularly liked "o" sounds. In the evening while I was practicing this sound outside, wild donkeys would approach me (see page 215–16 for a friend's full story about sounds attracting wildlife). Now I rise early in the morning so I can talk to the birds that live near me. I imitate their calls and when I do this, often they visit me.

We found other examples of ki everywhere! Ron and I massaged out one another's bound up knots of energy as we began to learn about the human body and how, often under stress, it would produce a knot of tension that could be easily addressed and dispersed. Ron began to develop a serious interest in chiropractic technique, and, as his practice dummy, I'm grateful he was talented at the manipulations of releasing energy. In these ways we began to understand more about the inner workings of our physical bodies, and how we hold stress and how it all was in some form of ki energy. We began to understand how to use the power in the movements of nature in our dealings with one another and others as well. We learned the power inherent in spirals as we discovered how to find the embedded spirals in Aikido movements and techniques. Everything seemed interconnected and networked together as one. And it all seemed to operate best if we were calm and relaxed.

I would continue to develop my skills, and work hard on learning Aikido technique. With its slow-moving, spiraling movement I found it beautiful to behold and exhilarating to perform. When I would manage to get the spiral just right, I could feel it—everything became effortless and moved like flowing water. Sometimes it felt as if I suddenly came upon a spiral in space waiting for me, and then it automatically engaged and moved me through the technique. There was so much to work on in Aikido class. But practicing Aikido didn't have to stop once class ended. I took particular delight in noticing this art at work in daily life.

## Warrior Nature

In 1978 there was not much Aikido in the United States, not even in California. Still, those who wanted to learn this Eastern art no longer had to travel all the way to Japan as the previous generation did, though they might have to travel to Los Angeles or a big city near them. We had been lucky that a student at the Claremont School of Theology was offering Aikido classes through Claremont's parks and recreation program. And although LA didn't seem so far away in those days—forty minutes down freeways that did not yet sport gridlock 24/7—we were content enjoying our Aikido training in Claremont as we got along well with our fellow students. After class, at what is euphemistically called "the second dojo," we would meet and communally share a pizza and a pitcher or two of beer. I even remember my brother meeting up with us once or twice when he blew into town. He knew where to find us, and our group was always happy to include him.

After three years, our little community Aikido class was paid a visit by the head of the LA headquarters dojo—Sensei Roderick

Kobayashi—who singled us out after class and insisted that it was time for us to prepare for our black belt tests at LA's Daiichi Dojo. And so there wasn't much choice as—three years in—we were still enjoying Aikido together and, although not rank hungry, we were hungry to learn the deeper lessons we felt lay ahead.

Our teacher in Claremont introduced us to a young man who was a student at California State University, Pomona, another university close by. He was studying Aikido at a club there and, like us, was also told to take classes in LA. And so we began carpooling together into the instructor's class at the headquarter dojo. And once we began classes there, we found a couple of other people who lived out our way and wanted to join the carpool. And then we found a few more people who wanted to join us for lunch after class before we drove back. They were kind enough to introduce us to LA's Japantown—Little Tokyo—both the restaurants there and the amazing Kinokuniya bookstore, which had books on every aspect of Japan and Japanese traditions. This included martial arts books, language books, cookbooks, and artbooks. I was a bookstore nut already, and so this became my favorite place. This was before Amazon, the internet, cellphones, DVDs, emails, even Borders bookstore! We were introduced to other black belts (yudan-sha) from different organizations at the Kinokuniya bookstore by the members of our lunch group. It wasn't hard to find them; on a Sunday afternoon we would all be jockeying for position in front of the martial arts book section to see what new books had arrived that week. It was a very active time for new books on Aikido, martial arts, and the samurai. We became familiar with the Kurosawa samurai movie fests in Santa Monica, where we would spot in the audience some of these same black belts we had met in the Kinokuniya bookstore. I took out a library card for the library in Little Tokyo, which had many more books on Japanese culture than my local Claremont library, and I began to travel into Los Angeles on weekdays. My Aikido world was opening. I was only years away from starting an Aikido magazine. My world was exploding.

### Prof B.

*When I finished my Ph.D. dissertation and passed the oral examination, my chairman threw me a party to celebrate my graduation as well as to celebrate my advancement to first-degree black belt* (shodan) *in Aikido. (There are ten degrees of black belt.) They happened in the same month. He asked me to invite whomever I wanted from both worlds, and he would provide refreshments and food for the party at his house. My chairman lived on campus in a small university-owned house. When my party was in full swing, his house was packed with people spilling out onto his small porch. I was thoroughly enjoying it—except for the sight of Prof B., who was crashing my party.*

*Prof B. and Ron were colleagues in Philosophy at the Claremont Colleges. They both enjoyed the philosophy poker group, which met every now and then, and they shared a class on probability theory, which included a field trip to Las Vegas. Ron was a brilliant blackjack counter—with his amazing mind and memory he could count a six-deck dealer shoe. And with his long ponytail down his back, he was easy for bouncers at the casinos to identify; they began to call him* The Pomona Kid, *and as time went on, he was suspected as a counter. He was no longer allowed into the games at his favorite casinos.*

*I myself had limited experience with Prof B.; my studies were not in his area of Philosophy. Also, he was an aging drinker who liked to have fun. There was something about him that put me on edge. And even though he was friendly with Ron, I had not invited him to my party, and Ron was fine with that.*

*Yet there he was with a drink in hand standing next to me. He began to needle me about my black-belt status, which I more or less anticipated; I took it in stride. There were few women in either Philosophy or martial arts at the time, and I wasn't afraid of some ribbing. Prof B.'s sarcastic remarks escalated to his poking me in the shoulder. But when he tried to grab my arm something in me suddenly* shifted. By this time he was having way too much fun with me. He had been an MP in the Korean War. But this evening he was way out of shape and resting on his laurels. No one was coming to my aid; they were too involved in their own conversations to even notice. "Whatza matter—Shodan Suzy—can't take it? Maybe we should test you out!?" With that he began to bring his massive body into contact with mine in an attempt to shove me off my feet. There was nowhere to move, there were so many partygoers all around me. My chairman's house was going to get trashed if this went on much longer, and I was getting very annoyed at Prof B.'s boyish behavior, so I said to him, "Let's take this outside."

My inner sage was screaming at me: "What are you doing? This isn't Aikido, and besides, you are just a new shodan! You might get hurt!" But I was way beyond listening to good advice as I strode to the door and down the stairs to the little yard outside. I took my place on the lawn with plenty of space around me so that I could watch his approach. I did my usual things to center myself and bring up my power. The party followed me outside to stand on the porch overlooking the lawn. Especially because this party was in my honor, I wore my most comfortable clothes: black karate gi pants gusseted at the crotch for easy movement, sandals, and a stretchy t-shirt top. I took off my sandals and waited in a ready-for-anything stance. I was centered and feeling strong. The lawn was small but large enough. Then once he took his place on the lawn, he gave me the once over and I heard him say, "You are frightening, I'm not sure I want to do this!" I figured it was more jesting at my expense, and I stood silently waiting. Aikido students are not trained to attack; it is often explained by saying that Aikido is a defensive art. This is always a smart understanding for beginners to have, but it isn't exactly correct. Still, I was waiting for him to attack. I was ready for the drama to begin.

But then something began to change. I noticed my gut feeling was changing, my annoyance at Prof B. was gone, and I began to soften and feel compassion for him. I noticed him shuffling around a bit, *looking here and there, wasting time, not knowing what to do. He wasn't facing me. I began to reflect on what I was doing. I studied him a bit: he was older, he had been drinking, he seemed uncentered from the get-go. He seemed very unsure. Suddenly I felt it was all over; I thought he was coming to his senses and that the situation could de-escalate, and he would go home. Then, as if that was all a calculated distraction from him, he suddenly said, "What the hell!" as he turned and lunged for me.*

*He was a hulking and pot-bellied 235-pound middle-aged man who was not quite six feet tall, closing the distance on me, a five-foot-two, 110-pound brand-spanking new black belt. I was not afraid; I do well under pressure, and so I was calm and focused. I was set on not getting hurt and now—after my assessment of him—I wanted to protect him as well.*

*Stepping to the side or getting off-line is a mainstay in Aikido. Then in addition to stepping off-line one is taught to take the attacker's energy with you as you go off-line. There is a judo throw (koshi nage) that Aikido practitioners love to do; it wasn't my favorite throw, and I didn't feel I was very good at it, but because of that I had been focusing on it at the dojo. I was able to get underneath an attacker because I was small and bendy—one of the many advantages smaller people have in Aikido. I grabbed his hand as I got off the line and bent underneath his body mass as it came hurling toward me. This throw is technically a hip throw, stretching out the attacker's center over your backside as you position yourself under them so that by straightening your legs at the right time you lift their feet off the ground, and with good timing you jettison them off your back into a flip onto the ground.*

*I had Prof B. across my back ready to go, but I knew he would be badly injured if I followed through with the throw, so I stopped with him balanced on my hips. I wanted him to understand that he was now in trouble, that I could throw him to the ground at any moment. I wanted him to see what a precarious position he got himself into.*

*I slowly straightened my legs to take his feet far off the ground as I lifted up his bulky body with my hips. He was heavy but not hard to lift. My legs were strong, and I had him positioned over my hips so the largest muscles of my body could handle the lift. He had no ground to stand on as his feet were now in the air. It is a horrible feeling not to feel the ground, and I began to hear him plead with me. My more ferocious side wanted to throw him for causing this disruption to my party, but instead my compassion surfaced, and I said, "Say uncle and I'll put you down, and then you must go home!" I still had control of his hand, and so in addition to the judo koshinage hip-throw position, I also had an arm-control lock that you often see law enforcement use in moving perps from one place to another. I twisted his arm slightly. "Uncle, uncle," he said. The group was still watching, and so I slowly bent my knees to place his feet on the ground. I let go of his arm, and with glassy eyes he sheepishly stumbled off toward his Claremont home just a block or two away. I was pleased that I didn't hurt him, and when I saw him leaving my party, I was even more pleased. I returned to have some fun at my party.*

The Prof B. story displays several important points about Aikido. One is the importance of staying calm: I had avoided anger and had the presence of mind to take Prof B. outside the house. Also staying calm helped me act appropriately when he did decide to lunge for me. So staying calm is important, and it's tied up with maintaining your center.

Another important point is detecting a fake from a real attack. This case posed difficulty for me: Inside the house it took me a while to see that Prof B. was not just enjoying some friendly ribbing, but wanted to do me some harm, to discredit me in front of all of my Aikido and Philosophy friends and colleagues. Thank goodness clarity finally came to me before he body-slammed me to the floor. Then outside he seemed to vacillate for a moment or maybe it was a calculated act to distract and soften me, but he ultimately did attack me.

What motivated Prof B. to show up at a party to which he was not invited, and then to attack the person in whose honor the party was being given? Good question! Ron and I had been studying Aikido for four years by this time, and our new interest was no secret to our friends and colleagues in academia. Perhaps it wasn't about me so much as he thought Aikido was fake, and Prof B. thought he would reveal this truth by making a demonstration of me.

Aikido does look fake especially in demonstrations. It is such a flowing art that its unseen power is often unappreciated until you experience it. O-Sensei had this problem; students interested in tough martial arts (which O-Sensei taught in his early years) were skeptical of O-Sensei's later performances. The late Terry Dobson was such a skeptic. Terry Dobson was an American living in Japan studying with the founder. Terry had practiced with the New York Giants and was a marine, a bouncer, and a huge angry guy. I met him as a much older man, and he told me this story.

During a public demonstration O-Sensei would typically speak to the audience about Aikido while some of his high-ranking students who were suited up and ready to be called on sat in a line on the floor, waiting for O-Sensei to nod their way to summon an attack for demonstration purposes. When that happened, the student he nodded to would spring up and attack O-Sensei, and O-Sensei would demonstrate a throw that was usually unbelievable to see. So unbelievable did these throws look that Terry felt these students of O-Sensei were taking falls for the old man, that they were complicit in a deception.

Not interested in studying something fake, Terry wanted direct confirmation that Aikido was real. During one demonstration Terry was suited up and sitting among the students in line, and he decided to discover the truth. Typically Terry was not one of the students that O-Sensei nodded to (which only fed Terry's suspicions), and so watching closely for O-Sensei to turn toward the student line, Terry didn't stand on ceremony, he rose and took the first opportunity to charge in with all he had. He said it was like hitting a brick wall; immediately he was floored. What O-Sensei was doing was not fake, it was unbelievable! After that Terry went on to help spread Aikido in the United States, opened a dojo in NYC, and even wrote several books on Aikido.

These stories about feigned attacks differ from one another. The dean was clearly bothered but not angry enough to follow through with physical violence. He wasn't going to attack me, but he wanted to intimidate me so, in fear for my well-being, I'd drop the matter and leave; it almost worked.

Prof B. was not perceptibly angry but insincere in that he was not really there to celebrate with me but to take me down a peg. What was false about this situation was his reason for being there in the first place. Thinking back on this moment now, I should have just poured my beer over his head when he first started his "attacks." Messy, maybe, but it might've been enough.

In the Dobson story, Terry Dobson believed O-Sensei's students were engaged in a deception—faking falls for O-Sensei out of respect for him. Dobson was mistaken; the students were not faking! But he had to attack O-Sensei himself in order to feel that energy and discover the truth.

It's not just philosophers who seek truth; I think we all do. Truth makes a difference. *Makoto* is a term that means both sincerity and truth: high values for attacks as well as for people. Attacks that are real are sincere attacks. It is not easy to come by a sincere attack as they take a commitment of energy to produce (remember the dean didn't pull it off). Sincerity in general takes a lot of effort, and so we must notice and be mindful of sincere people.

When training in Aikido you want sincere attacks so that you can practice how to handle them. Of course, at the beginning, attacks can be both sincere and very, very slow to allow you to stay safe while you practice your moves with calmness, but as you proceed and advance in skill level, you want the attack to be faster, so you know how well you're doing.

Sometimes people get the wrong idea about black belts. A student can earn a first-degree black belt rank in about four years. To be given a black belt they need to be actively training and show some comprehension of the technical repertoire of Aikido; the first three black belt degrees are usually about technical proficiency. This varies from school to school. And, although this may seem wholly focused on the physical aspect, a seasoned teacher can see if there is a deeper understanding of Aikido's principles informing the technique. As a student advances to the fourth-degree black belt and above, the focus shifts to these deeper lessons. The embodiment of these deeper lessons is what I'll be talking about in this book.

I remember my own black belts who traveled with me to Japan and were shocked that students there had earned a black belt in a single year! But often those Japanese students were training every day, in every class, instead of a twice-a-week schedule. Every school has its own standards for black belt. But one thing that black belts must cultivate is care for beginners. Often a black belt rank means too much to a person; they forget what it means, and their ego swells. And many, not believing they deserve that rank, take on the self-made challenge to prove they are deserving of it. This usually means they become hellbent on showing how badass they are; perhaps this was operating in the story from the last chapter. But this story does bring home how important getting off the line of attack is to your safety: we want to lose the deer-eyed response to an oncoming attack as soon as possible.

Of course, the next step is to learn how to connect with your partner, how to take your attacker's center, and how to use the energy of the attack to throw or pin them. Aikido presents a practice that can be exhausting for this reason. Attacking from the center takes effort, even when going slow. We always thank our partner for generating the energy they've put into an attack so we can practice our moves. This is part of the meaning to the respectful bow we give our partner at the end of practice. In this way, real, true, and sincere are the highest values.

Ron and I would run an Aikido dojo together for thirty-five years. He kept his professorship at Pitzer College up to the time of his death although instead of walking to class as he would before his illness, I would drive him. Ron even taught at our Mount Baldy Summer Camp the summer before he died. That he was able to find the strength for this is a testament to his Aikido training. I was proud that he faced the end of his life so gallantly—his was a warrior spirit to the end. Even though it's sad to lose someone, I like to reflect on what a wonderful model he was for those of us he left behind.

Our years in Aikido provided us with countless adventures and many deep lessons. We both felt that teaching Aikido students was much easier than teaching our university classes in Western Philosophy. One thing is that while Western academic classes prohibit touching a student, Aikido lessons demand close physical proximity. In an academic classroom, whether something was true could be argued over ad nauseum if a student weren't bright enough to follow an argument, but in Aikido a simple throw would settle the matter without question.

Looking for the deeper lessons in Aikido gave Ron and me much to discover together. It was not rare for us to fall into paroxysms of laughter at small epiphanies. And we learned that taking oneself too seriously was a death knell to truly teaching. Through our lessons, which were peppered with laughter and experimentation, students flourished, and we experienced tremendous happiness.

# FIVE

# Awakening to Makoto
## *The Principle of Heartfelt Sincerity*

> *Around two o'clock in the morning as I was performing ritual purification, I suddenly forgot every martial art technique I ever learned. All of the techniques handed down from my teachers appeared completely anew. Now they were vehicles for the cultivation of life, knowledge, virtue, and good sense, not devices to throw and pin people.*
>
> MORIHEI UESHIBA, *THE ART OF PEACE*

In the last chapter, I described how I began to see the broader applications of Aikido. Initially, it was the physical dynamics of Aikido that produced in me a desire to begin classes with Ron even though I wasn't interested in martials arts or Japanese culture. Certainly I believed Aikido would produce for me the power to set me free from my poorly chosen habit of smoking, and my underlying anger at the world along with it. I relished the feeling of training: those spirals, the continuous movement—so challenging to work with, so fascinating to see and to study—and I could feel the promise of this training when I felt my weight releasing downward toward the center of the universe, and my arms extending out toward the edges of the universe as I prepared my partner for a throw. But this promise I still identified as inherent in physical training alone.

After a while I began to feel at home with the movements of Aikido, and I could enjoy a faster paced practice while keeping my center. I loved training; once stretched out and with warm and bendy muscles, it seemed as if I could go on forever flying across the mat or practicing *suwariwaza* (training on your knees) until I had turned into a puddle on the mat. In fact, I could tell I was becoming proficient at keeping my center when I could get through a civil conversation with my adolescent son when he was behaving at his worst. In fact, Aikido helped me rekindle a strong relationship with him before he left home after his graduation by helping me learn the lessons of patience and openness. But, like all worthwhile lessons, it took a while.

Eager to share my findings, I was surprised that my fellow Aikido buddies weren't interested. They generally disagreed with the idea that Aikido could be an off-the-mat practice at all; they saw Aikido only as a collection of techniques, of martial arts moves. Even when I began to teach Aikido classes, my fellow teachers at the dojo would argue that one is "sensei" during class, but when class is over, and we step off the mat we are no longer "sensei." *Sensei* in this interpretation is nothing more than a person who corrects physical technique. I think my fellow instructors thought that anything else should be avoided at all costs lest one holds themselves up to be a kind of guru. These archetypes seemed to me extreme and not at all what I thought a teacher should be. Of course I've seen teachers who find an ego trip in teaching others, but only the most naïve or needy student would fall for that act. It seemed to me that any sensible person would find teaching a humbling experience, as they try to help another person learn. This does not involve self-aggrandizement at all.

A *sensei* is someone who is a teacher, a guide because they have, as the Japanese language suggests, gone before us. I heard a teacher once explain this by alluding to a sensei on the path before us. So that if we are following a sensei up the mountain path, we might only catch sight of the bottom of their foot as we follow and try to catch up. I thought this was a good illustration of sensei as it bears the reason for the respect for a sensei (that they are ahead of us on a certain path) without getting into the dangerous territory of ego, idolatry, and such. In this way, the sensei has gone before us; they are a sensei because they are ahead of us on the path of Aikido. The sensei of a dojo may have many assistants if the classes are large. And, although an assistant may be ahead of us on the path, we wouldn't call that person "sensei" any more than we would call teaching assistants in a university class "professor." *Sensei* is reserved for those who are even more steps ahead.

And so, to let the title *sensei* go to your head is to be avoided at all times by having humility, which is a large part of the art. But in those early days of practicing an Eastern art with such subtlety as Aikido, there were many misunderstandings and much to learn.

Teaching Aikido to a beginner requires turning back from your own physical training to slow down enough to help another along the way; it is still training, but of a different kind. It is training in teaching, in compassion. Remembering the personal difficulties one encounters along the way only helps to make you a better, more compassionate teacher. You understand how to slow things down without watering them down. So once someone agrees to be responsible for teaching an Aikido class, they do step into the role of a sensei. And most step into this role carrying the duties and responsibilities of a guide and protector for the students they are teaching, as in teaching a student how to deliver an honest attack: whether fast or slow, it should never be empty. Empty attacks, like empty social gestures, are fake, and Aikido does not deal in falsity. Teaching this is usually done by demonstrating an honest attack. But if you deliver an honest attack to the student at a speed they cannot handle, you most likely will injure that student as in the story I told on page 51; this is teaching the wrong kind of lesson. As a sensei, students copy you, and so teachers need to be exemplary all the time, on or off the mat.

No one taught me how to teach Philosophy; I was just led to a classroom and told to go in and teach the class. Of course being familiar with the material and preparing a syllabus were departmental requirements for teaching a class. But these are the formal aspects of a class for which all teachers prepare; it doesn't have anything to do with connecting with the students sitting in front of you. Given a room full of forty students teaching is not easy and the teacher who does it well is the exception (at least in my experience that was so). The task is to draw out a student's curiosity and interest so that you can make a connection with them and bring them along to consider things from a different point of view: in this way changing those opaque marble eyes into bright, shiny eyes. Ron and I used to talk about teaching all the time. He was a wonderful teacher; a brilliant philosopher in his own right, he could also attract a student to the excitement of learning. In a class of forty you're lucky if you can move one or two students in this way. Looking out over the young heads of a class, a teacher can see which ones are awake, receptive, and listening. You can see activity and feel a line of connection. Even from across the room, there is something good happening in the space between you and that student.

## Masakatsu Agatsu Katsuhayabi*

There is a principle you learn in Aikido: *masakatsu agatsu katsuhayabi,* which is often translated as "true victory is self-victory." Among other things, it speaks to the importance of giving an honest response, but let me explain. We might see this principle at work in developing the patience it takes to help a beginner, or to talk to an angry friend; in other words, this principle is about developing the sincerity to work toward your purpose and make it happen. A beginner needs a slow attack to give them time to feel the correct response, with the proper body turn and footwork while keeping their balance throughout. Doing all of this at once can be overwhelming and so giving a beginner an honest attack is to give a very, very slow attack. Even slow attacks can be centered and honest. The point is that while a beginner may not yet

---

*Katsuhayabi* can also be pronounced "katsuhaya*hi*."

have the skill to deal with a spirited attack, an attack that is watered down to the point of a limp arm will not teach them anything useful. A slow attack can still communicate strength and spirit.

O-Sensei was not the first person to think that such training might instill in a student the propensity to do what is right. Aristotle made this same point hundreds of years prior to O-Sensei. Aristotle's ethical system is often referred to as "virtue ethics" because he thought humans should cultivate themselves to be virtuous—in other words, to become someone who naturally does the right thing at the right time for the right reason. Done enough times, a person's virtuous acts will develop a deep-seated disposition to act in a virtuous way. Practice and repetition are how a virtue gets embodied in Aristotle's system. He thought if a person was educated to behave in the proper way, once he developed this disposition, he would spontaneously do what is right, and that this is how you make good people—by cultivating their nature.

As I listened to my Aikido teachers, I began to realize that there were philosophical principles like this one underlying Aikido too. In part, the principles of Aikido are there to help educate students on how to make their Aikido training safer. O-Sensei thought it was important to ask a student who wants to learn Aikido to discover a deep reverence for life, a compassionate outlook, and a spirit of loving protection for all creation.

As the Tokyo school grew, there were many students—Japanese and international—all training together. O-Sensei was not blind to the potential for difficulties given students' experiences with the war that had just ended; after all, he was teaching classes with students from both sides of the war. But to fortify honest training he could bring the principles of Aikido to the forefront of his art, and help students learn something about compassion, self-control, and sincerity.

As I learned about him, I thought O-Sensei was very smart. He didn't write a lot: some poems, diagrams of the universe's energy, and calligraphy—brushwork covering principles he found important. Looking at the various collections of his calligraphy that I have had the pleasure to see, versions of the principle *masakatsu agatsu katsuhayabi* seemed to be one of his favorites as they were among the most prevalent. He would give his calligraphy to his instructors and to promising students. I remember when a teacher gave me a calligraphy, it was a moving moment that summoned a deep dedication as a response. O-Sensei was filmed many times, so we can see his movements. But it is still incredible that without a lot of books and advertising, he attracted generations of young people and foreigners to spread Aikido around the globe. Although he was not a prolific author, he did lecture on and off the mat; he was a good talker. And as much as students just wanted to train on the mat, we are extremely lucky that there were students and others around who either understood what he was saying, or at least knew what he was saying was important enough to write it down.

Over the years, I have heard many Aikido teachers refer to the philosophical principle of *masakatsu agatsu katsuhayabi*. It was explained as *true victory is self-victory*, and after being alluded to, the class would usually go back to Aikido training. Sometimes a teacher would add something more by saying what victory was about, but as an Aikido student in the United States at that time, many of O-Sensei's sayings were captivating but not very well understood. I felt lucky that with my philosophy training, I had resources to fall back on—not Japanese—but ancient Greek philosophers as they too were concerned with many of the things O-Sensei addressed. There is a philosophical maxim—sometimes referred to as one of the three Delphic maxims of the seven sages—inscribed upon the Temple of Apollo in Delphi, Greece, which translates to "know thyself." I will discuss this famous maxim and its relation to O-Sensei's principle below on page 83.

Then much later in my training I learned that this principle was not of O-Sensei's making, but one derived from his studies of the *Kojiki*. Of course, immediately I secured a copy of the *Kojiki* and found that it is a lesson hidden in a fable that drives home the importance of self-control, and the development of a well-rounded and sincere person.

The stories of the *Kojiki* were passed on through the generations until they were recorded in about 700 CE. The *Kojiki* is the ancient book of the cosmogony of Japan, the book that lays out Japan's nature religion, Shinto. I learned that O-Sensei saw the teachings of the *Kojiki* as important. At first, I just thought he was religious, but over time I began to see that rather than writing his own books, he was making use of lessons and principles already available in a written book, which all Japanese were familiar with as a part of their education; O-Sensei was a pragmatist.

### The Cosmogonical Story from the Kojiki*

*There is a couple, Izanagi and Izanami, who are creator spirits. They create the pantheon of* kami *(spirits).† After giving birth to fire, Izanami (female) dies and is taken to the underworld. Izanagi (the male) goes down after her, trying and failing to save her. Afterward we find him performing a water misogi (purification) by the river's edge. He is washing off the stench and pollution of the underworld after his narrow escape from his search for Izanami. During this misogi some important kami are created like Amaterasu Omikami, the Sun goddess who is to rule the heavenly plain (Takamahara), and her brother, Susanoo no Mikoto, the Storm god who is to rule the earthly realm. Izanagi thus sets up the very antagonistic forces whose reconciliation is at the heart of this story.*

*That the father gave to his daughter, the Sun goddess, the heavenly plain, creates a deep jealousy in her younger brother, the Storm god. His jealousy festers. At a certain point, he becomes unhinged and commits travesties against the Sun goddess and the heavenly plain. Among other vile acts, he damages her crops and kills a horse, which in turn kills one of his sister's maidens. These travesties send the Sun goddess fleeing to seek isolation in a cave. But because she is the Sun*

---

*For my purposes here, I encourage those who are interested to read the entire story from the *Kojiki*.

†The Shinto term *kami* is composed of the words for both fire and water, and more specifically means something like energy or spirit.

*goddess, once she pulls the rock across the cave entrance, she deprives the entire world of light, and all is cast into darkness. As a result of all these bad acts, the Storm god is banished from the heavenly plain.\**

*Eventually the Storm god begins to realize what he has done, and he regrets his wanton ways. He wants to atone for his bad acts. He realizes that his sister is important to him, and that a life without her and her help with the cultivation of the earthly plain will make him miserable. He realizes that he needs to meet with his sister to apologize and set things straight. But rectifying the situation with the Sun goddess doesn't come easy. She no longer trusts him. The Storm god's bad acts have left him with an untrustworthy reputation.*

*With much difficulty, he manages to arrange a meeting. The Sun goddess is very suspicious of this meeting because her brother has been dishonest with her before, and she wonders if the meeting is another trick. So she chooses to meet in a remote location, and she shows up—her hair tied up and a quiver of arrows on her back—dressed and ready for a battle with her brother just in case. The Storm god has to convince her that he is sincere, that his desire to see her and apologize is not just another trick. He has to convince her that his apology is coming from his heart, that he is being honest and truthful. The Storm god has to convince the Sun goddess that he is makoto.*

Sincerity is the property of genuine heartfelt truthfulness. To be sincere is to be honest, to not hide or otherwise be false. To be sincere is to reveal your true feelings. So when the Storm god manages to be sincere, he is speaking from the heart; it means he has managed to work out his conflicting feelings and now can be straightforwardly honest. In other words, he is cleansed of his jealousy, which has matured him to value his sister. In the meeting that takes place the Storm god manages to show the Sun goddess his heartfelt sincerity. His display of sincerity actually creates the energy of heartfelt sincerity, which takes

---

*There is a lengthy but famous story, also in the *Kojiki,* about removing the rock from the cave entrance to release the light by drawing the Sun goddess back into the world again.

*Fig. 5.1. The kanji for makoto.*

the form of a kami, and this kami bears the name Masakatsu Agatsu Katsuhayabi Ame no Oshiomimi no Mikoto, which O-Sensei refers to as *masakatsu agatsu katsuhayabi*, an important principle of Aikido. The fable has many twists and turns and illuminating points about relationships and correctness of action, but for our purposes its import is that in the meeting with his sister, the Storm god contributes to the creation of the kami Masakatsu Agatsu Katsuhayabi. He brings that energy of makoto into existence by its very exercise, by his acting with sincerity. In so doing, the Sun goddess was struck by his honesty, by his genuine heartfelt truthfulness.

O-Sensei uses this spirit's name as a key principle of Aikido: *masakatsu agatsu katsuhayabi*. We might translate this as "to see the brilliance of truth one must first cut through the clouds of confusion within," or, "overcome the fighting spirit within your heart," or even, "discover your purpose and then succeed in your mission"—wonderful embellishments on the popular translation of "true victory is self-victory." The story told above is about the power of true heartfelt sincerity.

The brilliance of Truth can be found once we cut through the clouds of confusion within ourselves. Once again, I am reminded of an ancient Greek philosopher. Socrates's dictum *gnothi seauton* (know thyself) points to the importance of looking within. He said that "the unexamined life is not worth living." The aim of self-reflection is to find clarity within so that we are able to appreciate and transmit the truth of reality. And in seeing things clearly, we cultivate a transparency that reflects the truth. This may take a certain amount of internal struggle as our belief system does not always accept new things. Many times we think we clearly understand a situation only to find that our assumptions are wrong; we may have to change our thinking about things. In a subtle way, the epiphany alters our universe.

Reading this story in the *Kojiki* gave me a sudden jolt of realization, as if a thunderbolt shook me out of my slumbers. Not only was this principle named after a kami in the *Kojiki,* but, if my reading of the story was correct, this kami *was* the very energy of heartfelt sincerity that came into existence as a kami at the very moment when the Storm god was demonstrating it! That is, his heartfelt sincerity gave rise to something new in the world: a new kami. His heartfelt sincerity *was* Masakatsu Agatsu Katsuhayabi: the kami itself.

But as exciting as this realization was, it disturbed me greatly: I was told that Aikido was a modern martial art. But now there is an essential principle of Aikido from the oldest spiritual book of Japan: a book full of myths about how Japan and its kami were formed, as well as a book that sets down Japan's indigenous nature religion, Shinto. I understood that Aikido was a modern martial art. Now, after years of training in this "modern" martial art, I faced a conflicting proposition: that the amazing principle of heartfelt sincerity, which is fundamental to Aikido, came from the ancient past.

Of course, I could adjust my understanding about Aikido and view this principle as clarifying Aikido's philosophy. In fact, since I was a philosophy student, I found that wholly acceptable; it even made Aikido more appealing to me. Principles give to Aikido a kind of cohesiveness and meaning that makes Aikido a Way, path, or *do.* The Japanese have a name for a martial arts practice that is technical in nature: *jutsu.* But add to a technical system an underlying principle or philosophy and the whole system becomes a *do,* a Way: So when the founder first taught in a dojo at Ayabe, he called his art aikijutsu; then Aikibudo, then later it became Aikido. I liked that Aikido was a Way; I certainly felt my attitudes changing. Aikido now made a difference to me on a deeper level. But something still didn't sit right: *masaka agatsu katsuhayabi* was not just the creation of a philosophical principle by Aikido's founder but a kami from the oldest book in Japan! If Aikido is not a religion, what is a kami, a spirit, doing at the foundation of Aikido?

I was not interested in studying a religion and so it would be a problem for me if I found I had been studying a religion when I thought I was studying a modern martial art. But in those days, confirmation was hard to come by.

I began to hear the rumblings of ancestral forces enticing me to look deeper. It was time for me to seriously consider the source and learn of Japan's culture and history so that I could discover the truth. I began to learn Japanese. I read many books. I talked to many people. Every step took me deeper and deeper. I became interested. More than once, I interviewed the priest at Kumano Hongu Taisha about this particular story in the *Kojiki*. I still was unsure that one of O-Sensei's principles came from the *Kojiki,* and I wanted confirmation.

The priest said that many people come to the Kumano shrine because they identify with this fable; and he began to convince me that everyday people experience, in their own lives, difficulties not unlike what is described in this *Kojiki* story. The priest went on to say that it is not surprising to find a brother and sister disagreeing and at odds with one another. After some time passes, if the brother sees what he has done, and laments his bad behavior; he may want to make it up to his sister to correct the relationship. The priest emphasized that such problems are common and can be found in most everyone's life experiences. And so, in the case of the story, the task of repairing the relationship, of convincing his sister of his genuineness, of his true heartfelt sincerity is critical. I recalled in my own youth I had to rectify my rash behavior to restore important relationships, and so it made sense to me that such problems were common to the modern Japanese people visiting the shrine today. I finally realized that the story is a teaching moment for everyone, as it is about common everyday problems.

Indeed, in the *Kojiki* story, the elements are exaggerated because they involve spirits, and spirits don't act in insignificant ways. To begin with, there is jealousy, not over something mundane like being passed over for a baseball game ticket, but because of something big like not being assigned the part of the universe you wanted! Also, the Storm god misdirects his anger toward his sister when it is probably his father with whom he should be angry. Put simply, the Storm god is mixed up. Then, his bad acts get really bad; he doesn't just smart off to his sister, but among other vile things he skins her horse, and he kills one of her maidens! So not only did he misbehave in a moment of ire, but he totally derailed, lost it in a big way, and sullied his reputation big time. In the kinds of problems we mortals have, the elements are not usually as magnified like this. But, of course, it is the magnification of the story that helps to illuminate the elements of the problem. This story from the *Kojiki* is an overarching story about taking the opportunity to do the right thing for the right reason at the right time. Most of us can identify with it because it offers inspiration to the usefulness of moderating our own behavior. And that serves us well so that we do not damage relationships by mindless bad acts. And also if we momentarily lapse into bad acts, this story demonstrates how to recover.

There is another loftier reading of this same story, which is relevant here. This brother and sister—the Sun goddess and the Storm god—need to find a way to reconcile the natural antagonism that exists between them. Looking at the antagonism, not as a personal issue but as a cosmic issue, we can see first the antagonism, or opposition, as one between heaven and earth, the two domains that these kami steward. The Storm god finally taking his domain seriously sees the earth as needing the nourishment of the heavenly plain in order to generate life in the earthly realm, while the Sun goddess is completely self-absorbed with her own domain. And so he insists that the Sun goddess share her heavenly nourishment with earth. His insistence takes a disturbing course that causes the Sun goddess to seal herself away in a cave; it also gets the Storm god booted out of heaven. The myriad kami get the

Sun goddess out of the cave, and the Storm god makes his plea to her to meet and reconcile. Showing that he is sincere is what brings about the reconciliation, which results in heaven and earth working together to make earth abundant and to pave the way for heavenly influence to quell the discord on earth. I am told that O-Sensei saw himself as the Storm god sent to quell the discord on earth—which he sought to do by creating Aikido.

Such a reading can be extended to account for the critical place of Love O-Sensei saw in this reconciliation between heaven and earth. We do not want to be in a system where heaven and earth are at odds. Rather, with these two absolute powers caring for one another, and working together, that Love component becomes exemplary.

### Raddie

*In my "Rise and Shine" Aikido class for at-risk kids, there was a little boy (I'll call him "Raddie") who could really cast a dark shadow. He was a rascal of about ten who wanted to fight, was angry at the world, and (as my father would say—maybe about me!) was full of piss and vinegar. Raddie had been thrown out of the schools he had attended—all of the schools. He was at the last school that would accept him, and now he was selected by his teachers to be in my Rise and Shine at-risk kids' program.*

*Raddie could be infuriating, and during one class I sat him out so that he could "find his center." When I sit students out, they are to sit on the edge of the mat until they get a grip (find their center). Their signal to me that they were ready to join in class again was to sit at their center in seiza (sit on their heels). Raddie was whining as he sat on the edge of the mat. I was leading stretches with the rest of the students, and Raddie faced me while the other students had their backs to him. I quietly continued leading the stretches as I observed Raddie militantly untying his white belt (obi), which held his uniform top together, so as a result of this untying, his uniform fell open. Then his militancy escalated, and he rose to a standing position and waved his white belt over his head. My anger began to rise. But that day I reacted to something else: with Raddie's white obi sailing overhead like a white flag, he got my attention, and in that inappropriate gesture I saw that he wanted to be a part of the class. I invited him to join class. My observation was confirmed when I saw how fast his obi was tied around his waist, and almost at the speed of light he joined the line of students sitting quietly on the mat. Raddie began to slowly trust us, and he slowly became almost social. There were still times when he would call other students names. But I observed him once as he heard another student in class call a boy named Joseph "fat." Raddie looked so sad, and I heard him mutter "that's not nice," and then I heard him say something nice to Joseph. Baby steps. At the end of one of my classes I offered Raddie a fresh strawberry from a bowl filled with fruit that had been picked in a local strawberry patch that morning: they were red, gleaming, juicy strawberries bearing the full fragrance of strawberryhood. I found them irresistible and brought them to class. Raddie looked at the strawberries and sneered, "Those have gone bad, they're no good, they need to be green!" I made a deal with him: "Try a bite of this strawberry, and if you don't like it, I'll take it back, no problem." He took a bite, and then like magic the rest of the strawberry disappeared as he gobbled it up. I put the bowl of strawberries on the table nearby and told him to help himself. As I turned to walk away, I saw his hand reaching out for more.*

---

In this simple story, Raddie had honestly said what he believed to be true, that strawberries are best when they're green. And he delivered his opinion with great sincerity. Who knows how he came by this idea: maybe the only strawberries he had been given were ones that were hard and firm and tinged with green from stem to stern. The point is that even though he was being honest, he was wrong about the nature of things—that strawberries are ripe when they're green. Truth can be elusive. Becoming more educated about what's true can involve wonderful experiences, like eating a fully ripe and juicy strawberry straight from the strawberry patch; such a truth is not difficult to swallow.

Sometimes you hear "it may not be true for you, but it is for me" as a defense for a certain set of beliefs about reality that are being challenged. And it's true to a certain degree that one's reality can be markedly different from another person's. How can this be if there is only one reality, one truth? Drugs and certain physical maladies can skew one's perception of objective reality. Put another way, the fact that there is an objective reality independent of what one might see will account for misperceptions as when a drunk stumbles over a wrinkle in a carpet—they did not see it, but it was still there. That is, our own proclivities to see things can be just as unreal as when someone high on a hallucinogen sees pink elephants. Someone who has the proclivity to be fearful and paranoid may see the world in terms of potential attacks. Suppose Max hears disrespect for his mother when his friend says, "I thought your mother looked very nice last night in her party dress." Such an innocent statement might be heard by Max as one with sexual overtones, or perhaps as a sarcastic statement about her weight, or maybe one that questions her morals for being out at night in a party dress. Of course, we wouldn't naturally interpret the statement in these ways, but we don't have the proclivity for protective paranoia that Max seemingly has with regard to his mother.

I'm sure we all have been misunderstood at some point in time. If we're perceptive then we can fix it immediately, and then remember to take better care of how we say things. But if we're not perceptive, such simple misunderstandings can result in unplanned tension or even in an altercation. In making the comment about Max's mother, his friend might not notice that Max has taken great offense at his comment. A conflict that will seem inexplicable may be in store for Max's friend, especially if he gets slugged.

In these days of hypersensitivity, a simple mistake can lead to a tragedy. Someone who has a proclivity to anger may take offense at many things, and if this person carries a gun, the situation can turn dangerous in a flash. So one person's reality may not be another's. But it's important to know whose reality is based on the true nature of things. There is only one truth of the matter. In many cases there may not be anyone in the room who is able to see what's true, but that doesn't mean the truth does not exist. Jupiter may not be observable on a cloudy night, but that doesn't mean Jupiter is not there behind the clouds. When considering a person's frame of mind in making a statement, the truth may be undiscoverable by the information we have at hand; it takes a lot of sensitivity and information to understand another person's reasons for saying things, and to know how closely those statements adhere to reality—a good reason to temper our judgments. But there is a truth there somewhere. In cases of human crimes it is detectives that are given the task of discovering to the best of their ability what really happened. In cases of psychological distress it could be the therapists who can help a person get to the bottom of the matter. There are many reasons why a person may not see the truth. Still, clarity is an end worth pursuing. I daresay that this is why Socrates suggests that we must examine ourselves. This is a common theme with philosophers, and rightly so.

Since the proclivities of Max, in the above example, colored the meaning of his friend's statement about his mother, Max's perception of reality did not match up with his friend's. And if Max hauls off and slugs his friend, their relationship may come to a sudden close. Perhaps Max's proclivity to be overprotective of his mother exists because he had a past experience with a promiscuous girlfriend, and he hasn't sorted out his painful past experience with things as they are now. But the work begins with oneself. For if I can't see clearly then how can I reasonably criticize anyone else for not seeing clearly? And if I can't see clearly, how can I make good judgments? I might look for someone who seems to see clearly, be they a therapist or a wise friend. But if we know we are on solid ground, that we are seeing clearly, it makes it much easier to tell when another person is not. And that information might provide protection to us.

### Truckhead

*Some people are so mixed up they do not see clearly. A person like this came into my Aikido dojo early one evening as I was chatting with one of my senior black-belt students behind the registration counter. I had just finished teaching a class and was taking my time leaving. This man—I'll call him* Truckhead *for reasons that will become clear—entered the dojo and immediately interrupted our conversation by blurting out that he wanted to take Aikido classes. I looked up at Truckhead, but try as I might, I couldn't get a clear picture of him.*

*In most cases when I meet a person the space between us is transparent and clear and it is easy to make eye contact and notice the features of a person's face, like the color of their eyes. But Truckhead was not clearly visible; I could not get a clear image of him even when I looked straight at him; I couldn't even find his eyes in the cloudy nature of the space between us! It's hard to explain but the best I can say is that where his facial features should've been I saw nothing but a kind of blur, a faint image of his facial features all mixed up and ever-changing as if his face were a Picasso painting. It was as if a kind of vibration bomb went off in the space between us and stirred up currents that made transparent perception impossible. I looked at my black-belt student who was beside me. I could see him perfectly well. But when I looked back at Truckhead the hazy perception was still there. I see this as a kind of muddling. Over the years when I meet someone and experience this muddling, I have learned to proceed with care as something unknown is producing the muddle; it could be a strong emotion, and it could be an intent to deceive. For obvious reasons, I prefer not to deal with people who present this way. But sometimes you don't have a choice: I greeted him as a potential student while I became very mindful of every nuance.*

*Truckhead continuously and belligerently interrupted me as I tried to answer his questions. But when his interruptions verged into angry complaints and accusations, I took a moment to assess the situation. I wasn't sure whether he had the capacity to calm down and listen; his intensity and disrespect began to signal danger. And when Truckhead accused me of being involved in a kind of racket to cheat people (as he put it), my optimism vanished along with my patience with and tolerance for his crude conversational style. After all, insulting someone is an attack.*

*In the East there is a tradition of waiting at the gate, saved for people who are not ready to receive the formal training they seek. This was Truckhead to a tee; he was not ready for training at my dojo, and so, in my mind, he could wait outside the gate—which meant outside the doors of my dojo I ended the conversation in an Aikido-like way—by agreeing with him. "Well, it is clear that this dojo is not for you," I said. "I'm sure you'll find a place that suits you better somewhere else. Thank you for coming in. Good-bye." I turned and walked into the mat room to enjoy a few more minutes of the practice taking place before I gathered my things and headed for my car outside. But Truckhead appeared next to me on his knees, apologizing. He begged me to allow him to sign up for classes. What a sudden change. I guessed correctly, as I later learned, that Truckhead tried to circumvent me once I had left the entry room by asking my black belt to sign him up for classes; Truckhead was surprised to learn that he would have to have my permission first. So here he was begging forgiveness. Why would I agree to allow him into classes at my dojo? I could see that he would bring many problems if I did that. He was being dishonest—first accusing me of cheating him, and then with this fake begging asking forgiveness. It was clear he would say anything to get in. And while it is true that we teach people to be honest and sincere when they come in lacking, Truckhead's deception had an aggression to it that signaled danger to me. My thought that he should wait at the gate resurfaced, and I quietly told him that he was disrupting class and must leave. I sat there quietly as he continued to struggle for my attention until he saw that the students in class were beginning to stare at him. Finally, he left.*

*When I decided to leave, I watched for Truckhead. He seemed to me an angry person with a lot of personal issues whom I may have set off—even though that was not my intention. As I stepped out of the light of the dojo and into the darkness of the parking lot tarmac, I was suddenly bathed in the headlights of a truck; a truck had backed into a parking space just for this effect. Its engine was on and roared instantly once I was out in the open. Sure enough, it was Truckhead! Here's someone who can't let things go. He was so upset he couldn't get what he wanted that he had to make a last statement. Even though his truck came speeding toward me, it was easy for me to step back in between two vehicles for protection. It was all drama; Truckhead's tires squealed as he sped off into the night, having had his last word. I never saw him again.*

In this story, Truckhead was an insincere man who was full of fight. From the moment I met him, his presence created a muddled atmosphere: He accused me of cheating students, and then begged me to allow him to train. His "attack" with his truck was just as confused as his verbal arguments; more a gesture of having the final say. In the previous story, Raddie was also mixed up and full of fight. But he was open to the suggestion that he take a bite of the strawberry. And that openness served him well; I daresay his beliefs about ripe strawberries were changed on the spot.

Compare these experiences to one in which an adversary was focused and clear cut.

### Takeout

*After my class one evening, two Aikido students who were also staff members of my magazine,* Aikido Today Magazine, *were hungry. There was a good Thai restaurant just outside the city limits, not too far from the dojo. Going for a bite to eat sounded good to me too, and I knew this place well; Ron and I had frequented it many times, and we even took visiting teachers there. It fit the bill as it was open very late at night, and had good, fresh food!*

*The restaurant staff recognized me when the three of us walked in, and we were quickly seated in a booth in a central part of the restaurant. We ordered right away, and our chopsticks and water were on the table. Sally and I were on one side of the booth, Luke on the other by himself . . . but not for long. Out of nowhere, a tatted and dangerous-looking older member of a local gang—I'll call him Mr. Badass—slid into the seat next to Luke. It seemed from Luke's reaction and Mr. Badass' body position that he had shoved something into Luke's side. He was looking at Luke with a stare that was palpable from across the table. Mr. Badass was not facing me; in fact, he didn't even acknowledge either Sally or me, but there was no muddling present. Sally and I instinctively took our chopsticks in hand as we slid our hands out of sight and under the table. Everything about this guy clearly shouted "danger." He was very confident in himself: he didn't fidget, he had a clarity about him, he knew what he wanted, and he was determined to get it. He was older with many scars, and his manner was calm and smooth. There was no indication that Mr. Badass was in any way altered by alcohol or drugs. He seemed very centered. Looking past Luke I could see that the restaurant staff were all frozen in place with their eyes on our table; in fact, the entire restaurant was suddenly quiet and watching. This perception brought home how much danger we might be in; they seemed to know, and to fear Mr. Badass.*

*He spoke only to Luke. Luke was one of my black belts; he was a friendly guy with great energy. He also was very centered, imaginative, and unflappable. Mr. Badass quietly said to Luke, "Hey man, I need a ride to my car . . . it's just a few blocks from here." Luke did not flinch, but he didn't offer to give him a ride either. Luke remained calm and composed. He responded, "Oh man, we just ordered . . . our food will be here any minute." Mr. Badass seemed a little annoyed that Luke was not panicking or agreeing to go with him. Another seemingly long pause, and intensifying his already palpable stare, Mr. Badass replied slowly, "Hey man, my car is really not too far, you'll be back soon. I need a ride now." This was followed by an even longer pause from Luke who was keeping a very calm demeanor. Luke replied, "Hey man, I'm here with women, it's not cool to leave them alone so late at night. I need to stay here; I'm sure you understand what I mean." At that Mr. Badass removed whatever it was he had shoved into Luke's side, and he said with an almost friendly tone, "OK, man, I understand," and he got up and left as quickly as he had come. We all took a breath . . . in fact, the entire restaurant took an audible breath. Our waitress came over and asked if we were ok. "Yes," I said, "but please make our order for takeout!"*

This bad actor was completely different from Truckhead in the previous story. In the case of Truckhead, I was a seasoned Aikido teacher, and I could tell Truckhead was a problem from the start. If I simply gave up and signed him up for classes just to get rid of him so I could go home, I would have faced a bigger problem down the road as doubtless he would have caused trouble for all my instructors. You can't run a dojo in this careless way, making it easier on yourself in one instant only to push off many more difficulties to the next. How did I know he would be a problem? There was nothing sincere about him. Sincerity is important; if a person is sincere what they say and do comes from the heart, and you can trust what they say. The American judicial system determines this by having people take an oath: what you say outside the court is one thing, but with your hand on the Bible and uttering an oath of truth, it's entirely different. (Of course, if you still lie under oath, you're setting yourself up for very bad things.)

As I noted earlier, Truckhead presented as a muddled, confused, and conflicted person; he didn't really know what he wanted and was flailing around in anger. A real attack is a sincere and honest attack; it is invested with the attacker's commitment to strike. But Truckhead was all bluster, he was full of himself and did not have a good grasp of reality. He was unhinged enough to be dangerous, and without some great institutional power behind me to help in that very moment, I'm lucky I was mindful enough to pick up on it.

Unlike Truckhead, Mr. Badass was as transparent as you can get; he was crystal clear about what he wanted, and he joined our table with intense and focused energy toward Luke. Maybe we looked like easy marks that would follow his demands out of fear. Was he holding a gun against Luke? It seemed his request for a ride was just to get Luke outside where Luke might be robbed, or worse. There were a few wild cards in this situation. But with the honesty of Luke's responses, along with the deliberateness of Luke's respectful delivery, Luke's answers provided the driving force behind the peaceful resolution to the problem. Luke had chosen the correct response for this bad actor, one that was understood and respected. It was a kind of honesty or genuineness and meeting of the minds that happened between them. Luke, who himself was from a background where men are expected to protect their women, was appealing to Mr. Badass's honor as a man. Imagine if Luke had tried to bluster his way with threats and bravado. It might not have gone so smoothly. Honesty has a power of its own that can be felt even by dishonest people. It cuts through all the silliness.

People don't have to operate in these deceptive ways. Conscious deception only happens when a person has something they are trying to hide. In the case of Truckhead, I'm not sure he was consciously trying to hide anything. He may have just been an angry, irrational man who was having a bad night and looking for a fight; maybe his wife left him just before he appeared at the dojo. But, in the case of Mr. Badass, his true motivations seemed dishonorable from the start, and what was alarming was that he didn't care who knew it; he was forthright. But he underestimated Luke. His perceptions of the world were clear as well; once he realized Luke was not falling for his request, that Luke was not afraid and was calling for his respect, Mr. Badass cut his losses and took off. I think I even remember him saying "have a nice night" on his way out.

Honesty is underrated and too often discounted. It isn't shiny and fast like a false promise. But honest people can get things done more easily. I have made agreements on just the shake of a hand. This informal agreement of a handshake used to be more common, but so too were trustworthy people. Have we forgotten how to assess another person? I'm not talking about pedigrees or contracts, but a feeling you get from another person when you meet them. It's something a little different from intuition; it's something that passes between two people.

It is what happens in the space between two people that is important. With Truckhead and Mr. Badass there was palpable discomfort in the space between us, there was much alarming energy, and there were red flags signaling danger. The thought of being in a car with Mr. Badass was terrifying. Mr. Badass didn't smile, and whatever he poked into the side of my student was a clear-cut threat.

Paying attention to what happens in the space between two people is perhaps one of the most important lessons of Aikido. For the beginner, it comes slowly. However, over time an observant student will realize that what is between two people facing one another is not empty space. Maybe you can't see any objects there, but there certainly are energies moving around us everywhere we go. Learning about our physical universe is just the first step to the many lessons available to us with regard to seeing reality. Learning about energy and how that energy manifests forms the deeper lessons of Aikido. Making the energy good between two people is the sign of Aikido mastery.

# SIX

# Honoring the Gems
# of the Past
## *Preparing the Path Forward*

An old philosopher's trick is to foster confusion in a person to get them to listen. Confusion is born of conflicting, incompatible elements in a worldview. And so, when confused, most people seek the comfort of a resolution, and a wonderful learning opportunity unfolds. Now I was confused. I wanted to learn how an art with a kami at its foundation could be anything but a religion. I wanted to know how an art based on something from the ancient past could be viewed as a modern martial art. But finding clarification was not easy.

Although Aikido instructors didn't talk much in class, I had heard instructors talk about the samurai. At first, I blindly tossed it off as a guy thing, a fixation on ancient warriors that fortified their martial arts interest. But instructors would talk about how dressing in our Aikido uniform linked us to the samurai, that the wooden sword (*bokken*) we train with is a replica of the samurai sword, that the staff is even more historical when viewed as a spear like that of Izanagi's when he is creating the world, and that Aikido techniques come from the samurai's sword and staff arts. There even was some talk about how the etiquette and morals of the samurai gave rise to what we practice today as a part of Aikido. Certainly the etiquette involved in handing someone a bokken or jo, or the bows of respect expected at certain—and often numerous—points could be traced back to the rituals of the age of the samurai. But clearly there were more ancestral forces at work besides the ancient book, the *Kojiki*; I knew O-Sensei had studied several sword forms that come from the samurai along with the open-hand techniques he studied with the son of a samurai.

Were there other things from the ancient past that figured into Aikido? I began to look at everything with new eyes. With all my practice in awareness I had entirely missed that the art I had been studying had these hidden aspects operating in plain sight. My refusal to learn about Japanese culture was not helping me to distinguish what was traditionally Japanese from the modern art of Aikido.

Aikido practice kept me physically fit. Ron and I had quit smoking some years ago, and by this time, I had my Ph.D. and was teaching philosophy at a local university, and we were now happily married. But I no longer saw Aikido as just a fun practice with my husband. It was that, but in addition I felt Japan's ancient past reaching through time to transform for me this modern art into an ancient jewel. Where did this notion that Aikido was a modern martial art come from? My study had just begun; I felt I was on a mission.

## Aikido: The Modern Art

For reasons having to do with the presence in Japan of occupying forces after World War II, it was prudent to present Aikido as a modern art without overt ties to Japan's religious or martial past. There were problems with Aikido's having too close an affiliation to Shinto and also to the samurai sword arts. For instance, there was a ban on martial arts. And there was great skepticism about Shinto in general even though it was a particular Shinto sect—State Shinto—to which the government and Emperor Hirohito subscribed. The warrior arts and the link to anything Shinto (like the *Kojiki*) were frowned upon by the Western occupying forces after Japan surrendered in 1945.

In a brilliant move to save Aikido, and to assure its eventual spread around the world, Kisshomaru Ueshiba, the founder's son, in effect westernized Aikido to be more palatable to the West as well as to the occupying forces of the West in Japan already. What I mean by this is nothing deep. To be awarded permission to offer classes, Kisshomaru Ueshiba had to cast the Aikido program he was proposing into a Western mold. O-Sensei's dojo had no dressing rooms and no posted city permit; the training space was connected to his family's living quarters. But Western institutions were run differently: classes were open to the public, students needed to register for classes by filling out forms, the administration had to provide class descriptions, testing requirements, syllabi, curricula, and faculty lists that help make programs and classes transparent. I believe that at this time, techniques, such as that which O-Sensei invariably called *kokyu nage* (breath throw), became codified to make a more complete system. This was a strategy—to bow to the Western occupation's conditions to get permission to move forward in offering Aikido classes to the public. In doing so Kisshomaru was able to keep the doors open and keep the art alive.

It wasn't long after this when the Ueshiba family, headed in this project by Kisshomaru Ueshiba, began to actively spread Aikido worldwide by sending their instructors abroad to teach Aikido. Books were written, and seminars became abundant on distant shores—all to introduce the world to this "modern" martial art. Kisshomaru Ueshiba found a way to keep the dojo open, transforming the educational model of Aikido into something more familiar to the West. We are tremendously grateful for this, of course. And we mustn't lose sight of the fact that he was saving his father's art for the world; more dedication cannot be imagined.

Kisshomaru Ueshiba was a well-read man, educated at Waseda University and designated Executive Director of what is now known as the Aikido Foundation. He did attempt to explain some of the subtleties of his father's view of the world in the books he wrote about

Aikido. In 1984 Kisshomaru published a book, *The Spirit of Aikido,* where he offered a global and historical exegesis of ki in an attempt to clarify some aspects of his father's views. In the streamlining of Aikido, Kisshomaru Ueshiba managed to create an art that was appealing to Westerners while maintaining the central features and a few esoteric aspects of O-Sensei's art—like ki energy, spiral movement, and the philosophy of yin and yang. Kisshomaru Ueshiba was wise. Although Westerners might have benefitted from a deeper presentation, there was the risk that many of these elements might've been off-putting to a Western mind at the time, not to mention the risk of complete censure by the Allied occupation immediately after the end of the war.

Today when a new student joins a dojo it may seem very modern, as most mat spaces are kept clean and uncluttered. Westerners, fascinated by Zen Buddhism, fashion their dojo after Zen's austere aesthetic: polished floors, and a single, simple flower arrangement on the front wall below the founder's photograph. Incense may burn nearby. Classes begin with a traditional bow of respect before warm-up movements. Then students partner up and engage in the technical lessons offered for that class. Western dojos are designed not to distract; it is an important shift from the noisy, busy world outside the dojo door. Aikido instructors when they do talk to the class typically focus on some element of technique: timing, posture, distancing. Deeper lessons might include breathing meditation. For years this is the Aikido I knew, and it was enough for me; that is, there was plenty to digest: correcting poor postural habits, stretching out stiff and overused muscles, finding my center, learning how to quiet myself, and trying to understand strange instructions like "inhale your partner," and "use your ki energy."

## Aikido's Ancient Influences

It becomes evident that in contrast to modern Aikido is the world that gave birth to O-Sensei's art. Almost two centuries ago, life and the beliefs that went with it were very different. In contrast to what I'm calling the modern art of Aikido is the world that gave birth to O-Sensei's art. It was a world of imperceptible energies, kami spirits, sacred swords, strange, winged, long-nosed creatures were said to teach swordwork in the darkness of the mountains, the power of ki energy, the sacred power of sounds, words, and waterfalls, and the belief that with hard training one can become cultivated and transform to the highest form of a human being and possibly even beyond. There was a hint of magical energies too, of time travel, mind-reading, summoning powers greater than we know, and seeing the future. Kisshomaru Ueshiba kept as much of this as he could, but the rest needed to go into the closet to give Aikido the chance to grow with the support of the Western occupying forces and the guarded curiosity of Western people. At that point in time, it would be folly to try to pass by the Westerners talk of the samurai and Shinto. Yet, as we will see, these are two undeniable influences in O-Sensei's world, as his son recognizes in the following passage:

> Aikido is essentially a modern manifestation of the Japanese martial arts (*budo*). It is orthodox in that it inherits the spiritual and martial tradition of ancient Japan, first recorded in the eighth-century literary and historical works, *Kojiki* (Record of Ancient Matters) and *Nihongi* (Chronicle of Japan). This doesn't mean that aikido blindly carries on the tradition of the ancient fighting arts, merely preserving and maintaining its original form in the modern world (Ueshiba 1984, 14).

## The Significance of Origins

One might wonder of what import old stories are to a modern martial art. Isn't the mere allusion to the past enough to sate our interest in origins? Why look deeper?

When my son started his business, which now is very successful, I gave him a framed photograph of my grandfather, a stern but successful Nebraska judge, lawyer, and businessman: we all referred to him as "EB" as his name was Ernest Bert Perry. In those days, without the convenience of an iPhone, it was customary to have formal photographs taken. In this posed photograph of EB he stood impeccably dressed with his no-nonsense command evident, and his intimidating energy seemingly emanating from the photograph, his eyes boring caverns into the viewer's head with a quiet disarming Mona Lisa smile. I found the photograph a little unsettling: it was a photograph that stirs you up even if you don't know and love EB as I do. I gave this photograph to my son as he was growing his business; I thought some motivation from his great-grand-father would be meaningful to him. I was right. I saw that grandad's photo was honorably displayed by my son's work desk, and my son told me that every day he would be stirred into action by EB peering at him from across his small apartment. He commented on it, "I look at EB's photograph, and if I'm languishing on the couch, I get right up and get to work. It's almost as if he's talking to me." Now my grandson, who often visits his father's apartment, comments on EB's photograph as well.

There comes a time, even in the most independent and stubborn young person's life, where it is comforting to know you have a family with a history. It can make quite a difference to a young person's sense of longevity and place in the world. Without family reunions and albums available, a young person may feel set adrift in the world, unattached like a lone ship in a boundless sea. Doubtless why the Ancestry website is so popular, and calls what it does "finding anchors for your soul." Being given a photo of an ancestor is to be given a bigger picture of the world; it makes a person a part of a tribe that has roots in the past, a part of a bigger and older family. With this perspective, a person may feel differently about themselves just by knowing they are a part of a larger family, and not battling the world alone.

For Aikido, photographs of O-Sensei function the same way; an image of O-Sensei gives Aikido a sense of history, direction, and purpose. Moreover, he fits the part especially well for us Westerners: a wise old Japanese man with a white beard. We all love what he was about and point to him with pride because he pins down the beginning of Aikido for us. And so being able to trace the art back to a historical master makes our training seem more respectable or legitimate in many ways. Even if we've never met the man, by being a student of his art we are a part of the Aikido lineage. I'm no longer by myself but part of a larger world community when I look at O-Sensei's image. Many arts and professions are big on lineage, and it's not uncommon when two people meet that a bit of lineage is trotted out to find a connection. It's very common in Aikido circles for students to cite for one another their lineage back to O-Sensei.

Often modern practices come from old traditions, and so they may become more meaningful if we learn about their origins. Such understanding connects us more strongly to what came before. It makes the modern practice more colorful, it gives it texture, and it provides insight. It's time to see how our current practices started, how they came to be as they are from ancient beginnings, and to acknowledge these beginnings unabashedly as a part of our history and thus as a part of the formation of our art. This does not mean that if we discover a religious aspect operating in the origins of Aikido that we must become religious. But religions and Philosophy, although not the same, pay close attention to systems of thought. And Philosophy can appreciate the origins of religion without participating in its dogma. So this is how I'd like to proceed, with curiosity and appreciation for what went before from a wholly philosophical point of view. Now nearly eighty years since the end of World War II, O-Sensei's art in its fullness and depth can be examined.

O-Sensei presents a striking contrast to today's Aikido leaders as he was a man out of an older time, raised in a traditional Japanese culture and vested in the ancient arts, in esoteric practices, and in rituals of the warrior. He could build towns with his hands as he did in Hokkaido, he farmed in Iwama to feed the starving neighbors who took refuge in his Tokyo dojo when they lost their homes in the fire bombings of the war, he traveled by foot over mountain ranges, he fought in wars, and he faced a firing squad in Mongolia. He was at home standing under waterfalls and traveling through the wild spiritual mountains of Japan. How many of these have you done! Life is so different today.

Once established in Tokyo as a teacher, his dojo was attached to his modest family home, and when his dojo and home were bulldozed to make way for the three-story concrete building that is today's Aikido World Headquarters, I am told by someone who was standing next to him at that moment that Morihei Ueshiba watched through tear-filled eyes. His world was being moved in directions that were not comfortable for him. But he was a man who embraced change; he was a man of the moment. Invincible.

The West was once again ushering in significant changes: Tokyo was being rebuilt after the war. Japanese were wearing Western-style clothes. But Morihei Ueshiba continued to wear the traditional clothing of Japan in his natural embrace of the world he knew best. It was clothing that he had grown up with and was comfortable in, clothing from the time in which he flourished. On one of my trips to Japan, I had the pleasure of interviewing Ayako Iwata of Iwata Shokai, the woman who made his Aikido uniforms and hakama, and she said as O-Sensei became elderly, and still dressed in his thick cotton *kosode* (crossover jacket), she would line it with a soft material so that the thick cotton fibers wouldn't irritate his aging skin. He died a very old man in modern times at the age of eighty-six, happy to see his art expanding to the West, for it would take the participation of everyone—peoples East and West—to attain world peace. We're still working on that.

I am told his classroom lectures and public demonstration talks centered on principles illustrated by stories from the *Kojiki,* as he knew their import would help to cultivate people to a higher, more responsible level of existence. And although he was not a prolific writer, he did design some diagrams of how he saw the world, and he wrote some *doka* (poems). In his classes he did not teach in a step-by-step fashion but demonstrated amazing feats that no one has been able to duplicate since, feats that displayed some of the harder-to-understand aspects of Aikido: invincibility, nonresistance, oneness with the universe, even a demonstration that seemed to defy time-space, and a memorable demonstration of horizontal extension with a *jo* (staff) caught on film.

He demonstrated the incredible powers of Aikido, which was always an enticement to young students as they ogled at the possibilities for themselves. His explanations of his demonstrations were of the energetic powers of the universe, and of the kami spirits from the *Kojiki;* he believed that world peace was possible, and he believed that Aikido could deliver it. His calligraphy inspired his students even though they may not have initially understood the ancient secrets present in them. He taught that techniques of Aikido are prayers for peace as well as purification from the everyday filth of this earthly world: Training everyday keeps a person bright and healthy.

> The purpose of Aikido is to elevate ourselves from the world of matter to the world of the spirit. Matter descends, the spirit ascends. Aikido is a wonderful flower that blooms in our world and bears great spiritual fruit. Aikido should be the basis of our lives, and we should strive to establish true goodness, true love, and true sincerity everywhere (Ueshiba 2007).

O-Sensei was a visionary. He enjoyed meeting students from all around the world, and he thanked women for training in Aikido. He was not a bigoted, sexist, foreigner-hating, and bitter old man. He embraced Aikido students of all nationalities, genders, and spiritual backgrounds. My friend, M, who lived in Japan for many years, told me of a class she attended during a bad snowstorm in Tokyo. The trains were not working, but she slogged through the streets to get to class anyway. Besides her, only one male student showed up that day, but there was a group of Japanese women dancers who were staying at the dojo. O-Sensei cheerfully came onto the mat to teach this class of women dancers, along with the two Aikido students who made it to class that day—a rare and unpredictable surprise for everyone! He taught them Aikido and thanked them for studying Aikido too. He brought out a scroll depicting the Sun goddess in an illustrated story from the *Kojiki* and talked about its meaning in support of women.

I believe that O-Sensei saw universal truths being expressed in these *Kojiki* stories. As every Japanese person is part-Shinto, they have heard a certain number of stories from the *Kojiki*. Although O-Sensei was a spiritual man, I see him as someone who used *Kojiki* stories, not for religious indoctrination, but in reference to something already familiar to his students.

## A Comparison of O-Sensei and Aristotle

O-Sensei was undoubtedly a man of Japanese culture and steeped in Eastern traditions, and, although there are differences, he bears some striking parallels to Western philosophers. There is a great difference between the views of Aristotle and those of O-Sensei. For one thing, Aristotle was a prolific writer and so we can read about his views. O-Sensei was not a prolific writer, and he spoke in parables to illustrate his view of things. In order to more deeply understand O-Sensei, we must then study the stories he thought were important to his art. Principles of self-cultivation tend to contain timeless truths; that is why writers from the recent past, like O-Sensei (1883–1969) and distant past, like Aristotle (384–322 BCE), can be relevant to us today. Truth knows no space-time constraints.

Light symbolizes truth because it reveals reality. And since the beginning of time, light has been the ultimate goal for thinkers. We use the phrase "light at the end of the tunnel" for a sought-after destination, or the promise of arrival to a final state; cartoons use lightbulbs as a symbol for ideas; the Statue of Liberty raises her torch to light the way, and her crown with seven sun rays as its aureole further signifies the light of liberty and enlightenment. For the ancients, too, some form of light or truth constituted the final end, the ultimate purpose to life.

Plato, Aristotle's teacher, presents in *The Republic* the Allegory of the Cave, in which he illustrates how we are freed from the shackles of ignorance by emerging from the darkness of the cave into the light. You will see in chapter 9 the description of Fudomyo and how this image of enlightenment, that of freeing oneself from ignorance, is central to

Eastern Philosophy as well. There also is a cave story of Japan's Sun goddess whose very being is light, so when she closes herself off in the cave to retreat from the world, it goes dark. Part of this cave story is the reference to moving the rock aside to reveal the light—that is, moving the rock away from the cave opening (a version of cutting through the darkness), and enticing the Sun goddess out into the world again so that there is light. You sometimes hear an allusion to "moving the rock" in connection to bringing forth the light. In Aikido, it is the sword that reveals the light of truth by cutting through the dark clouds of confusion.

Truth is a very useful quality to pursue, but it can be elusive. You may think that if you are honest and sincere in your description of your feelings, that you are dealing directly with the truth. And while it may be true that you are honestly describing your feelings, it's possible that you still may not be dealing with truth or reality in a deeper sense. Remember Raddie in the strawberry example I used in chapter 5? He initially believed something that was false until convinced by the truth about strawberries. In such cases, then, we learn about the person who is sharing their truth, but maybe not much more than that. The best way to escape ignorance is to talk to an honest person who has a firm footing in reality, for they do not "block the light;" in a sense they are the light. In fact, find a wise person and they will be transparent like a window to truth, with nothing in between like prejudices or preferences that create falsehoods. In this way we might say they are the universe!

And so we can open that closet door to learn more deeply about the origins of our many current Aikido practices. In the next chapter, I will talk about the significance of forests, mountain wizards, energies, samurai, vibrations, and the philosophy of yin and yang. And in the chapters ahead I will describe how the forest was necessary to the practice of becoming a warrior, and the home of the mythic figures known as the fathers of warriorhood: Fudomyo, Sarutahiko no Okami, and Sojobo, leader of the *tengu* (the mysterious winged teachers of sword, and protectors of the mountains). And in chapter 9, I will focus on the traditions of the iconic Japanese warrior, the samurai.

Quelling the discord on Earth was the primary focus of the kami once the Earth came into being. O-Sensei dedicated himself to this end, creating an art he believed could bring world peace if enough people practiced it with the principles of self-cultivation and loving protection for all living things. He provided a practice that would support this. He developed movements that would help cleanse us of everyday pollutants, and he promoted a principle that would help to uncover our natural goodness. Together the human race would have the means to be exemplary stewards of the land, helping to quell discord where it is found. We might explain this world peace as the love that is produced by the reconciliation of heaven and earth working as one. This is the story of the Way of Aikido.

# SEVEN

# The Practice of Purification (Misogi)

## *Slowing Down, Letting Go, and Opening Up*

Many *torii* gates serve as huge entryways to a shrine, although torii gates are found elsewhere as well. Shinto torii gates are often painted red, made of two upright pillars with a rope or at least one cross piece at the top. A shrine may have one gate or many gates leading to it.

Shrines mark the grounds of Shinto, Japan's nature religion; and temples mark the grounds of Buddhism, an import religion originally from India; as a rule, Shinto doesn't have temples, and Buddhism doesn't have shrines, although there was a time in Japan when they were mixed. I have visited many shrines and temples in Japan, and I can appreciate the philosophy behind these religions without being religious myself. This is my orientation in this book.

I find myself thinking a lot about the three gates at Tokyo's Meiji Shrine.*

---

*Whereas shrines are typically dedicated to a particular kami (like the Sun goddess) that is enshrined on the premises, Meiji Shrine is an anomaly as it is dedicated to Emperor Meiji and his wife, the Empress Shoken.

*Fig. 7.1 A basic torii gate.*

The first gate marks the physical entry point—the stepping-off point. Tokyo's Meiji Shrine offers a dramatic example of the stepping-off point as it is literally a step or two away from the urban sidewalk with all its distractions in the heart of downtown Tokyo. And so, to visit Meiji Shrine, you chose to take that step off the urban sidewalk to step onto the wide and light-colored gravel path that is the entrance to the Meiji Shrine. And as you do so you've passed under your first gate, which marks the beginning of your journey to the shrine: the departure from the mundane. And that departure is made all the more dramatic by the contrast of the concrete hardscape amid cars, buses, noise, foot traffic, and the polluted essence of city life with a greenscape just beyond the gravel pathway ahead of you. Right away a noticeable shift happens, and the immovable hardscapes of the city are replaced by a visual field alive with the movement of gentle breezes and the quiet rustling of trees and shrubs as the breeze passes through them. As you move along this gravel path you become part of an organic world. Relaxation occurs as you begin to walk more slowly, to wander a bit to see what's on each side of the path.

By the time you reach the second gate the scenes and sounds of the modern city are hard to remember and impossible to hear. You are deep in green meditation; you have become part of a world that moves more slowly. So slow that you are easily able to appreciate details previously missed: like the striped pattern on a leaf, or the color of a particular insect. It's as if you've been lifted up and transported to a forest. Many forms of shrubs and trees grow there, and there is a rather large pond. And like the populations of birds, butterflies, and insects that you find around the trees and shrubs, bodies of water have their own populations of birds, ducks, fish, and water plants like lotuses, worlds upon worlds of wonder.

If you've been enjoying your walk with a friend, as I was when I was there, your conversation at this point turns to your immediate surroundings. If you were talking about a book you were reading, or a great Indian restaurant you've visited, once under the second gate everything is focused on what is immediately present, you are in the here and now. The shift is that pronounced and yet you may not notice it as a change; it is that subtle. Pronounced but subtle, as if something overwhelming but undetectable has made itself known. Time fades and sophisticated conversation takes on elementary guttural exclamations like "ooh" and "ahhh," as your eyes grow big noticing some new detail emerge from the space around you. A little further on and you begin to see the abundant gravel of the shrine grounds, and the old dark brown buildings rising up under the impressive roof in the clearing. As you walk on you begin to penetrate the layers of shrine buildings searching for the innermost sanctum: the seat that holds the sacred relics.

The third gate is the one that takes you to the heart of the shrine where, for the most part, the sacred energies (kami) are enshrined. And the many shrines I have visited all seem to be breathtaking at this arrival point; you can't help but stand in boundless awe. I'm not sure exactly why but that is the nature of the third-gate state; a deepening of one's awareness. Some of these shrines are thousands of years old, and so the perception of the shrine before you opens doors to the past. Like the photograph of my grandfather EB, or certain photos of O-Sensei—the person depicted comes alive, bringing with them a hint of the mores of the time. You can see it in their dress, the way they hold themselves, and also in the background of the photo. "Old fashioned" we might say; mores change of course but it can be refreshing to be reminded of what the world was like when a historical figure was living. Doubtless why people in modern times visit these historical shrines so often. The history of these structures can transform one's experience to something deeply personal and yet otherworldly. So, the *third-gate state* has come to mean to me "directly perceiving something that is at once in the here and now as well as something timeless." I think of such a thing as perceiving truth.

I have experienced this third-gate state many times, whether it is standing before an inner shrine, or practicing Aikido on the mat where a movement suddenly is so in tune with the world, it is as if you've stepped into a spiral in space. Sometimes I even experience this state while cooking, or gardening, often moments where I allow myself to closely observe or acknowledge the form of life I am handling. This happens in realizing the change in a flower or herb we've grown from a small seed or the earthy fragrance present in the food stuffs we are combining. Even during conversation, a sensation of one moment—be it a sound like a lawnmower you hear in the distance or the tone of your friend's voice—may vividly bring back some element of a past experience. It seems that the third-gate state experience has three necessary conditions: slowing down, letting go, and opening up. Boundless joy is a buoyant feeling where your mind clears, and you know nothing but the moment; you are not cognizant of time, or lunch plans, or who's watching you, thinking of how you might document the experience for publication or how to best take a selfie. Rather, it is clearly and distinctly perceiving the world. O-Sensei's "I am the universe" is a third-gate state. It is such a pleasurable feeling that you don't want to do anything to disrupt it. But once you reflect on your experience, and how not to disrupt it, it is gone. The third-gate state requires complete immersion; being one with the universe is euphoric but fleeting for this reason.

## Forests

In our modern world, we can find epiphanies in urban settings, whether it's sitting alone in a quiet room or next to the clean expanse of a beautiful wooden conference table in the boardroom, or even negotiating the noisy but intelligent chatter of students in a college classroom. There are many places that can support our personal cultivation. Of course, most of us live in urban settings, and so our daily training takes place there. Aikido dojos often provide an oasis of calm from the surrounding urban world even during classes, and doubtless one of Aikido's most attractive elements is the thoughtful design of urban dojos all over the world. Walks to a shrine or even through a park or garden may have to wait for the weekend or a vacation. But a nearby neighborhood Aikido

*Fig. 7.2. Mountains in Yosemite National Forest, California. The National Park Service says it's "not just a great valley, but a shrine to human foresight, the strength of granite, the power of glaciers, the persistence of life, and the tranquility of the High Sierra."*

dojo can offer a temporary respite to an overworked self even if you're not a student there. There were people who would visit my dojo just to sit for a moment. They would sometimes bring a friend. I remember one Karate sensei I knew who showed up with his visiting teacher just to show him the utter beauty of my dojo.

O-Sensei stood in the forest: With one foot in the past, and one in the future, he was a visionary astride time and space. He spent much of his time in forests: working to save trees and shrines, creating a community in Japan's northern region, and training himself much like the warriors did before him. It is clear that he enjoyed practice in nature. There are many photographs of him doing just that, and his direct students have tales about him waking them up and taking them deep into the forests at night to train with a sword. It is not hard to understand why; in such organic settings it is easier to see the universal truths of nature: the spiral nature of water's movement in a stream or sea, and the telltale signs of wind as it rustles through the bamboo leaves. Aikido's movements are the movements of nature, and so where better to learn about them than in their native setting amidst the timeless elements of earth, air, fire, and water. Forests were very important to O-Sensei; and because of this I think of forests as O-Sensei's dojo. His son, Kisshomaru Ueshiba, writes about him:

> The mountains of Ayabe offered an excellent gymnasium for study and practice. The Master selected a suitable place, hung seven or eight sponge balls in a circle under the trees and with a nine-foot practice spear, beautifully thrusted them in turn. His various skillful movements were engraved on the memories of the students at his side (Ueshiba 1978, 153).

Although forests may summon up images of ancient, towering, old growth trees from the distant past, I don't mean to suggest that O-Sensei himself was a relic of the past: O-Sensei's mind was a truly timeless mind. He was familiar with ancient traditions as well as the needs of the future.

*Fig. 7.3. O-Sensei in the forest. O-Sensei would often use a tree as a training partner. He would protect the tree with armor if needed. He didn't go through life mindlessly; he paid attention even to trees.*

My friend M led me to the places that most inspired O-Sensei, and so we were in forested areas most of the time we were in Japan. These were the forests that O-Sensei visited frequently. I was lucky enough to visit the forests of the sacred Kumano mountains, which were the backdrop to his child time home of Tanabe and important sites like Nachi Falls, Shingu's shrines, and of course the ancient shrine deep in those mountains, as well as Mount Kurama, Tsubaki Grand Shrine, and the Ayabe forest near the Omoto kyo grounds. They are all awe inspiring, but for slightly different reasons. Through the Kumano mountains, many make a pilgrimage to visit three sites: Kumano Hongu Taisha, an ancient and most-important shrine, Kumano Nachi Taisha, a shrine next to one of Japan's longest waterfalls, and the red-painted Hayatama Taisha in Shingu. The Kumano mountains are home to the three-legged crow, which is said to be the messenger of the gods. Mount Kurama is the dark forest where the Tengu Sojobo, protector of mountains and trees, lives, and where the saga of Minamoto no Yoshitsune's warrior training begins. Tsubaki Grand Shrine is the place where the earthly kami—and father of martial arts and misogi—Sarutahiko Okami stepped off the heavenly bridge. There is a waterfall for misogi practice available on the grounds, which O-Sensei used many times.

Mountains are regarded as sacred by the Japanese. They are to be protected and preserved from development. Standing in the dappled light of the forest, it is easy to see why. As you enter the forest the scent of cedar trees hangs in the air, and the air itself seems soft and moist from the trees limiting the drying sunlight. Forests are special places, and many people these days go to the forests to experience a "green meditation," a form of relaxation. Doubtless our relaxation is an effect of the abundant oxygen the trees give off as their byproduct. And it's unbelievable that we can enjoy this necessary element while returning to the forest trees our own byproduct and a necessary element of life for them: the carbon dioxide we exhale. What a brilliant symbiotic relationship we share with trees in forests. A recent study, "The Old Man and the Tree," by Jonny Diamond in *Smithsonian Magazine, Science,* found that trees over 150 years old are more effective at absorption than newly planted young trees.

Of course, trees provide shade, which cools us from the heat of summer, some trees provide food, and other trees are good windbreaks. Recently, Jianfeng Zhang showed that a heavily forested area will produce negative ions that have been shown to provide calming properties that help to balance the stresses and pollution of our urban existence (Zhang, 2020).

For this reason, I imagine that is why most brainstorming workshops are located near forests, wilderness areas, or seaside environments even if the workshop planner is not familiar with this research. Forests, wilderness areas, and the seaside are simply pleasant, relaxing places to be. They are the destination of vacationers who already know such locations are good even without the research. The more trees, the better precipitation an area enjoys: moisture attracts moisture. And, of course, trees are home to much wildlife, which provides entertainment and amusement with the antics of birds, butterflies, squirrels, lizards, and so on. Where fields have hedgerows, birds and insects make their homes, and fertilize the plants below.

You may become religious when faced with the beauty of a well-formed old-growth tree. As they become rarer in our modern world, they are all the more treasured. In Japan it is common to find a Shinto rope (*shimenawa*) wrapped around a tree or rock; the shimenawa marks it as sacred (touched by the kami), its beauty a sign of its divinity. The exemplary trees and rocks that are most respected by the Japanese aesthetic reveal an undeniable beauty in some aspect of their physical being: their size, shape, or color. And it is believed that those that possess such extraordinary beauty do so because they possess the kami spirit. Today most countries revere old-growth forests; in California tourists visit the huge redwood forests of Northern California, and the giant sequoias of Yosemite National Park. Such forests help with climate change mitigation. They are considered sacred by most who see them partly because of their uniqueness and age: our world does not support longevity, and so where it's found it seems like a little piece of magic on display. The trees are wondrous beings that have witnessed an ancient past from a world unknown to us. A bristlecone pine, 4,800 years old—which means it was born before the Egyptian pyramids were built—is still alive in California. Their beauty is undeniable although not fashionable as they reveal to us at once the fortitude of their inner spirit and the many travesties they have endured to just live for such a long time. O-Sensei, too, is like these forests with his roots in a distant past. Yet he has created an art like Aikido for the modern world. It was his hope that people would learn to live together in peace and loving respect for the living world.

How is someone who chooses to go barefoot through a forest different from a person who puts on hiking boots? The booted person, by covering their feet, protects themself from some of the elements, but in so doing they inhibit the foot from experiencing the sensations of the mountain floor. In contrast, the person going barefoot is wholly experiencing the mountain floor.

Today there is a movement of earthing and adherents of this way of life argue that the soles of our Western shoes cut us off from nature's vibrations. Moccasins, as footwear, may be a middle ground: they are made of leather and if they are without an additional sole, they enable us to have some foot protection while still being able to receive the earth's energy (those vibrations from nature) through our feet.

It seems impossible to be aware of all of our effects as we move through the world. But like absorbing the earth's energy when we walk barefoot, I can feel many subtle things if I am receptive and not consumed by thoughts of other things. My teacher and I used to talk about how our body is an information tower: We have senses that perceive shapes, colors, sounds, smells, and so forth. We have skin and nerve endings on our appendages to help us receive information. We have learned what kinds of information to pay attention to and what we can more or less ignore. As we become older, this list becomes vast, and items may shift from one list of what we can ignore to another list of what's important.

But our attitude is also critical here. If I view myself as apart from the world and as inessential to it, I will be blind to much of what is going on. Or if I allow myself to become angry not only will that color how the world looks to me, but the energy I put out will be of a certain form. Remember O-Sensei's declaration of "I am the universe": if we absorb and connect with everything and with an attitude of loving kindness we can move peacefully along.

Population growth has placed demands upon how we live. So much of the wildness of the natural world has been replaced by the wildness of urban settings; a deadly trade to be sure. Humans have created vast networks of communication, especially in our urban areas. The city offers us lessons in living with other humans. It can be joyful, and it can be dangerous. Humans have created symphonies and freeways, art museums and educational institutions. We have created laws and governments to enable each one of us to be helped from prejudicial and unjust treatment, and for the most part, we all agree to abide by these human laws. They are our protection from the bad acts of our neighbors. But there is another system that safeguards us, that emerges in times of crisis and disaster, and it comes from deep down inside us. It is the love for one another that shows itself when a stranger is trapped in a burning car, or is injured and cannot walk. You can see love at work when the chips are down, when some deserving person or community needs help and we come to one another's aid. A samurai virtue, benevolence, points to the expectation that a samurai be magnanimous, that they take pity for the conquered and the weak. This may seem a little different from love as it is couched in the reality of social status, but the similarities outweigh the differences: it still involves lending a helping hand to someone who needs it. So preoccupied with making a success of the human experiment, it seems we did not imagine that trees, in their natural forest setting, behave as a community too. Today we are discovering, through the study of forests, that there exist even deeper parallels to our own communities.

In the mountain forests, a community of trees will help one another, not only with healing, but with issues of defense. It has been shown that the mycorrhizal fungi, a symbiotic energy form that exists among and connects the forest tree roots, provides a network of communication that helps one tree distribute healing energies to another tree's damaged root zones when that other tree communicates that it is in trouble. In *The Secret Network of Nature,* Peter Wohlleben found that trees can release toxins in self-defense to ward off insects and other critters, toxins that make insects and critters so sick they do not come back to visit that tree again.

These are just a couple of ways in which we can see the forest as a community of trees in a deeper sense. There are even hints of how tree communities and human communities have a relationship beyond the chemical exchange of gases, and the stress-reducing properties trees have for us: for example, we use their wood for the potential warmth stored inside, we make incense from the bark of fragrant cedar trees for use in our meditation practices, paper has provided safekeeping for our important ideas over the centuries, and even mushrooms—which are often medicinal and nutritious—grow best in the forest. Some of our strongest medicines are found deep in the forests as well. Even our lovely orchids, which we can purchase today at Trader Joe's grocery store, came from the interest of the English aristocrats who collected orchids from the West Indies and Chinese forests in the early eighteenth-century. Humans have had a long and healthy relationship with forests.

Although mountains and forests may exist together, you can only see a mountain vista from outside the forest—but when hiking inside the forest you can enjoy the details of the forest floor and trees. Mountains present incredible vistas that can be especially appreciated from afar, when you see the various peaks rising up from the ground into the sky. Such sights offer an expansive view of geographical landscape, best seen in the daylight. And these perspectives offer a therapy for the over-worked mind of the urban dweller. As a girl from the Northern Plains living in Los Angeles, this was made clear to me every year, as Ron and I headed out for an Aikido camp in the Colorado Rockies each summer. We would drive on the highways of Utah, Arizona, and New Mexico and, although we did visit and train deep in the forested mountains, it was the space we experienced on our drive there that opened before us in amazing vistas that gave us such renewal. Forests are dark places because the trees growing tall block the sunlight, an advantage of faster-growing trees that prevent the slower-growing species from gaining a foothold. For a time I lived in the forest of Mount Baldy (formally known as Mount San Antonio) where you could catch a glimpse of the vista through the trees of the valley below . . . and of course from the top of the mountain. A completely different kind of orientation. I have often wondered if those who have grown up in wooded areas similarly found in later years a relief upon returning to the woods from a time spent in the open plains.

Walking through the forests we can appreciate all the life that is sustained under the canopy of trees: communities of insects, animals, birds, and fungi are well and alive in the forest. While you're in a forest it is difficult to see clearly past your immediate position. In the darkness of a forest, many critters are watching you, undetected, as you move about their homeland. And here, in the forest, the ground is not a hardscape but presents itself as dark and spongy in the filtered light of the tree canopy, so caution needs to be taken for snakes and roots and other things that may off-balance your step. The forest is not static; trees are not just vertical growths that stand without movement like our cement city pillars. There is much movement of smaller branches and leaves when a breeze moves through, and I've even seen tall trees "dance" in a much-needed snowfall, and smile with upturned branches waving in joy after an abundant rain or even an earthquake that sends energy up from unknown places.

## Forest Guardians

On our many trips to Japan, my friend M found in me a willing and eager partner to wander through some of the sacred forests O-Sensei frequented, forests of well-known and protected mountains. Forests where young warriors would go for training, hoping to be educated in the ways of the staff, sword, strategy, and magic by the mountain protectors, the tengu.

Mount Kurama is a popular day trip, twenty minutes by train from Kyoto to Kurama, the little town at the base of the mountain. Once, on our way to spend a day in the forests of Mount Kurama, we stopped off to visit the shrine/temple there—Kuramadera—that dates back to 770 CE. Kuramadera was built to protect Kyoto from evil forces from the north, according to Chinese geomancy. Mount Kurama is known as the abode for gods, demons, and superheroes. And we were initiated into this spooky world by a huge, larger-than-life, red-faced carving with an enormous nose that greets all visitors as they exit the train station.

This face was representative of the tengu said to call Mount Kurama home. The tengu are a fabled type of creature that were said to inhabit mountains—like Mount Kurama and the Kumano mountains—as protector spirits of the mountains and forests. In the ancient world a young man wanting to become a warrior would seek training here, hoping to be educated by the tengu who could impart ancient lessons. Such a creature might teach you swordsmanship and magic as the mythical king and lord of the tengu, Sojobo, did for Japan's legendary warrior Minamoto no Yoshitsune. With a human face, albeit red with a long nose, tengu have the feet of crows and feathered wings. Sojobo is thought to have the supernatural abilities of invisibility, shape-shifting, flight, and being able to see the future, all abilities eyed with envy by young warrior wannabes.

## The Legend of Sojobo and Yoshitsune

*Yoshitsune ended up at Mount Kurama as a baby who was delivered to the temple there to be trained as a monk. His warrior father, who was head of the Genji clan, was killed in 1159 CE by the opposing Taira clan, and so sending Yoshitsune to the temple saved his life. Yoshitsune happened upon Sojobo, who lived in that forest, and an epic training began: Sojobo taught Yoshitsune martial arts, swordsmanship, and magic. Through his training Yoshitsune learned to exceed the limits of human power, and ultimately, he avenged his father's death by defeating the Taira clan. This story has been immortalized by Japan's woodblock artists of the past (and today's anime artists as well), see fig. 7.4 on page 124. O-Sensei was once a young man who practiced with the sword and staff and was familiar with these legends. He also spent quite a lot of time training in the area of Mount Kurama.*

*To spend time in the mountains was an important rite of passage for young men wanting to be warriors, who hoped for an epic training like Yoshitsune's with Sojobo. Among warriors, this is well-known lore: the tale of the battles between the Taira (Heike) and Genji (Minamoto) are on par with the Trojan War as described in* The Iliad. *Moreover, both legends were kept alive by oral history and, in particular, by blind bards who would sing the stories around the fire until they were finally written down.*

*Fig. 7.4. Sojobo (right) instructs Yoshitsune (left) in Swordwork by Tsukioka Yoshitoshi.*

It took M and I all day to hike through the dark forest of Mount Kurama to the little town of Kibune, where we would enjoy filling our famished bodies. From the Kurama temple area we had made our way over the twisted and enormous network of eroded cedar roots that rest in a tangle above ground, but—contrary to expectations—we did not travel in Yoshitsune fashion—jumping over the roots as he practiced his martial exercises to help him develop quickness of foot and balance of body over uneven ground. Nevertheless, Mount Kurama with its legends and stands of cedar and cryptomeria trees produced a wondrous experience for us as we slowly moved through the perfumed but treacherous forest. We passed small temples dedicated to various ancient figures like Fudomyo, patron god of samurai and mountain warriors. (I will talk more about him in chapter 9.)

Of course, there are other forests that drew O-Sensei's interest; one of the forests is in the Kumano mountains, and M and I would visit there every time we set foot in Japan together. O-Sensei's hometown, Tanabe, has a picturesque setting on the shore of the Pacific Ocean where the spiritually mysterious Kumano mountains rise up in protection behind it. What a wonderful place for a young boy to grow up. O-Sensei had spent much time in the Kumano mountain forests as a young man; he is said to have made the journey by foot from Tanabe to the jewel of the mountains: a Shinto shrine called Kumano Hongu Taisha, now a World Heritage Site that is located deep in the range, a hike of about two or three days from Tanabe.

The ancient roadway to the mountain shrine is called Kumano Kodo. It served as an imperial pathway for the famous pilgrimage to the ancient three sites: the shrines of Kumano Hongu Taisha, Nachi Taisha, and Hayatama Taisha. There was a pilgrimage around the peninsula from Kyoto to the Kumano Kodo—there is now a highway close by that most people use—to get to the shrine, probably the most important of the three spiritual sites. Although the imperial palace was at this time in Kyoto, the pilgrimage would walk all the way around the peninsula to avoid going through the dark and scary forests. The imperial entourage incorporated many people, including horsemen, maidens, cooks, and royalty, and the rock paths you see as part of this ancient roadway through the forest creates a new understanding of what happened there so many years ago. They are built with such care: wide and flat to accommodate communal walking and also men on horseback. And where there is an incline the design of gradual steps made easier passage for ladies in formal wear with mosquito netting hanging from their broad-brimmed hats. I found it truly illuminating. But there is a beauty above and beyond this where one can easily imagine the inspiration the ancient roadway gave to those many generations of pilgrims who walked along the path. When I was there, portions of this pathway still existed, including marvelous rock paths and steps in the forest. During the time of my visits the path, mostly blocked by downed trees and storm-strewn vegetation over the years, was impassable. And like most people, I was forced to take the road to the shrine. But today the path has been cleared, and I hear it is very popular with global hikers who flock to the ancient highway to enjoy an adventure hiking an old road among the cedar trees and bamboo groves. Clearing this ancient roadway was one way in which O-Sensei's hometown carved out its economic survival after its youth fled to the urban areas in previous years.

In short, the forests of Japan are where we find Morihei Ueshiba. He adventures through the forest as a young man, wandering deeper and deeper into the mountains. I can picture him hiking to the famous mountain shrine Kumano Hongu Taisha, where his mother prayed for a son before his birth. Many years later, when he was living on the Omoto kyo grounds in another part of Japan, O-Sensei would spend time in the mountains there too. These were the mountains of Ayabe, and my friend M and I, on my first trip to Japan, visited this area, where we were shown to the O-Sensei memorial in the Ayabe mountains.

As you can see, there is much about mountains and forests in the story of Morihei Ueshiba. Besides his childtime romps, you will see that he was politically engaged in a couple of movements that saved mountain shrines and trees, and also led a community of people into the wilderness of Hokkaido to create a town far away from his hometown of Tanabe. And he never let go of the importance he saw in mountain training: as an older man he is said to have led his live-in students up into the mountains in the dark of night to practice swordwork, or in the daytime to stand under waterfalls. In general, these mountains support wildlife like monkeys and wild boars, both of which can be vicious. If O-Sensei didn't meet a tengu, he may have had to discourage a wild beast if he faced an encounter deep in the forest while walking alone.

According to legends, another important kami—Sarutahiko Okami—the father of martial arts, came to Earth in the mountains near the Tsubaki Grand Shrine (where he is enshrined). There I saw a sign by a rock where Sarutahiko Okami is said to have stepped down off of the heavenly bridge—for Sarutahiko Okami was an earthly kami.

The world was much different when O-Sensei was young. Not so long after the reign of the samurai, Morihei Ueshiba's world as a young man would've reflected much of the samurai culture, the lore that comes from the *Kojiki* and the mythology surrounding it. There were warrior icons like Sarutahiko Okami, a symbol of misogi, and Morihei Ueshiba visited his shrine often. In fact, O-Sensei even arranged to have this earthly kami enshrined in his Aiki Shrine, which he built on his property in Iwama quite a distance north from Tsubaki Grand Shrine. Even so, it was so important to him that he arranged for Yukiteru Yamamoto, (95ᵗʰ Guji of Tsubaki Grand Shrine) to make the 300-mile journey and perform the honors of this enshrinement of Sarutahiko Okami in the Aiki Shrine. Rev. Yukiteru Yamamoto Guji would've transported part of the relics of the kami all this way with his entourage of assistants to help with the ceremony. O-Sensei didn't do small things.

Tsubaki Grand Shrine itself is surrounded by hillsides of green tea plants. On my second trip to Tsubaki Grand Shrine, as the bus began the incline to the shrine, I saw the many tea plants thickly growing on the hillside. Closer to the shrine, I saw even more tea plants. I wondered, without finding out for sure, if all the wonderful green tea served at the shrine came from these very plants. For a bus ride, the atmosphere of the mountains surrounding the shrine was most pleasing as it lent a wondrous quality experienced when going deep into nature. At Tsubaki Grand Shrine, after a day of tea ceremonies, interviewing the son of the Guji that brought Sarutahiko Okami's relics to the Aiki Shrine—Rev. Yukitaka Yamamoto (96ᵗʰ Guji of the Tsubaki Grand Shrine)—and experiencing waterfall misogi, I went outside after our dormitory dinner with one of the students to enjoy some fresh air and conversation about all that we were experiencing. Sitting on a stone bench as it became dark, there was a very thunderous, piercing screech, and what sounded like the flapping of enormous wings. Knowing that Sarutahiko Okami, the father of tengu, is enshrined on those grounds helped our imaginations soar. And that is one function of these myths: to open the imagination of people so they may be inspired to go beyond what is commonly accepted and recognized.

## Misogi (Ritual Purification)

*The person who has bad energy and the person who has a fighting heart from the beginning are already defeated. So how can one's bad energy be taken out to purify the heart, making one in harmony with the activity of the entire universe?*

O-SENSEI, "TAKEMUSU AIKI," 1976

O-Sensei said Aikido is misogi. Most definitions of misogi say it is a Japanese Shinto practice of ritual purification, equivalent to *shugyo* from the Buddhist tradition. As we have discussed, misogi is now a modern practice derived from Shinto beginnings, and by practicing misogi, a person's endurance of a prolonged physical effort burns off impurities from within.

In Aikido the term *misogi* is often used for waterfall practice, or some sword and staff practices. O-Sensei thought Aikido training itself was a misogi. Misogi refers to a practice of purification that is usually an intense practice that forges a person's capacity for a stronger center, greater endurance, and improved self-control. In doing so, bad energy and inner conflicts are burned off. So we can talk about misogi as a practice that clears away the obstacles to greater self-cultivation. A common image of misogi is the pounding of the steel used to make a katana (the samurai sword). It takes countless repetitions of folding and pounding the steel, time and time again to pound out the baser elements in the steel so that the blade will be refined. All of these practices of misogi are described as a cleansing because their intense nature dispels the baser qualities that inhibit our cultivation (or the refinement of the steel); they are, in effect, pounded or washed away.

In this book, I am looking at the modern applications of Aikido and tracing them back to the ancient practices that O-Sensei was fond of. Partly by examining where a tradition comes from, we can more deeply understand its meaning and significance. In this way empty forms of tradition are brought to life. Standing under waterfalls is done all over the world by people from many walks of life. It is done for cleansing, and there are many woodcuts of ancient Japanese warriors sitting under waterfalls, probably for the purpose of purification as well as cleaning the body.

As mentioned, Shinto, the indigenous religion of Japan, is a nature religion. Religion in Japan differs a little from what we are used to in the West. In the West, people through their family tradition or by their own choice may subscribe to a religion. But in Japan, most people are both Shinto and Buddhist. Shinto celebrates weddings, while ceremonies for death are Buddhist. It is said that many Japanese see these two religions as providing the ritual ceremonies for major life passages, and not so much as doctrines of faith. Of course there are shrines (Shinto sites of worship) and temples (Buddhist holy places) where religious people can participate in prayer and ceremony. However, Shinto and Buddhism are incompatible at a certain theoretical point, and yet the Japanese have no problem observing both. So, we mustn't get too bogged down in trying to fit these Asian rituals into a Western religious standpoint lest we miss their essence.

Shinto provides the cosmogony of Japan in the texts of the *Kojiki* and the *Nihongi*. It views humans as good from birth. Its philosophy of life celebrates and holds in reverence this very world of nature, sounds, colors, and forms, and it finds beauty as the presence of the divine. The sounds of Shinto are the heartbeat of the drums, its shrines fly brightly colored *noren,** and spirituality is seen in all natural forms as energy or kami. Buddhism, although older, is a foreign import from India, and it is very different in its symbolism and basic beliefs: polished and empty floors, black robes, shaved heads, and silence except for the hollow sound of a bell are well-known signs of this practice, often found in the images of temples. It maintains that we strive to transcend the suffering of this illusory world through meditation through which we

---

*Noren are fabric dividers that the Japanese use to separate spaces. Usually they hang in doorways of shrines as well as in everyday living spaces.

train to cut our attachments to this material world. Although these are extremely simplified characterizations of two world religions, it should suffice to demonstrate their contrasting natures as well as some of the symbolism we see in dojos in the West.

Misogi shows up as a Shinto practice of ritual purification when one of the creator kami—Izanagi—finds the need to purify himself by the river after he escapes from the underworld; he is washing off the putrefaction he encountered there. Izanagi's misogi gives birth to many kami, but most importantly, when he washes his face, he gives birth to the Sun goddess and to the Storm god who we encountered in chapter 5.

But for us mortals, it doesn't take a journey to the underworld for us to need cleansing. Life on Earth is messy and dirty, and so in our everyday activities we inadvertently collect dust, toxins, and a whole slew of filth that begins to stick to our skin and hair; it begins to cover up and dirty our natural material self. News of current events, or just dealing with angry and fearful people, can bring a negative frame of mind to any of us; this is another form of collecting impurities, as a negative frame of mind can color our interactions with others, make us unpleasant people, and hide our natural goodness. In the West we take care of this by cleansing ourselves in a shower or soaking in a bathtub to relax and clear our heads to make us feel better.

So, although misogi is best known from the Shinto stories in which someone practices ritual purification, because it is often practiced under a waterfall, we connect misogi to the forest. Of course, the forest is always inspiring for practices like this. But misogi can happen most anywhere. As I will describe, Aikido has jo and sword misogi that students can practice in a field or a dojo. And let's not forget that O-Sensei thought Aikido practice itself was misogi.

To stay under the cold pounding sheets of water coming off of a mountainside takes a strong center to be sure. And to help find that center once we step under the waterfall it's useful to have a chant to help us focus. In this way, we learn how to find stillness under the pressure of the pounding cold water, and this in turn develops endurance and fortitude. As a result, anger and fear are cleansed away, and replaced with a surge of limitless and boundless energy. This purification practice is called *waterfall misogi,* a practice that is meant to develop the will

*Fig. 7.5. Misogi at Tsubaki Shrine waterfall in Japan.*

or spirit to move beyond the body's comfort zone, to push the student to new capacities of endurance, and to clear away any thoughts of defeat and weakness.

## Waterfall Misogi in California

My good friend, M, took me on my first trip to Japan. We visited the places that were of spiritual significance to O-Sensei. There are photos of O-Sensei practicing waterfall misogi at Tsubaki Grand Shrine and at Nachi Falls, one of Japan's longest waterfalls. And we visited both.

This reminded me of a waterfall on Mount Baldy, down the road from my mountain cabin in California. It is not nearly as long as Nachi Falls, but its last and longest drop is a respectable 150 feet. This seems almost insignificant compared to Nachi's 436-foot drop, but it was enough to help me renew myself through the arduous task of caring for my late husband during the years he battled cancer before his death. It was the one thing I would do for myself every week. On Wednesday morning, I would take my depressed, depleted, and desperate self, get in the car, and drive fifteen minutes to our mountain cabin by the waterfall.

From the small foothill town in which I live you see a mountain range looming to the north, revealing, sometimes until May, a snow-capped Mount Baldy, the crown jewel of the San Gabriel Mountains in Southern California at 10,064 feet. It is part of the Angeles National Forest (established in 1908), which covers more than 700,000 acres primarily within Los Angeles County. Those that take the time to notice this mountain range as they drive along the flatland's roads are given some moments of inspiration. But admiring the mountains from the flatland and being up in the mountains are two different things. It is a different world up there, forested and wild. I love the mountains, and once I moved to Claremont at the base of these mountains, I would find many excuses to be in them: hikes, solitary sitting, Aikido training, or finally living in my mountain forest cabin with a waterfall on my road. Joy.

Once I reached the cabin, I would check my gear for all the needed elements, and then I'd take off walking along the unpaved road behind the forest gate, 6,400 feet high in the mountains. It is a road that ascends gradually to go over the top of Mount Baldy to the desert on the other side, passing through the ski area at its top. No one makes this drive as the road is rough and gated at both ends, and besides the Mount Baldy Ski Area people discourage traffic that is not their own. But, because the road serves as a back road into the ski area, many hikers and skiers do walk it, and I see them coming and going year-round sporting water bottles in the summer and skis in the winter.

But a little way from my forest cabin, there is a hidden and extremely rugged mountain sheep trail that heads in the opposite direction, hugging the side of the mountain as it winds around it. This trail is well-traveled by mountain sheep as well as by humans who know about it. Given the severe weather on the mountain and its overuse, this path is always changing, getting more and more dangerous to pass. At one point, there are only a couple of rocks poking out of the mountainside to offer you a place to step to continue on to the waterfall. With one hand on the mountain side these two steps allow you to round this point to the last bit of path that takes you straight to the bottom of the falls. Turning around this point is frightening, as one misstep or slip will easily take you forty feet down a rocky cliff. But once you round this point you are welcomed by the deafening call of the waterfall and the moist air billowing up around you. Before that turn the denseness of the mountainside muffles the sound completely. Once I spotted a mountain sheep hiding behind a bush when he heard me walking this path.

At the base of the falls the water plays over a rocky field before it forms a downhill stream that ultimately provides well water for the flatlanders below. But being so close to the falls, this water provides wonderful drinking water at my cabin, and so we call it "Mount Baldy champagne." Making your way across this rock-and-water filled field you face a great challenge: maintaining your center while walking on the slippery, mossy granite rocks. And as you close in on the very rocks where the falling water lands, its roar is deafening, and its mist is almost opaque. This is a place where all kinds of creatures come for water. Once, through a fog in the middle of winter, Ron and I stood on the road where the sheep path begins for maybe the last time together there at that spot. It was an overcast day, and we couldn't see the falls because a cloud had moved in to sit right in that basin. I was moved to voice an ancient Japanese prayer (*amatsu norito*) when a beautiful beam of sunlight suddenly came from out of nowhere, parted the fog, and shined down on a creature neither of us could identify at the base of the falls. Then almost as suddenly, the view was gone as the fog filled the basin again. We were provided a glimpse of an amazing sight that was burned into my brain. We never figured out what that creature was, just that it was larger than a human. This is an inspiring place, but it is also dangerous.

Its basin is rocky and so you step carefully. The water is cold and the first time you step under it, that contact on your skin is unexpectedly heavy on your shoulders, sending your center up to your throat, and making your "chant" an awkward high wail before you jump away. But practice makes it easier to stay and stand under the sheets of pounding icy water while chanting, keeping your center strong. The chant helps to focus your attention away from the shock of the cold water, and it helps to build endurance and fortitude. Once I get started, the cold water and its heaviness begin to feel good; it pushes out of me my stress and tightness and makes me feel light and free.

When I head home, I feel renewed. I feel I can do anything. There is an exhilaration to be had once you have been under the falls. A kind of calmness and quiet pervades your entire body. And you are lifted somehow out of the heavy dark energy that stress can so easily produce. That is, you feel the tremendous centering that connects you to the ground below while simultaneously there is a lifting, reaching, or maybe even soaring feeling throughout your entire being like a bird with tremendous wind under massive wings moving upward in the sky. There is no feeling like it! All your worldly cares vanish, and you are boundless.

But there is another feeling that happens here, and it is the feeling that you are one with the universe. It's not a power in the sense of a physical strength, but it is the power to be filled with acceptance, which I take to be the feeling of nonresistance. Difficult as my life was during my husband's illness, I was able to accept it without ill will, without resistance. And by just facing reality in this way it did seem to make things easier to endure. I think without the resistance I was able to conserve my energy to do good and useful things. This misogi would always send me back down the hill being grateful that I could help make Ron's life a bit easier, and comfort him with my companionship. After all, the universe holds within it multifarious kinds of conflicts, which get worked out in one way or another (if we're lucky), but we must never view the universe as rejecting anything; it just is. The sun makes no judgments about who gets light; it shines on every single one of us.

O-Sensei experienced losses in his life too; the death of two sons and, of course, his father. Doubtless he was faced with many hardships as he took on extraordinary missions during his life. But Aikido is an art that is designed to increase a person's capacity to do more if they study sincerely. O-Sensei had a tremendous capacity for accomplishing tough things. Developing the self-reliance necessary to be able to walk the wild and craggy mountains, sleeping and eating in this rugged environment, and perhaps having to face off with wild creatures were some of the capacity-building lessons he came by in the forest dojo early on in his life. But we also see in films and hear from his students about his attraction to teaching them sword and staff work in the mountains as well. Did he come into contact with tengu? One wants to know. In O-Sensei's time tengu were legendary creatures that figured in stories like Yoshisune's. Young men wanting to become warriors would spend time in the mountains hoping to meet a tengu. At least, I like to think he was ready to meet one! And, if he did not, then we can think of this readiness to meet a tengu—being aware and mindful in an environment that held many distractions and that must have been exhausting—as itself a capacity builder.

O-Sensei described a particular moment he experienced as a kind of enlightenment. After defeating a challenge from a kendo master, O-Sensei describes his experience this way:

> I felt that the universe suddenly quaked, and that a golden spirit sprang up from the ground, veiled my body, and changed my body into one of gold.
>
> At the same time my mind and body became light. I was able to understand the whispering of the birds and was clearly aware of the [divine kami], the creator of the universe. At that moment I was enlightened: the source of budo is [divine love]—the spirit of loving protection for all things. Tears of joy streamed down my cheeks.
>
> Since that time I have grown to feel that the whole Earth is my house and the sun, the moon, and the stars are all my own things. I had become free from all desire, not only for position, fame, and property, but also to be strong.
>
> I understood: budo is not felling the opponent by our force; nor is it a tool to lead the world into destruction with arms. True budo is to accept the spirit of the universe, keep the peace of the world, correctly produce, protect, and cultivate all beings in Nature. I understood: The training of budo is to take [divine love], which correctly produces, protects, and cultivates all beings in Nature, and assimilate and utilize it in our own mind and body.
>
> O-SENSEI IN KISSHOMARU UESHIBA'S AIKIDO

Is enlightenment a religious experience? It seems like a silly question to ask. Enlightenment is a moment of complete transformation. Whether you attribute it to a deity or not, it is to experience a life-altering change. Certainly we take an enlightenment experience to change a person for the better. And many train seriously hoping one day they will experience enlightenment.

# EIGHT

# The Way of Protection with Maai

## *Timing and the Power of Distraction*

At first the red-tailed hawk was sitting on one of the two palm trees that tower over the front of my house so I can only see the tops of these tall palms if I am in my backyard. But as if he flew closer for a social visit, the hawk alighted on my backyard oak tree not far from where I'm standing. I always know when he is around by the great shadow that passes over me as he glides by (hawks don't flap their wings like other birds), or by the massive wingspan that catches my eye just too late to see all of him well. And sometimes the crows tell me by their ruckus, which is punctuated by the quiet that descends over the backyard as the squirrels and birds hide from this raptor for good reason. Of course, the critters are hiding from the hawk, not from the crows whose noisy caws are like an alarm for them but a feigned attack to the hawk. This quiet time is not relaxing; it is like the quiet that precedes a tornado as it moves across the Great Northern Plains in the greenish-yellowish sky. Unusual how a great power can be preceded by such stillness.

The crows rain down on the hawk in a burst of activity, cawing and swirling around him. The four or five needle-nosed crows look like the Indian thunderbird drawings as they swoop down toward the sitting hawk. But the hawk does not flinch; he doesn't even seem to register that there's any threat or irritation as he quietly waits in meditative silence for the crow storm to blow over. The hawk is a threat to the crow, and so when a hawk enters crow territory, the crows kick up a territorial fuss. The crows keep this up as long as their energy holds out, and then they retreat. The hawk takes his time, and when it suits him, sometimes forty-five minutes later, he unfolds his massive wings and glides off to another tall tree. And when that happens, when that powerful raptor silently glides away from the yard, birdsong erupts in a kind of fiesta as palpable relief emanating from the trees, and then my little fountain is once again ringed by tiny, yellow-breasted finches singing songs of gratitude for life.

Given our discussion of feigned attacks so far, we could analyze this scene accordingly. The crows are not like the bird police or like the kamikaze: Police would arrest offending perpetrators, and kamikazes strike their mark. I think of the crows as a community warning siren: their noise draws the attention of critters and creatures like me, alerting us that a bird of prey is nearby. But, for all the commotion and dive bombing, the crows do not actually attack the hawk, as the hawk is more powerful. And so the crows offer warning attacks, which are really fake attacks, impressive if only for their agility and perseverance. The hawk has a great center, a pronounced but quiet presence, and the advantage of size and might; the hawk has no reason to be concerned. It is the crows that need to be careful, and they are: they keep their distance, coming close to the hawk in their dive bombs without getting too close. Keeping the proper distance ensures their safety.

## Maai

In Japanese martial arts, this kind of distancing is called *maai*, which denotes the proper distance between me and an attacker. But distancing happens everywhere: birds sitting on a wire equally distanced from one another, schools of fish swimming as a single body, flocks of birds soaring over fields, even the intuitive distance we keep from strangers—close enough for a comfortable conversation but not close enough for discomfort.

I cannot express enough how important maai is. Of course, the martial arts training applications of maai are easy to understand. When a person first begins a martial arts class, it is viewed as special and so lessons of maai seem to present something new to the beginner. But beyond this, viewing how a concept about timing and distancing affects other aspects of life—the space between birds sitting on a wire, or driving in traffic—gives us a much broader understanding of how these martial arts terms function around us every day. And to understand how we may already use maai in our daily lives may allow us to draw on those experiences and make us much more competent in class.

In the case of training, it is easy enough to get the outline—two people training, each a separate entity—but, as all Aikido teachers are aware of, given differing moods, skills, and dispositions, the blend of the two people into one is not easy. Simple again, but not easy. And, of course, nothing is static; everything is changing, and change creates differences in timing and spacing so that the intervals are continually in flux. Practicing how to make the correct adjustments given this dynamic situation is what training is all about.

I remember noticing maai outside of class when I was at an Aikido camp in Colorado's Rocky Mountains. Because the mat was filled with Aikido practitioners, the movement of the class as a whole was rather seamless. That is, the circular whirls and falls that—over time—grew in their intensity and speed still did not result in collisions. But when I went down to town to get a few supplies, a man in the grocery store ran into me with his shopping cart and I was bumped into more than once by others there even though they had much more room in the store than we had on the mat. Clearly, practice and education make a difference. My example illustrates that study of concepts without practice or training alone is not enough to bring one's awareness to our use of space and time; it takes practice and training to become aware of your relationships to others and to things as we move about through space.

I wonder if maai could be a helpful concept in looking at much more mundane considerations like the prow of a boat in the water, the hairs of an ink brush in its bamboo pipe, or a hat on the head of its wearer. Wouldn't maai be at work even when the fit seems tight? If the water did not part when the prow of a boat separated it, travel would be very different. When the glue holding the ink brush's hairs melts or breaks, that ink brush will not help the artist create a masterpiece. And if a hat does not fit the head of its wearer, the wind may easily relocate it.

But one might ask, if maai is a concept that applies to such mundane objects as an ink brush or a hat, wouldn't the concept be so broad as to be meaningless? When I begin looking at the world in terms of time and space intervals, nothing seems to escape consideration. It does seem like a reach to talk about maai and calligraphy brushes, for example. But maai is partly about intervals of space that will always exist to some degree between two categorically different materials. Yet the "fit" of these two materials is what makes a good or bad brush. And it is the fit we're concerned with in Aikido, as the true meaning of the *ai* in *Aikido* is about fit and appropriateness. So it would seem the prevalence of maai would be all the more important. I know I'm pushing the envelope here a bit, but if we're talking about self-protection then noticing where the concrete is crumbling on an overpass might also be important. Here we'd be talking about the poor mix or "fit" of crushed up rocks and water! Maai is not just an exotic term for an element of practice in an Eastern martial art, it is something that exists around us everywhere and so, understandably goes unnoticed. The sooner we become aware of this, the more sensitive we will be to our surroundings. And this has got to be of prime martial arts importance.

It has been my contention that we need to become aware of what is around us, especially those things that are so familiar to us that we've ceased noticing them already. How can this awareness help us? In the case of the connections like the brush hairs and the bamboo pipe—or perhaps the fit of a hat on a head—we don't notice maai perhaps because the fit is so close that the two different substances seem as one. But where the connection or fit is difficult to maintain, it can shed light on the nature of the connection itself; maybe the hat is too small, or maybe the ink brush needs some repair glue before it falls apart. It seems that people who may seem to be prescient in that they fix something before it falls apart—or catch something no one noticed was flying their way—may just be people who are more perceptive than the rest of us. Or in the case of timing, by observing traffic, we can determine how an impetuous person driving a car differs from a prudent one.

A study of this kind ultimately allows us to improve our own practice, whether we're trying to find a hat that fits or make our way through a crowd on the street. When we are participants on the Aikido mat, the practice tests our level of understanding regarding maai. Reconstructing backward—as I've tried to do above—our Aikido practice teaches us how to better observe the world around us.

Then, in terms of maai, everything counts: the observable distance from us to our partner, the quickness or slowness of our partner's movements, whether our partner is holding something and the specific nature of that thing; whether there are prevailing winds, and if so, their direction; whether there are extenuating circumstances such as the visibility of anger in our partner's face or body, or some other liability that might alter the interaction. Just as the observation of a neighboring car's tires being low may affect our decision to remain driving next to them, if we see that our partner's ankle bears a brace indicating potential weakness—or perhaps we see that their bokken is too heavy for them, or that it's broken, or that their grip is in some way compromised—we may alter our attitude and movement.

This is not to say that we take in their information by one sense alone (such as vision), but like an information tower—we may absorb all that we can by being completely receptive to what is around us. It is clearly evident, then, that someone who is distracted or otherwise caught up in thoughts, worries, or emotions will not make a good information tower. But two information towers working at 100 percent can partner up to an incredible and joyful practice.

In practice maai does not begin when you step on the mat, but when you wake up. Once you bow yourself onto the mat (if there are not sweeping or other dojo housekeeping duties expected of you), you typically line up with the other students to be ready for the beginning of class—like birds sitting on a wire. When the sensei arrives, bows to the class, and sets a lesson, the class is set in motion. Constant training with partners affords a wonderful opportunity to study maai to perfect our performance in the everyday world.

An historical picture of maai appears when we consider an early samurai battle between Nobunaga Oda and Yoshimoto Imagawa. In the battle, Nobunaga Oda ultimately overcame the superior army of Yoshimoto Imagawa by using his scouts' discovery that Imagawa's guard was down: he was resting nearby celebrating with only a small fraction of his force. Oda seized the opportunity to get close to the leader. That is, he could win the war by taking out the enemy's leader, and with Imagawa's massive army elsewhere, the probability of a success was increased.

Talking about this as maai might not be a standard interpretation; we would more regularly refer to it as *strategic thinking*. But to use this illustratively as a macrocosm of the microcosm of maai, strategic thinking and maai are similar. Consider another example where maai describes the use of the rising sun at daybreak to—in effect—blind an adversary unthinkingly facing East.

Maai also varies from culture to culture: When the United States began to send diplomats to countries with which we were—at the time—unfamiliar, we found that in some cultures a person stands much closer to another person than we do in this country. These cultural differences sometimes made negotiations more difficult, as no one had a clue what was going wrong in the interaction. It was found that maai was the problem: when one person stepped into a U.S. diplomat's personal space, that diplomat would intuitively take a step back into a more comfortable maai for him, but unbeknownst to him that step back produced a less comfortable maai for his contact, who would in turn intuitively take a step forward to return into what was his comfortable maai—and so the dance across the room began.

Also the importance of punctuality for a meeting differed between cultures causing misunderstandings until the cultural differences regarding time were discovered. Seems like a clear example of maai to me. Once the reason was discovered there were some interesting studies about maai to help our diplomats along. Seemingly subtle aspects of our space-time relationship with another being might be more important than we know.

In Aikido the distance or maai between me and my partner is typically striking distance: that is, the space it would take if I stepped in to deliver a strike or a punch. Prior to this step, neither person can reach one another. When you pair up for Aikido training in class, it is this distance you take when you bow to your partner. Unless a person is familiar with attacks and knows how to deliver a punch or a strike, figuring out how much space it would take to deliver an attack takes some practice. But this soon becomes second nature, so that when pairing up with a partner the proper space is automatically observed. The maai for Aikido may be different from other arts; for instance, judo players start much closer, often holding the lapel of the other person's uniform. But judo is a grappling art, and so their maai is to begin next to one another.

Anyone who drives a car well already understands maai because good drivers know what constitutes the safe distance to keep from another vehicle, and how to maintain that distance between your car and others as you change lanes, catch an exit, and merge amid the constantly changing traffic. In the story above the crows "attacking" the hawk veer close enough to make their displeasure known, but not close enough to violate the hawk's space and cause a fight. They keep the proper maai while they are dive-bombing the hawk. I've seen photos of a baseball umpire and a player locked in this kind of maai: in each other's faces, but not close enough to cause real problems (most of the time). These are both examples of fear at work: the hawk and the umpire hold a power, a threat over the "attacking" crows and an angry baseball player, which prevents the fight from developing further.

The aggression in another's heart accounts for a great many difficulties we experience. Why feign an attack at all? From a "psych out" in a sports match, to straightforward deception in a human transaction, human behavior often involves deceit. People are often capable of talking a good game with no intention of following through. In finance we call such people scammers; in romance they are Romeos, cheats, and players; and in physical confrontation they are called bullies. Such people are imposters; the name suggests falsity and deception. No matter their reason, what they bring is empty, and false. This is to say that what promises or agreements they make do not run deep, and they do not come from the heart. They are not people we can count on.

Of course, we all know there are these kinds of people in the world. Imposters are dangerous and can cause injury to people with their deception, and so identifying them before they do harm is of interest— especially with regard to physical attacks. If I can stay away from a person that is deceptive, I do. For a deceiver is a crazy maker, a high maintenance person. It takes energy to be around people you cannot trust; you must be on high alert at all times. I'm too lazy for this. Still, we don't always have a choice, and you may have a colleague who fits this description, in which case it's best to proceed cautiously. The quote, "Keep your friends close, your enemies closer" (paraphrased from Sun Tzu's sentiments in *The Art of War*) is especially useful. Such crazy-making personalities are good fodder for the movies, but I think we would all rather avoid them in real life. In Aikido terminology, these individuals lack truth and sincerity, or makoto.

## Truth and Grounding

Why is truth such a big deal? Even when there is no issue of deception and two people disagree openly, the truth will settle disagreements—if you can discover it. If your navigator disagrees with the direction you've taken, you're lucky if you have a map, an accepted authority that will settle the matter. Otherwise the disagreement may turn into an argument or a fight, one that might damage the relationship, if not physically harm you. Truth provides a firm ground from which people can agree, actions can be taken, punishments and rewards can be handed out, discoveries may be pursued, relationships can be begun. If there is no truth to be found, if we cannot find agreement, then proceeding is like trying to walk on shifting sands.

So truth provides a firm ground from which great endeavors can be launched. It is like the ground on which we walk: essential. Ground provides us (literally) with a rock to stand on. I was surprised to find under my mountain cabin, which was built in 1929, that one of the main supporting timbers rests on a flattish, large rock sitting on the ground. I was used to seeing the square concrete footings contractors use, and it concerned me until I realized that the mountain is where this rock came from (and probably the basic substance of the cement too), and so my cabin quite naturally was sitting on a rock that was sitting on a mountain: a good paradigm for something very immovable. The post with the weight of the cabin pressing down insured that it would not move anytime soon.

Truth is like this rock; it's something we cannot question, something so intrinsic to our being that, once discovered, we walk and talk from that perspective. If you're not sure about the veracity of what you're saying, you may still be discovering what is true; it can take some time. But once there is no doubt, as in the proposition "I exist," you have found a truth to build on. It functions as conceptual ground, as immovable, as a worldview.

We call "being true" *sincerity*. Whenever I would interview elderly Aikido sensei in Japan, not only was it a year's investment just to set up the physical meetings, but once I was there sitting in front of the venerable sensei, they would put me through more tests; they had no interest in sharing their stories with someone who was not honorable, and who might put their stories to questionable use. And since I was virtually an unknown to them, they were testing me to see if I were sincere. This property of sincerity or truth in a person is, again, what the Japanese call *makoto*. It is extremely important. Someone who is makoto is an honest person who speaks from the heart, and who tells the truth. You don't doubt their word because they are known to be reliable—in short, they are someone you can trust.

Sometimes Aikido instructors lead exercises that ground us, that firmly connect us to the earth's energy—such exercises can help us have both feet on the ground, making us more immovable like a mountain. Such grounding is a sign of being down to earth, or reasonable. Its opposite is to have our head in the clouds, or to be an airhead or spacey. So if you were to hand a sword over to your partner, which would you wish they would be? I would choose that they be grounded in earth's sobering heavy energy rather than "ungrounded" or unhinged. The grounded person's attack may be more powerful, but I would have a better chance of predicting it than I would an attack from a crazy, unhinged person. I would be a fool to give a sword to someone who was not grounded in the ways of the sword.

In the following story, the space that delineates the maai is filled with energy and tension. Also, we see that dogs, too, respond to what is happening in the space "in between."

### Rocket Dogs

*I grabbed my umbrella on the way out the door to take my pup, Ame, for a walk to the nearby city park as it seemed about to rain. As we waited for the streetlight to change, I could hear the two dogs barking from the corner house we had just passed. They were big dogs with deep-throated voices. I had been happy to see they were in a fenced-in backyard when we passed by. Ame and I crossed the busy street with the light and headed down the block. About halfway down the block I noticed barking that became louder, and the unmistakable clipping noise and heavy panting behind me meant one thing: The dogs had gotten out and were coming for us! When I used the world's best self-defense movement, and* turned to look behind me, I could see the dogs running down the sidewalk straight for us; their fur was flying away from their faces, their ears were pulled back to streamline their bodies, and they were moving like rockets down the sidewalk. In the distance I saw the dogs' human run out of his house, but he was still across the street and over a block away, so he was not close enough to grab them, and they were not heeding his calls. There was no one around to help me, and Ame—in her young and innocent mind saw them as potential playmates—was no help to me either. An ugly picture began to form in my mind.

Ame was young but too large to easily throw on my shoulder to flee, and, even if I could've outrun these rocket dogs, I doubt I would have an easy time getting Ame to join me. As I was beginning to consider the fetal position for survival, I remembered a lesson from my Aikido class about keeping calm and allowing other options to open up. And it's true that when we accept too strongly one reading of a situation, we create a kind of tunnel vision where we can see only one possibility. I took a deep breath to calm myself.

Strangely, I found myself turning quickly to face the racing dogs while I held my pup back. I aimed the pointy end of my umbrella right at them, and then, just as all hell was about to break loose, I pressed the umbrella button. WHOOSH! It immediately sprang open to its full size, providing me and Ame with a shield! Not only did it cut off Ame's perception of her new "playmates," but it clearly confused and paused the forward movement of the two oncoming dogs. They were startled! They stopped. They looked around. The sound and sudden diminishment of their visual field stayed them. They had no idea what just happened. Reality for them altered. The pause was just long enough for the dogs' owner, who had been running down the sidewalk like a madman, to reach and get control of them. Once Ame and I were on our way again, I found myself laughing out loud. How the nature of a simple walk to the park can change so suddenly from peaceful to dangerous to comical! Sometimes life is grand!

Recounting my story to my Aikido sensei in class later that day, he said that the umbrella move was also a good example of proper maai: If I had opened the umbrella too early, the dogs, seeing it from a distance, would simply have run around it. To be effective I had to open it at just the right time—just before being mauled and eaten—to startle them and make that sudden movement work for me. Aikido seemed very cool!

When we face another being, we face a living, breathing, functioning entity that puts out sounds, smells, and energy; the space in between us is not empty space. Much is happening in this space, vibrations are going everywhere; it is boundless, even though you may not see it. We may inextricably be drawn to or repulsed by another person, and this may be an immediate and natural response; just by coming face to face with another, a lot of information is transferred. We may not know how to effectively understand this experience, but it's important to figure it out.

### Classroom Chaos

*When I was a university professor, I had just switched campuses to take a part-time post at California State University, Los Angeles (CSULA). I was not new to teaching university classes, as I had completed about eight years at the sister campus in Fullerton. It was the first day of classes and I was assigned to teach an introductory ethics class. Walking up the stairs at Martin Luther King Hall I found my classroom easily enough. But as I opened the door I almost turned around and went home: I saw some young Asian students cowering under their desks because of the ruckus being caused by two loud, large, tattooed men, whose comments, postures, and irreverent remarks signaled their overt disrespect for most everything in their immediate vicinity. They were sitting at desks in the middle of the classroom enjoying the power of scaring young college women. I felt at any moment that their overt disrespect would turn toward me, their petite, young ethics teacher! They seemed angry and I wasn't sure if they had been drinking, but I knew I would be in trouble if I didn't manage to get control of this class right away. I had to avert their attention before they had time to dig* in and ridicule me as the young woman who was going to teach them ethics! Gathering my courage, I stepped inside to take my place at the lectern in the front of the room. I introduced myself.

It was a defining moment: I could see that the men were waiting for my next move and so, looking right at them, I asked if there were a couple of strong guys in class who might help me. They immediately volunteered and I asked them to come up. As these two hulking men stood my inner sage started up. "Are you nuts?" it said. "What are you doing?" I was going to demonstrate an exercise I was familiar with from my Aikido classes. It was true that if I didn't pull this off my class would be lost in mayhem and very difficult to recover. But I shook this defeatist attitude out of my head, re-centered, then filled with confidence I took a breath and welcomed them up. I admired their strong arms, a sure way to their hearts, but I didn't need to rely on deception: they were very impressive arms; these guys looked strong.

There was a practice I learned in Aikido, a demonstration of energy control. It was something I had been tasked to perform in countless Aikido demonstrations being the small woman in our Aikido group. So, with the confidence that I could pull it off again, I instructed these students to lift me up by my arms: one on each side. They had no problem. The first time I let them demonstrate their strength as they could easily lift me up very high. The second time, however, I focused my energy downward so they could not get my feet off the ground. Feeling overly confident, the third time, I again let them lift me high, and while I was up, I focused my energy down and brought them down with me. They just looked at me with their mouths open; they were in disbelief. I thanked them and asked them to sit down. The young women had come out from under their desks and were now sitting with visible relief. The class unified around the surprise of what they had just seen. And in that confused and undefined moment, I said a few inscrutable things about energy and proceeded to teach my class on ethics. Everyone was quiet and very respectful.

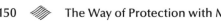

In order for my energy demonstration to save my class that day, it had to happen while everything was still in flux, in order to set the scene and define the class dynamics with me as teacher and them as students. To wait would have given the men time to define their leadership role in class with me scrambling to reassert myself. Doable perhaps but difficult. Distraction is the power an entry can offer; because it interrupts the attacker's focus, it disrupts their energy. Like changing the topic in a difficult conversation that is about to produce fighting energy, distraction can relieve tension by dispelling the energy so it can shift to something else. Such an off-ramp is often also a relief for the attacker, who may feel committed to a certain course of action once it has begun. And so part of maai is timing. And this kind of immediate entry that works to interrupt another's action has a name: *irimi.*

As I exited the room at the end of class, the two men ran down the hall after me. "Professor Perry, Professor Perry, how many years did it take you to learn that?" They were my star students all quarter, they became friendly, and they once even visited me during office hours. I developed a fondness for them.

I am reminded of another story about this sort of thing. An Irish Aikido sensei told me about his encounter with a thief in his Dublin apartment when he returned home at the end of a busy day.

Once he opened the door to his apartment, and caught sight of a thief going through his stuff just as the thief, hearing the door open, looked up at him. "How about a cuppa?" my friend said. And that was the start not only to a good cup of tea shared with an initially scared and off-balanced person, but to a peaceful resolution that could easily have gone another way. I bring this up because it focuses on that initial moment when two people meet. I'm sure my Irish friend was not happy to see that his apartment had been breached, and that someone was touching his stuff with a mind toward theft. But my friend had talents for helping those who were down and out, and so when he opened the door, he saw something else: someone down and out in life to the point of desperation, someone who needed help. And it was this perception that my friend acted on.

We can imagine that critical meeting when the door opened, and all was laid bare: probably the space in between the thief and my friend was full of the thief's fear. We might imagine him wide-eyed and momentarily frozen. When my friend offered a cup of tea, I imagine that the fear was replaced with relief. This struck me as a great story, and one that stood apart from most stories I hear about confronting a thief. Since I first heard that story, I have wondered if, given a similar scenario, I would have the presence of mind to see more than inevitable conflict upon opening the door and catching a thief. We are so programmed sometimes that it stifles our imagination.

These last two stories begin with a person opening a door. What the person sees is telling in terms of their response to the situation. In the case of my classroom, my overriding perception was one of rescuing the poor students underneath their desks by immediately diverting the attention of the bad actors to establish some semblance of order in the room. In my Irish friend's story, his quick focus on changing the room's dynamics was an effective way to calm the bad actor in order to help out. In both cases, there is an embrace of energy in order to change it, to transform it.

I think how we initially react has to do with how we cultivate ourselves. These days it's difficult for most people who watch the news—full of stories of bad actors and innocent victims—to have anything but the anticipation of conflict at the top of their mind. But many people these days are taking control of what they spend their time watching. That is, given the aim of the news, and its off-balanced way of presenting the world, "news fasts" have become popular to ensure a balanced system. This is also true with movies, television, and books. My mother reared me on murder mysteries. But over the years the graphic nature of some of the television crime shows has become difficult for me to watch, especially those based on crimes against women: it turns my stomach and stays with me for longer than the program. Once I realized what I was doing to myself, I signed off from some particular programs altogether. Humans are sometimes portrayed as so monstrous that it's not a surprise that we come to expect bad things from strangers. But if a person orients themself to a more positive perspective, it would stand to reason that their initial perceptions might be more positive too. I find I enjoy the very old shows that now air as reruns; their innocence is refreshing and the material very funny.

Before, I have used the common translation of O-Sensei's principle; that is, true victory is victory over oneself; but another translation of this principle has to do with destroying the aggression in another's heart. And this too describes what happened in the two stories above. The men in my class became friendly when given something they found interesting, and when my Irish friend offered the offender a friendly off-ramp of tea, the conflict and bad acting disappeared. True victory.

Maai especially applies to our interactions with wildlife. As our world overlaps with more and more wildlife encounters, there is talk about more face-to-face meetings between humans and other animals like bears or wildcats. In a case like this it is easy to see the communication happening in what we thought was empty space, probably because fear abounds. They say animals can smell fear and other states of being. Animals, then, are sensing what is in the space between. If the bear or wildcat is hungry or protecting their young, we may be in real danger, especially if we are afraid because fear, as an animal detects it, is an opening for further aggression. Here again, getting control over ourselves so that our initial response is not one of overwhelming fear would serve us well when we meet up with a large frightening animal. Watching coverage about animal life helps to allay these fears; such programs help us learn how to read animal behavior, which is the first step in communication.

But more and more stories are also told of peaceful encounters between humans and such animals. The ancient experience of wolves and humans becoming companionable around the fire gave us our good friends, dogs. Would that we might find our way to more friendly encounters with those who we, today, think are our enemies. It is a way toward living in peace.

## The Technique of *Onami*

Conflict is an essential part of the creation of a wave: water moving onshore meeting with undercurrents moving in the opposite direction provides us with the basic image of the colliding energies of a wave. But nature's resilience is in finding a solution that works to resolve conflict. In the case of waves, where they meet, they don't resist one another, there is no fight. Instead, the meeting of these two forces results in a kind of horizontal spiral, the lifting of shore-bound water up and over the outgoing undercurrents creates a circular movement in the interval, a resolution—a wave. The forces find a way to co-exist, even to create something new out of their combined energies.

There is a technique in Aikido, called *onami* (great wave), that imitates the behavior of a wave. In this technique, a circular movement is used to resolve the conflict of two opposing energies: the incoming attack and a forward entry into the attacking person. Most Aikido techniques are like this and use a circular motion to resolve conflicts. No matter the kind of attack—a punch, a strike, a grab, or an armed attack with one or multiple attackers—the basic recipe is the same. We do not resist one another in training but embrace the energy offered to us. It may sound scary, but slow and sure acclimation to the various types of attacks—which is what training is about—allows one to see the attacks as energy. Here is an example of the power of perception. With this perception, moving out of the way and embracing the energy becomes second nature to a student. Maybe like catching a wave in that a surfer avoids the danger of the incoming wave by riding it so that dealing appropriately with this incoming energy becomes enjoyment.

# Budo

Aikido is a budo, and the first Western translation of *budo* belies our preoccupation with competition, as we translated *budo* as "martial art." But as far back as the fifteenth century, Europeans use *martial* to refer to things pertaining to war or battle. Doubtless because the word comes from the Latin name for the god of war: Mars. And so the die is cast.

It's not surprising that Western scholars, in translating a text, translate it from what they know. Their own cultural perspective does not always get put aside, and so initially texts often have a rather egocentric translation.* And, as we have seen, in the early days of foreign diplomacy, our diplomats would initiate contact with their foreign counterparts without understanding the details of the culture they were visiting. It was still uncharted territory to them.

And so it is not totally surprising that the translation of "budo" gets off to a poor start when the West translates *budo* as "martial art." The stage was set for years of misunderstandings. The translation "martial art" does not do justice to the founder's important message. O-Sensei himself comments on this point, saying:

> . . . martial arts contests are about winning and losing, but this is not the truth of BU. The truth of BU is whatever is absolutely invincible and the absolutely invincible is absolutely not fighting with anything. Victory [katsu] is overcoming the fighting spirit within your heart and accomplishing your mission [of not fighting with anything].
>
> O-Sensei, "Takemusu Aiki," 1976

Clearly O-Sensei's understanding of the etymology for the character *bu* was based on linguistic elements that, when taken together, give us

---

*This happened in the early days with scholars whose faith in Christianity colored the way they translated Plato and Aristotle.

*Fig. 8.1. The kanji for bu.*

"to stop the spear" or "to not fight." Scholars have inconclusively argued about this etymology; even so, as we're trying to understand O-Sensei's views, it seems only reasonable to adopt the etymology he thought was right. So for our purposes, "budo" is "the way of stopping the spear."

Samurai in ancient Japan might be viewed as similar to our law enforcement in that their job was to keep the territory they were protecting safe and free from invaders. And so I'm also drawn to translating *bu* as "protection," which would give us "the Way of protection" as a translation for *budo.*

The *do* in bu*do* means Way or path; it is a familiar kanji found at the end of many names for arts like Aiki*do,* cha*do* (the way of tea), sho*do* (the way of the brush), and ju*do.*\* And so forth. In each of these words, *do* means "the Way." *Do* is a significant concept in that it signifies the idea of a life's path or orientation, as when a person says, "I'm studying Aikido." A serious student of Aikido finds an affinity to the path of aiki, and that is why their study of Aikido is more than just a practice of technique. It's not a religious notion, but it does seem

---

\*Jigoro Kano, an educator, took up the practice of jujutsu (the samurai battlefield fighting techniques) to learn how he could help his students to deal with bullies. Here is an instance of the importance of *do* as Kano's aim was to preserve the principles of maximum efficiency with minimum force, and mutual welfare and benefit he saw at work in jujutsu to form the basis of his new art: judo. Here *do* signifies that the purpose of the art is to practice a principle through a body of technique.

particularly philosophical; the way of aiki requires a person to be honest, sincere, and to not engage in gratuitous violence or deception. And, because it's a Way, or a path, it takes on the seriousness of an attitude, or an outlook on life so that walking this path through life* is part of what it means to be on the path of aiki. In the same way, students of budo are studying the way of protection: how to keep yourself safe but more importantly, how to keep others safe as well. And so, because he says Aikido is a budo we begin to see how O-Sensei saw Aikido as a path that leads to not fighting, a path that leads to protecting peace. O-Sensei says,

> The Way of the Warrior has been misunderstood as a means to kill and destroy others. Those who seek competition are making a grave mistake. To smash, injure, or destroy is the worst sin a human being can commit. The real Way of a Warrior is to prevent slaughter—it is the Art of Peace, the power of love.
>
> MORIHEI UESHIBA, *ART OF PEACE*

---

*The etymology of this character shows a warrior in a headdress walking such a never-ending path.

## NINE

# The Sword of Truth
### *Cutting through the Darkness*

*It is the way of budo to make the heart of the universe our
own and perform our mission of loving and protecting all
beings with a grand spirit. The techniques of budo are only
a means to reach that end.*

O-SENSEI IN KISSHOMARU UESHIBA'S *AIKIDO*, 1978

## The Sword

This chapter is about the samurai sword and how it relates to Aikido
training. The sword is a symbol for cutting through the darkness to
reveal truth or reality.

It took me years to warm up to the sword, perhaps because it is an
obvious tool of violence with many rules about how a person is to move
with, handle, care for, store it, and so forth. Today—nearly forty years
later—I love both the jo and the sword. The sword allows me to demonstrate a movement with a lasting impression: the sword's blade, hilt,
and cutting edge clearly marking a path through an Aikido technique in
a way that helps imprint the movement on the student. That is, because
there are so many protocols with swordwork: the sword is bladed on one
side with a tip at the end, you must hold the sword in a certain way, the

footwork is mandated by the sword strike you want to do, the moves to provide the particular cuts involved can be remembered as a kind of formula. Even when standing with the sword drawn and held before you, the blade side is down, both hands are in use—right hand in front of left— and elbows are kept in. The tip is in front of your vertical center and the sword held a few inches from your body with the tip leveled at the throat of someone (real or imaginary) standing in front of you. Possibly the most difficult part is the most important: your arms and shoulders are relaxed, your body is aligned with your feet under and your shoulders over your center. Eyes are quiet but observing. At camps I would enliven afternoons by creating a kind of sword story, a battle, where a student uses a pre-scribed sequence of sword strikes to move through oncoming attacks by several other students. This is a fun but difficult practice as finding just where the body needs to be at any one time in the midst of the "battle" was challenging especially when on the slope of a mountainside, or atop a large log resting on the mountain floor.

So after many lessons with the sword—how to disarm a sword from an attacker, how to cut properly with a sword, how to use a sword's hilt in practice, and how to practice misogi with the sword—it became more attractive to me. At one point in our training, Ron and I would drive into Culver City to take *iaido* (the art of drawing the sword) classes, but when the teacher called me to take a black belt test in iaido, I declined. I didn't care for this sensei, and I really didn't want any rank from him. Giving rank is like branding a student; they're yours in a way. For a time we followed a Japanese Aikido sensei who held many high ranks in many martial arts, among them Aikido and iaido. In fact, as traditional iaido forms don't look like Aikido forms (iaido moves are often done in suwariwaza and, because it is a whole martial art unto itself, the move-ments are not Aikido movements per se), this teacher became popu-lar with Aikido students because he had put together a system of iaido moves that were Aikido techniques. Also, he was kind. In a seminar up north, I cracked the end of my *saya* (scabbard) with a too-spirited movement right in front of him and I noticed he lurched forward to console me, but then pulled back not wanting to embarrass me. And at another seminar, as we were collecting our things at the end of class, we couldn't find Ron's jo. Someone had taken off with it. Not a thief really (seminars like these tend to leave you mindless and struggling to do even the most basic things like walking, remembering where you left your things). Probably someone just picked Ron's jo up by mistake. But the sensei noticed and when it was decided that the jo was nowhere around, he gave Ron his own.

We immersed ourselves in the sword and its many arms of practice. We were fans of Akira Kurosawa's samurai movies, which include many samurai characters bearing and using swords as well as the movies produced by Katsu Productions that featured Zatoichi, a blind masseur and swordsman. What made these movies attractive to me was the subtle humor used in many scenes. I came to know the characters well and developed favorites by noticing how their swordwork was an expression of their noble (or ignoble) character. Also I noticed that how they carried themselves was an expression of their swordwork. During the college's summer breaks, when things quieted down, we would reserve the Pitzer auditorium for "Samurai Film Night" and draw in quite a crowd; intended expressly for our students at the dojo, there were others who always wandered in to enjoy a free film.

## The Bokken as a Training Tool

On a purely physical level, I found training with a bokken (wooden sword) would tell me where I needed some improvement in my technique. Holding onto and extending a piece of wood out in front of our body adds weight and dimension to our movements, and that extra weight amplifies everything that needs work in the expression of a technique. A great learning tool if your ego can take it. Practicing with the bokken is a way of correcting ourselves with regard to posture. Using your arms to lift it will tear up your shoulder as well as make your lower back very tight and painful; too much of a forward lean and you may hit yourself with your own bokken. Similarly, if you lose focus, a moment's distraction can throw off your timing so that you are more likely to get hit, which is always a problem when you stand too close to another (this involves an understanding of maai). At seminars I often saw poor space management on a crowded mat when an overexcited (or poorly trained) student would let the bokken's tip move too far behind him on a strike and hit the top of another student's head who was training behind him.

Most Aikido students become familiar with the lessons of the sword through practice with a bokken, and in turn, such practice helps us to fine-tune the open-handed Aikido techniques. By polishing our skills of focus and center, bokken practice helps us to cultivate our perspective on a broader scale. Although there are many schools of sword that are distinct from Aikido, bokken is a tool many employ in Aikido classes for the reasons mentioned above.*

As I illustrate in this chapter, the abrupt nature of attacks can bring up our fear, and lack of confidence can make for a real chaotic ordeal. To this end, I describe how various practices with the sword prepare us to endure such unexpected moments with a calm, broadsighted focus.

## *Katsujinken* (Sword to Let Live) versus *Satsujinken* (Sword to Kill)

When I first began training with a bokken, I was taught the distinction between *katsujinken* and *satsujinken:* the former means "the sword to let live," while the latter means "the sword to kill." I'd never thought much about swords, but my teacher thought sword training was critical to learning Aikido, and so we trained a lot with wooden swords. The wooden sword is a replica of the samurai sword (*katana*) in its traditional proportions, and because it's made of wood it adds some

---

*I have good friends who do not use the sword or staff in their Aikido practice.

weight to your movements. There is a lot of etiquette in the handling of swords: how to care for them, how to handle them, how to cut with them, how to draw a sword from a saya, how to return it, and various ways of getting the "blood off your blade" (these movements are vestigial but used as a flourish in returning the sword to its saya. I knew many fellow students who spent a great deal of time figuring out how to make their sword "whistle" when making a cut). And a whole field of appreciation exists for the artwork you can find on antique sword's *tsuba* (handguards), saya, and even *ken* (blades).

The "sword to let live" versus the "sword to kill" demonstrates a lesson in attitude and purpose. The lesson is that a sword is to be used to protect life, not to take life. The same lesson extends to Aikido technique; not one lesson I took over my forty-six-year study urged me to engage in gratuitous violence. But, in order to understand good swordwork, we studied how to make strikes to various parts of a body. It is like a medical student who learns the many ways someone can die in order to save lives, or a law student who in the course of learning to protect people's rights must learn the innumerable ways a person's rights can be violated. Ultimately, the choice to respect and protect a person's life is the intended course of action in these studies, and in medicine and in law, violations will result in the loss of a license to practice. In Aikido, good teachers will refuse to teach those who choose harm over protection. Even so, learning how to protect includes learning how to kill.

Why teach students how to hurt others if you don't want them to? As in medicine and law, to use a discipline effectively you must know its full power—the good and the bad. I suppose you could say that to produce beauty or beautiful things, we must understand ugliness; or for those who disarm bombs, it helps to know how bombs are made. Learning the power of misuse in these areas helps us know what to look for in protecting other people. It is not the subject matter that kills or harms a person, it is another person's intent. Education is not just about technique, but also about proper use.

### Grocery Store Katsujinken

*My late husband, Ron, was a true scholar and could often fit the description of the absent-minded professor; his focus was of amazing proportions but often was directed toward his work more than to the everyday world around him. One winter evening Ron drove up to the neighborhood grocery store to buy some broccoli and paprika for a dish he was making. After he parked the car, and walked up to the front door, he was faced with an angry man jumping up and down in front of him. As Ron approached the door of the grocery store, he was astounded when this man hauled off and slugged him in the jaw. Getting hit in the face is a shocking moment. It can be painful and disorienting even when no real damage is done. But, as a person's whole head is shaken up by the contact, it presents a chaotic moment.\**

*Ron was a gentle six-foot-one man; when he returned home, he told me the story, and how he had spontaneously lifted this man off his feet and pinned him to the cement pillar at the grocery store's outside entrance so that he could talk to him without getting hit again. He wanted this man to quiet down. The man accused Ron of taking his right-of-way near the stoplight across the street from the grocery store. Ron was a careful driver, but I could imagine that he might have unwittingly taken someone's right-of-way if he were lost in thought. Once this became clear to the angry man who was still dangling under Ron's strong grip, he immediately apologized to Ron for hitting him, and the episode ended just in time as the store manager arrived. He had seen Ron lift and pin the angry man and may have thought Ron was responsible for whatever had happened.*

---

\*In fact, it is such a disruptive experience, a visiting Aikido teacher once wanted us to hit one another in the face just to experience it so we would be familiar with that experience. I declined. But I am not convinced that getting beat up in order to learn how not to get beat up is reasonable.

*This meeting could have ended differently if Ron had not acted with calmness and reserve. No one wants to get hit, but typically we know when a strike is coming. If Ron had been more alert to his surroundings, he might have known too. But I was impressed that when Ron did meet with a punch to the face, he handled it so well—he didn't return the punch, for example, and he did not lose his calm demeanor. Ron was strong and fully capable of getting angry; it could've ended badly for the angry man. But Ron had the presence of mind to get to a safe place—which in this case meant holding the angry man off the ground—where he could talk quietly to the man. Both factors helped to resolve the situation quickly.*

*This is perhaps the most important aspect of maai, for when there are problems of conflict there are typically a few moments that figure as the prelude to that moment of conflict. If we are aware of what's happening, we may save ourselves. Doubtless Ron didn't expect any problems on his way to the grocery store, certainly not the angry man who followed him to the shopping center and slugged him. Today we hear of many such incidents that end with someone being shot.*

*So Ron's quiet response to getting hit was to lift the angry man up to quiet him and to talk to him. This is an instance of katsujinken: Ron is an agent of peace in this story. Had he slugged or otherwise injured the angry man, that would've been a display of satsujinken.*

Not all Aikido teachers teach swordwork. Many of our teachers who trained in Japan were not taught with the bokken. Recall that after World War II, when martial arts was banned by the Allied occupation of Japan, it was anything Shinto and any links to the samurai or samurai arts that needed to go into the closet. This meant that there was no swordwork taught in the Tokyo dojo, and so if you trained at Aikido

World Headquarters during this time, as many of our Aikido leaders did, they may not have been trained in swordwork, at least not at the Aikido Headquarters, which was an urban dojo open to the public, another threat to maintaining safety, which I discussed in chapter 2. I am told that the teachers might demonstrate with a bokken, but that bokken were not used in class by students.*

The bokken has many lessons for the beginner Aikido student. As described, once we learn how to balance, to center, and to move from our center while maintaining our balance, adding a sword or bokken will change the physical dynamics of all movements. The student who slowly goes through the motions of learning how to handle a sword, and how to cut with a sword will at the same time practice better posture, good maai, keeping soft relaxed arms, soft eyes, and a strong center. Those who jump in too soon and cut wildly with a bokken may get injured; hitting yourself in the head with the bokken is painful, and hitting another is blameworthy and dangerous. I have seen both. And so the etiquette of handling a sword, even a wooden one, is about caution: never touch the blade, even if it's a wooden bokken. (I've taught many sword classes, and it is uncanny how many beginners will hold a bokken by its blade.) We learn how to handle a real sword by handling a bokken as if it were a sharp piece of steel. And those who practice with a *katana* (steel samurai sword) almost always begin with a dull-bladed *iaito*, as the samurai sword was known for its extremely sharp cutting edge so that learning sword cuts with a live blade poses great dangers. And, like a gun, you are responsible for your sword, especially if it's a live-bladed sword. This is true even when you are not around, as the sword is fascinating and shiny, and it must not be picked up by an interested child or unprepared mind.

---

*I have heard that a particular teacher would come every week and teach sword even though he was not supposed to. Part of this story is that some student would be assigned as a lookout to alert the teacher if they saw O-Sensei coming back to the dojo. In the outlying rural dojo, such as at Iwama, this was not necessarily the case.

That said, practicing with an iaito is not something most students experience in an Aikido class. For a few years, Ron and I took an iaido class in Los Angeles with some other Aikido black belts to see what it was about. The lessons of iaido are in drawing your sword, cutting, and returning the sword to the saya (scabbard). The class was exhausting if only because the energy and focus required was so detailed that one's mind became overwhelmed. For instance, thinking I was doing ok, the instructor would invariably come by, take a look at my body position, and say: "You dead!" Then, with what seemed to me an infinitesimal adjustment to my foot or hand, he'd smile and say, "You live!"

The iaito is much heavier than the wooden sword, and by handling such a sword your attention is called to the importance of the sword-making craft, as an inexpensive sword with poor balance is difficult to use. Samurai held the swordsmiths in high regard and paid them well to make them an exceptional sword: the samurai's sword was their protector, their companion, and their best friend—the friend that might save their life. For the samurai, the sword was their survival. The best swordsmiths were treasured as they were not mere steelworkers but something like magicians! When making a sword, the smiths would shut the doors of their foundry so they could forge the sword in secrecy, bowing in their special uniforms before the small shrine inside the foundry to call down the kami to imbue the sword with the proper protective spirit. Even today the few good swordsmiths left in Japan do not tolerate an audience.

The sword we practice with on the mat is a bokken, the fabric of our hakama is not the silk of a samurai's formal wear, but cotton or polyester, and, unlike the samurai, we don't carry a sword for defense around with us on the streets. (Of course, there are always a few wayward students who get too enamored of the samurai fantasy.) But despite the difference from its traditional role, swordwork can impart critical lessons for the Aikido student. Proper posture and extension allow a student to perfect the way a single cut is accomplished, as the arms must be empty of muscle tension to allow the shoulders to relax into the body, and to allow the movement to come from your hips. Also, the alignment of the sword with your center is critical so that you are moving as one piece—not separate body parts going in different directions. Learning how to do this takes time, and one must heed the guidance given by a complaining lower back and sore shoulders. But with perseverance, proper sword strikes can become effortless, and in turn, contribute to making the techniques of Aikido much easier to perform. Not so surprisingly, these deeper lessons about movement make your everyday life easier as you learn how to use your body more effectively in moving around through space. Swordwork also enhances a student's center by cultivating the awareness and posture to handle the power needed for a quick response to a sudden attack.

## Fudomyo

Fudo shin/fudo tai (immovable mind/immovable body) was presented to me as a principle of Aikido when I began training, and we would use it in practice in every class. Here in this principle of immovable mind, immovable body we are reminded of Fudomyo who, stable as the rock he sits on, is immovable in body. And an immovable mind is not captured by a thinking mind but maintains an unobstructed awareness.

I began this chapter with the distinction between the sword to let live and sword to kill—a beginning lesson about attitude for the Aikido student. The symbolism of the sword is vast in the East, and I'd like to mention a figure I was told was one of O-Sensei's favorites: Fudomyo. Fudomyo (a prominent deity in Shingon Buddhism) is a patron god of samurai and warriors. He is depicted as standing or sitting on a rock while surrounded by flames. The rock imagery shows warriors the importance of standing firm and strong in one's beliefs and being true to oneself. The flames are flames of purification. Fire, by nature, is a kind of cleaner; we use fire to purify the needle we will use to extract a

*Fig. 9.1. Fudomyo, a patron
god of warriors.*

sliver from our finger. Also, we use fire to destroy the bacteria in food
we are about to eat.

But Fudomyo's role is to slay inner demons as well, we all have
obstacles that prevent us from reaching enlightenment. The lotus flower
(a symbol of enlightenment) is often depicted on his head. He holds an
upright sword in one hand and a noose in the other so that he can bind
up and destroy the demons of ignorance. Fudomyo's sword symbolizes
wisdom or cutting through ignorance. We might say he represents purification, a kind of misogi, burning away impediments and defilements,
the barriers to self-cultivation.

*Bushi no ichi gon* (a samurai's word) was sacred because it represented truth. For a samurai, *nigon* (deception or lying) meant death.
And this is why Fudomyo, who cuts through ignorance or falsehood,
is a patron god of samurai. Aikido students often view themselves as
participating in a tradition that came from the samurai, and given the
above descriptions, it's easy to see why.

# Sword Misogi

There is a misogi, or purification practice, with the sword that, in the spirit of Fudomyo, will cut away inefficient body movements to make your cuts pristine; it is like being consumed by flames in that it will heat you up. But in addition to cleaning up sloppy body movements, the misogi—like all other misogi—cleanses our inner self as well. Like being under a waterfall, the stress, the inner conflicts, the bad attitudes we may pick up during a day or a lifetime can be released in a misogi. This leads to the cultivation of our being to a higher level. And we are made stronger and more centered for having practiced it. To complete this misogi takes tremendous fortitude and a strong center. I'm referring to a practice of 1000 sword cuts with a sword. Ron and I would often practice 1000 sword cuts with our students on special occasions. In films of O-Sensei, you can see him practicing multiple cuts with a bokken outdoors or in a forest. Whether he would do 1000 sword cuts is not clear, but the practice of many sword cuts helps a student to learn the essential skills of cutting with a sword.

The *shomen* cut is a vertical up-and-down sword cut, and it is perhaps the most difficult cut to master because the overhead-arm-position required for the strike down is an unnatural movement in certain respects. It is at once simple but not easy to do correctly. There are many details to practice: elbows in, the upper stopping point, the release into a cut-down, and the position of your wrists as you handle the sword. You must never let the wrists break their line, and the "catching" of the sword at the finish of the cut, not to mention how this strike integrates with the rest of the body, is also crucial—as, like all movement, it must come from your center. Our anatomy makes this cut difficult because of the many ways a person can improperly use their body to make it happen, including ways that compromise another part of our body like our shoulders and our back. Lifting with the upper body instead of lifting from our center can overwork the neck and shoulder anatomy and produce stiffness and tightness in the important muscles and ligaments that support our head; this, in turn, can lead to problems like headaches and insomnia. Or overusing your lower-back muscles to lift overhead contributes to tightness in the lower back, which may lead to many maladies like pain, sciatica, and ambulatory problems. It takes time to learn how to move well. We don't come with an owner's manual, but learning how to use the body properly will buy us much in terms of our health and general well-being. Too many of us use drugs to relieve the pain and incapacity of an overly tight body; better movement can address some of these problems more naturally.

Multiple sword cuts help us master the shomen cut as our body tells us when we're doing it wrong; all we have to do is listen and change our movement appropriately. The body is not subtle: If we do 1000 sword cuts using our arms instead of our center, we will not be able to lift our coffee cup to our mouth the next day. Sword cuts may seem like an upper body kind of exercise, but in Aikido all movements employ the entire body, the center being the source of all movement. It took me years to learn that our legs and our arms meet above our waist point, about midway up our spine.

Another lesson to be learned with this 1000-cut practice has to do with our breath and our voice, as someone usually leads the count to 1000. In a class with students cutting in unison, there is usually a shout everyone makes at the same time, at the time of the cut. It is called a *ki ai* and it's a shout that emanates from your center, and rides on your exhale. One of the enticing aspects of the 1000-cut misogi is this sound of everyone moving together, and ki ai-ing together. Like a choir, the mixture of voices into a single communal voice presents a palpable power in the room. For the leader who is counting to 1000—often in Japanese—the focus is demanding and debilitating. The leader can detect the group's fatigue as their ki ais become weaker—usually around strike 400. It is a physical drain to carry a class that has lost their energy, so upon hearing the start of fatigue in the class shouts, the leader has a vested interest in encouraging everyone to engage. Accordingly, they will invest a little more to reap a little more, increasing their own vocal volume or timing of the cuts to wake the students up. Or they may introduce a new pattern to perk up the class. All this without stopping. Toward the end of the 1000 sword cuts, it is the leader's voice that may become fatigued and strained, and at that point, in an intuitive reciprocation, the students join in to support the leader who brought them so close to the end that their motivation to finish pushes them to engage. This giving from both sides unifies the whole and makes the practice inspiring. I often led a 1000-cut misogi when I was feeling conflicted inside about something because misogis are so good and effective at resolving conflict; I always felt buoyant at the end.

Of course, part of this buoyant feeling may have something to do with pumping air through your system when you inhale to bring the sword up, and exhale on the cut-down. There were practices of cutting multiple times on a single breath if you had some breath stamina. Surprisingly, the calligraphy brush is very much like the sword: inhale and raise, exhale, and bring down the brush to paper and stroke. Sometimes you do multiple strokes in one breath. I'll talk about that later.

As we've discussed, although Aikido is a modern martial art, its practices are couched in ancient ways. The Aikido uniform includes the hakama (trousers), the distance (maai) used in open-hand training is sword distance, and even the posture required for throwing arts is the upright posture of a swordsman. When we learn to bow from a seated position, or seiza, it is with keeping the samurai's watchful eye seeking signs of attack as we bow instead of looking down. We also learn how to "walk" on our knees (*suwariwaza*) and do the Aikido techniques from this lowered stance as the samurai were trained to do if caught in the corridors of the palace.

The samurai provide a strong draw to Westerners, especially those interested in sword arts like Aikido. The image of the samurai is one of respect (at one point in Japanese history they were higher than the merchant class), extreme discipline, strength, courage, and loyalty—the image of the true warrior. Aspects of samurai life that most support this image are the composure and quiet but deadly and watchful eye they used as they moved through life. The high-position samurai had dedicated their life to their warlord, and so they didn't have time to attend their child's birthday party if indeed they even had a family. When you are loyal to this degree you do not load your life up with other attachments or commitments. And so the dedicated and loyal samurai strives to stay in the moment and not to get attached to other relationships or material objects. He had dedicated himself to protect.

Each samurai knew their place as boundaries were extraordinarily important: in battle a samurai would pair up with a similarly ranked fighter from the opposing side. And their failures to impeccably observe boundaries often resulted in ritual suicide (*hara kiri*, "gut cutting") as, in shame and reparation, they would take their own lives in a ceremonial display of apology. Rogue fighters were not tolerated in a warlord's regime. Their life was dedicated to the warlord, and that job of protection was their only mission in life. Of course, this was the ideal samurai—but I'm willing to bet that some lived up to it.

*Fig. 9.2. The kanji for do
(the Way).*

Today we don't pledge our loyalty to a warlord, but to principles that outline a way of life—like living with loving protection for all living things or knowing that true victory involves clearing the hatred from our heart. Committing ourselves to a life with honorable principles is, then, itself a way.

Katsujinken (sword to let live) and satsujinken (sword to kill) present a worthwhile distinction for Aikido students to understand because Aikido students are not vested with the powers to protect by killing, as the samurai were. And I daresay that our current issues with firearms and law enforcement are probably similar to issues with the samurai during this era. While the issues around practice are a little different for Aikido students today, because we do learn skills that when put to bad use can injure others, this distinction still helps to frame the practice with the proper mindset or attitude.

The cherry blossom signifies the life-and-death nature of being a samurai. Like the fighting skills of a samurai, the cherry tree takes time and effort to grow and produce a flower bud. It opens to much public celebration, shows its best display of beauty, and then suddenly falls to its end. This is emblematic of a samurai in that they train to perfect their skills, doing their best to celebrate their skills in battle, displaying all that their training has produced, only to face being cut down in battle if their luck runs out. We might see in this a lesson about being aware or mindful of each moment as if it were our last. As I said above, a samurai was to shun attachments as with martial arts training and participating in battles, samurai had little time to build a family. And so we can imagine that this lifestyle was the epitome of living in the here and now.

The tea ceremony is strongly tied to the samurai for this reason. The tea ceremony comes from the Zen tradition and is meant to celebrate life by celebrating a moment. The tea ceremony is a meeting with a motto: *ichi go ichi e* (one moment, one meeting). The saying captures the importance of celebrating the moment, the here and now. Even though the line of tea masters were Buddhist, approaching a tea house has similarities to approaching a shrine: the gravel path takes the guest to predesignated points of beauty—a tree or a flower—as its design twists and turns toward the tea hut. There often is a waiting place, a simple structure with a built-in bench, where you can sit until called by the tea master. The traditional tea house is a simple hut with a small entry door that a samurai would have to crawl through without his sword, a true act of humility like the simplicity of the hut itself. Still another preparation the tea master makes for the guest's visual stimulation is a selection of a calligraphy scroll for the day, which is hung in the hut's main wall alter (*tokonoma*) perhaps with a flower on the shelf. And although you find a tokonoma is usually a part of an aristocratic Japanese home, it also features prominently on the main wall of most Aikido schools, where you also will find the founder's photo and calligraphy on display, often alongside a flower and incense.

When the tea ceremony begins, the tea master sits before you and makes—in a special bowl called a *chawan*—a drink called *matcha*. In Japan, balance often is highlighted by an asymmetrical presentation. For instance, matcha is a very bitter powdered green tea, and to offset this difficult taste, it is traditionally offered with a small, intense sweet to eat just before you sip your tea: the sweetness in your mouth in combination with the bitter tea brings a balance a moment later. (The popular matcha drinks do not come close to the experience of drinking a cup of traditional ceremonial matcha.) Sharing a cup of tea is to meet a friend for a moment—hence the saying, "one moment, one meeting." It may be a fleeting moment, as—especially with the samurai—there may not be another. This is how the samurai lived their lives: no plans for a cruise in the spring, or saving for a fancy car; they lived for the moment, in the here and now, not distracted by the past or the future. Everything is in this present moment. This Zen thought is codified in the tea ceremony. One can't help but think of O-Sensei's "being one with the universe" in this idea of accepting reality as it is at that moment: clear eyed and unafraid. This is the non-resistance O-Sensei speaks about: it is to accept what is, to accept reality. True warrior training is about truth and reality; it is about survival. Of course, not knowing any samurai personally, I think much of this is idealized to create a strong image of the warrior. How many samurai lived up to this ideal is not known, but ideals provide goals to strive for in a lifetime.

TEN

# The Wizard's Magic Spear
## *Calling Down the Light*

The jo symbolizes the wizard's spear in the same way that the bokken symbolizes a samurai sword. But unlike the detailed history of the samurai sword, which is well-documented along with the samurai history, the story of the wizard's magic spear is shrouded in the past with no real documentation. But this is to be expected as mountain wizards and the warlord's samurai are categorically distinct creatures; the wizards are hidden in the mountain forests and they are at once creators of worlds, guards of the heavenly bridge, and teachers of the chosen few—not your normal run-of-the-mill person. Even the images of wizards are from prints of imagined creatures—related but still very different from humans. We see the jeweled spear in the hands of Izanagi as he stands with Izanami on the heavenly bridge creating the world, it is held by the wizards Sarutahiko Okami as well as the Kurama wizard Sojobo in the famous Japanese prints from the past.

Even the form of the Aikido jo has rather magical, shape-shifting properties. This shape shifting nature is found in its various forms. Its history is as a spear, even a jeweled spear in Izanagi's hands, but in Aikido it is a fifty-inch wooden staff, and there are Aikido practices for long six-foot staffs. Even in the famous print of Sojobo and Yoshitsune, the wizard performs a clearing movement, but the jo he holds is a branch with leaves. And in my following story, it is a nasty looking spear-like weapon. The sword is not like this at all, although there are some stories of jeweled swords, its form rarely changes so much. And while this is an educated guess, it is a lore that links well the few elements we do know. It also balances well with the sword.

## O-Sensei's Jo

I remember that just before my second and last interview with Kisshomaru Doshu in his home in the building next to the Aikido World Headquarters dojo, I was shown upstairs to the "museum" on the third floor. In it there was O-Sensei's training bokken and jo as well as his hakama, his *aikidogi* (uniform) and other artifacts. But even today, over twenty years later, what I remember most is a spear I saw in a glass cabinet there. I have a clear image of that wooden spear honed into an extremely mean point. I must admit, seeing this jo opened my eyes.

When I was introduced to the jo and bokken in Aikido class, I immediately gravitated toward the jo; it seemed so much less threatening. The sword has so many restrictions: it is bladed on one side, the tip and the hilt are used for different purposes, and although it is a vicious weapon, its use is limited compared to the freewheeling jo. The jo truly is a magic wand! I enjoyed freely whirling around with the jo extended from the length of my arm in a space-clearing move. I found the quick turns to address an attacker from various angles around me fascinating. The jo could move high and low, in a thrust, in a powerful spiral angle, end over end, or turning and using the jo's other end—all snap decisions that make practice with the jo smooth and unpredictable to all except the bearer.

Most Aikido practitioners who use the jo are more familiar with one that is blunt at both ends. It is common, however, for a student to be instructed—as I was many times—that the jo is really a spear, and so one end must be regarded as being pointed even if it's not. When designating one end as the spear-tip end (often on which end a student inscribes their initials) the jo is still regarded as having the versatility of using either end in practice: the tip is used for poking and the other end can strike or thrust. The jo offers endless possibilities. And so the jo's power is quite amazing.

Unlike the sword, the jo is a great equalizer, as Aikido techniques (and takeaways) can be practiced with a jo. As a smaller person I would often find myself in a class with towering men. These kinds of classes provided me with excellent training as I would have to do a technique well in order for it to work on someone much taller or larger than me. But when given a jo to use, the leverage and extension made that hard work easy (another aspect of the jo's shape-shifting ability). I made friends with the jo right away. I would walk with my jo and in desolate places practice a few moves; no one noticed my "walking stick."

From my conversations with O-Sensei's direct students, as well as from countless viewings of O-Sensei's films, I saw that the founder opened his Aikido demonstrations by holding the jo vertically in meditative stillness. Then, as he began to move, the jo rose upward over his head, still vertical in his hands until it was inscribing a growing spiral. Like the antennae found on a shrine roof, the vertical nature of O-Sensei's opening was to establish a connection with the divine realm. And so while the sword cuts through the darkness, we might say the jo seeks to open the light of the divine.

I remember being taught how to feel the energy moving through a wooden jo. Holding the jo about one-third of the way from either end, I would tap one end on the ground, and I could feel the vibration running through my hand. No other place on the jo would produce these vibrations. But holding it in the right place, the sweet spot, I could witness the jo's liveliness. What I felt as a vibration was a wave of energy moving through the jo, demonstrating that the jo was capable of conducting energy like the energy in the countless worms I found one day covering my foot as I was teaching some students this tapping lesson. The worms had answered a call I didn't realize I was making. So the jo affords us communication with other forms of life.

In the early days of running *Aikido Today Magazine,* I would meet up with various sensei from Japan when they visited California—either to take a class with them or to interview them (or both). I remember that there was one jo *kata* (jo sequence) that they all taught. Whether it was Koichi Tohei in his days of representing Tokyo's Hombu Dojo, or Morihiro Saito coming from a small town in northern Japan, they both had learned the same jo kata. Much later in my training I again encountered this kata as a part of a larger, seventy-five-step kata called *misogi no jo,* which was created by one of O-Sensei's oldest and most venerable students, Rinjiro Shirata. Shirata was encyclopedic in his presentations, and this quality drew many students to him in his later years. *Misogi no jo* is a compendium of O-Sensei's jo movements. But because it began with a quiet, four-directional thrusting pattern, and then quickly moved to circular strikes before finishing in a wild series of full-flying spiral movements, its build-up was undeniably powerful as it circled through the many movements Shirata saw in O-Sensei's demonstrations and teachings. As was Shirata's plan, a student learning all seventy-five steps of this kata would be familiar with all of O-Sensei's jo movements, from staid thrusts to a most wild moving jo fully extended from one hand in overhead spirals—which created tremendous power— and ending with that spiral toward the heavens in a loud ki ai. And as the pattern builds into this wild part, that power is experienced by the person attached to the end of the jo.

I used to practice this kata a lot. More than once, I drove J to Arizona to teach *misogi no jo* and often he would ask me to take a group of students aside and teach them a certain part. This was prior to the DVD Ron and I made of "Misogi no Jo" and so I scrambled to memorize the movements on his visits to my dojo. One balmy summer evening, just before class was to begin, I was practicing with A, one of our senior students. Ron was in the dojo office, and so A and I were the only ones on the mat. This was one of the first dojos Ron and I had put together so our *shomen* (head wall) was rather bare and elementary; it did display a photograph of O-Sensei over a shelf with a small horizontal

*Fig. 10.1. I demonstrate with my big brush at Blaine Library's Cultural Arts Night.*

bell. This shomen also exhibited a piece of calligraphy of "Aikido" brushed by our first teacher. It was not calligraphy that inspired either of us, however, because of the surprise invoice our teacher insisted we pay for his "gift" to our new dojo. I was quite surprised that when I told my philosophy students at CSULA that I was retiring to open an Aikido dojo, one of my philosophy students—a Sri Lankan Buddhist monastic—presented me with a beautiful, framed calligraphy artwork of "Aikido." It was striking and I felt, in my students gifting it to me with no strings attached, it represented the proper energy of an honorable gift. I wanted to swap out the two pieces of calligraphy right away but the act of taking down our own teacher's piece was still beyond our loyalty to him. Ron and I decided the best thing to do was to wait until the cheap little threads holding it on a nail gave way. We reasoned that the universe would tell us when to change out the artworks.

At any rate, as A and I began to practice *misogi no jo,* we eventually arrived at the wildest parts—the last movements—but before we could reach the end, out of the corner of my eye I saw the jo leaving A's hand as he wheeled around in that extended powerful spiral! With that power, A's jo headed across the mat in front of us, straight for the shomen. Time slowed to a crawl as we both stood in horror watching the jo travel end over end powered by that awesome spiral. We both were afraid it would hit the photograph and break the glass on the photo of O-Sensei. The jo kept its horizontal orientation, still moving end over end until it finally reached the shomen. It landed straight across the hanging calligraphy scroll that our teacher had "given" us. The force pulled the scroll off its holding pin and the calligraphy wrapped itself around the jo as it descended downward ringing the bell as it headed down to the mat. With the initial amazing *thwap* against the wood of the shomen and the loud ringing of the bell, Ron came running onto the mat to see what all the commotion was about. He arrived to find A and me standing in awe. Together we all approached the shomen slowly and looked at the calligraphy on the ground wrapped around A's jo and then we all fell into hysterics. Ron and I looked at one another with a single thought between us: A and I went to the house to get the calligraphy my philosophy student had just given me for the dojo. Ron prepared to hang it upon our return before that evening's class. The jo here does seem magical and mysterious, although I don't usually view things in this way, it was clear even to me that time: the universe had spoken! I remember an important sensei telling me that the jo is like a magic wand.

## Sarutahiko Okami

Sarutahiko Okami is a well-respected earthly kami who is seen in stories guarding passage on Ame no ukihashi—the Floating Bridge of Heaven—the bridge that connects the heavens to the earth. (For instance, he helps the Sun goddess's grandson descend to earth and he meets up with Ame no Uzume in another *Kojiki* story.) But more importantly for our purposes, he is the patron kami of Aikido, and he is viewed as a symbol of misogi. Sarutahiko Okami is enshrined at Tsubaki Grand Shrine as well as at the Aiki Shrine. He's often depicted as carrying a jeweled spear and described in this way:

> The length of [his] nose is seven hands, the length of [his] back is more than seven fathoms. Moreover, a light shines from his mouth [and nether end]. His eye-balls are like an eight-hand mirror and have a ruddy glow [like the] eyes of the serpent slain by Susanoo. (Herbert 1967, 356).

The priest at Tsubaki Grand Shrine in Japan received O-Sensei many times as O-Sensei was a frequent visitor. As I arrived there, after the 95th Guji, Yukiteru Yamamoto had died, it was his son, Yukitaka Yamamoto Guji, who offered me and my friend M a welcome. We enjoyed a misogi under the waterfall every time we visited. It was made all the more special when Yamamoto Guji told us that O-Sensei practiced misogi there many times. When O-Sensei constructed the Aiki Shrine on his property in Iwama, he arranged for Yukiteru Yamamoto

Guji to install some of the relics of Sarutahiko Okami there. It was a grand project, and its realization was a cause for great celebration. (Annually a great celebration at this shrine is still observed by the current Ueshiba head of Aikido.)

A famous story, which took place on the Floating Bridge of Heaven, is the story of the cosmogony of Japan, in which Izanagi and Izanami create the world with a jeweled spear.

In this 1800s print, we can see the two creator spirits (kami) at work. In this picture they are creating the earthly plain with an Amenonuhoko

*Fig. 10.2. Izanami and Izanagi creating the universe from the Floating Bridge of Heaven.*

(heavenly jeweled spear) standing on the famous Ame no ukihashi (Floating Bridge of Heaven). Churning the water with their jeweled spear, its drops of salty water fell from the tip and formed the land.

Although magic and mystery are represented best by the Aikido spear, there is some magic with the sword as well. The sword is a symbol of the famous Japanese magical sword: Kusanagi no Tsurugi (the cloud gathering sword). It was found by Susanoo no Mikoto after he slew the multi-headed Orochi serpent. And it is the sword he gifted to Amaterasu Omikami in the story I discussed previously.

But the lessons of the jo are very different from those of the sword. In the recordings of O-Sensei's movements, we see him making great spiral movements with the jo prior to and sometimes after his demonstration. Like the upward-facing antennae on the roof of a shrine, a Buddhist temple, or even a Christian cathedral, the jo can be seen as an antenna, when held vertically, calling on the powers that be to shed their light on us. Thus, the vertical realm—like the Ame no ukihashi—is regarded as the connection to the divine realm. The horizontal realm is the realm of our material community: humans, animals, and so on. Trees and mountains are part of this community, but their vertical nature demands our reverence as mountains and forests have been viewed from ancient times as having something to do with the divine.

Unlike the sword, the jo is symmetrical (unless we view it as a spear) and so it can move end over end. If we do view it as a spear, then one end is pointed and sharp while the other end is still useful as a blunt end. It makes the jo the commander of large movements, of creative impulses, and of clear connections to the world of the divine. Where the sword cuts through darkness, the jo summons the divine light. It does in many ways point us to the mystical side of Japan.

## Nonresistance

O-Sensei says again and again that he is the universe, and so when someone wants to attack him, they are attacking the universe—that is why they are defeated before they begin. Attacking the universe can't be easy; I wouldn't try it. But it seems it would be very useful to know how to become one with the universe. We can find some insight from my waterfall story from chapter 7. As you may recall, the waterfall story was about letting go of stress and strain. I needed to learn how to let go, to not resist, to not hold onto things. And it is just this sort of thing that also is required in the practice of randori.

Of course, this is never easy, and so there was a learning curve. For instance, I found that if I had a momentary doubt as to whether I was in fact letting go, it would interrupt my ability to just let go. Similarly, tightening a part of my body against the claps of water would interrupt the process, and send me back to square one. Either one wholeheartedly, in every aspect of their being, does not resist or does resist. As we get closer to unifying with the universe we begin to fully receive. If we can experience this receptive state, we have reached the state of nonresistance; a place where self-doubt and physically pulling away won't happen at all. At that point one experiences oneness with the universe, or unification. Seemingly impossible to maintain as we struggle with the distractions of self-interest—Is someone watching? Is that a bear over there?—it is the goal of the true warrior.

In order to know the truth of the matter we must be able to see what is real. And this involves nonresistance. Easy to say, but difficult to do. Once we try this simple exercise, we will be astounded at how many assumptions and interpretations we supply in the most innocent of circumstances. For example, in just opening our eyes in the morning light, if we are truthful about what we see, we will describe just the many colors and shapes in our visual field. But we have been taught that certain shapes and colors are called a *tree,* or a *window,* and so forth. We usually explain what it is that we see not by our raw sensory sensations—as in, "I see a blotch of green"—but by our learned interpretation—"I see a tree." Of course, it would be difficult to live in our world, and successfully communicate with others, if we had to talk in terms of raw sensory data. But the point is that we are far from recognizing that we've made a jump from that raw data ("I see a blotch of green") to a specific learned concept ("I see a tree"). And so we naturally operate in a world that is a step away from reality not realizing the judgments that have taken us there. A world in which everything has an explanation and fits neatly into a world order we have learned to call "reality."

We see a straight stick, we put it into the water, and although the sensory information says it is a bent stick, we "see" a straight stick that's in the water. Of course we all know that it is the water that creates a deceptive appearance to the stick. But how many other perceptions do we explain away without truly seeing what is there? It takes work to protect our valued worldview, and part of that work is in constantly interpreting what our senses tell us so that our perception fits with our expectations. And so we jump from what is actually before us to an educated guess of what is before us based on past experiences. How much easier would it be to just allow things to be as they are! To just receive without interpretation. Many people spend a lot of money and time learning how to do just this in meditation workshops.

Looking at my pup, Ame, as I write this, I notice she is a perfect example of nonresistance or acceptance of what is: she is reclining on the cool cement of my patio, the gentle spring breeze moving the tips of her long white fur as it travels across her body. Her head is up but her eyes are closed. She just is—she is so still, so content, so accepting of the current moment, she could be mistaken for a statue, but her ears are up and in a moment she might spring into action to chase a squirrel who has come too close or to snap at a bee buzzing near her head. Right now she is just part of the patio. And this is what humans aspire to experience when they meditate: To just be.

We can see that, without our interpretation, incoming information is, by nature, chaotic. No doubt why we're strongly motivated immediately to interpret the information; it is comforting to make some order out of the chaos. People do not seem to enjoy change, although life is change. When there is no change, there is no life. But is resorting to our quick explanations of what we see the only choice? Why no, it's not! If we boldly accept the chaos of what is, without providing our usual, ready-made explanations, we may begin to discover other things: we might just see an order present itself without our having to manufacture one. This is the kind of perception scientists train to cultivate so that they are seeing clearly. And it would be good for us all to follow in that aspiration. But as long as we make the interpretive leap, we miss those opportunities.

We have eyes, but do we see? We might say truly seeing is to receive. It is the master of Aikido who can operate at this level. Most of us sense the incoming energy of an attack and name it: "It's a straight punch," "It's an overhead strike," and so forth. This is what we're trained to do. So this naming of an attack produces the response of a technique that we have been taught to perform in such cases as if the name and response are tied together, which in fact they are.* But the master doesn't need to identify the form of the energy that is coming; the master allows the energy to be unnamed and responds to it spontaneously. So "appropriately" or "fitting" is what *ai* means here. When we add the kanji for energy—*ki*—we get *aiki* which (as been stated previously) can be translated as "harmonious energy." And aiki refers to what is manifested by the person being attacked. *Aiki* could also be translated as "appropriate energy."

We have many attachments as all of our material objects have lines of energy attaching to us. This goes for relationships with living beings as well for simple material objects like books, rings, and cars. This is a good and necessary thing for human development as bonds bring us feelings of well-being. But when someone is ascending, as in a hot air balloon, the tethers are cut. And so if we are to ascend, like the balloon, some of the many lines of attachment must be broken because we have outgrown our need for them. Some we hold dear, and others we let go. By reducing our material footprint we become

---

*Technique names in Aikido follow a formula: attack name first followed by the technique name, as in *munetsuki kotegaeshi*. *Munetsuki* is a punch, *kotegaeshi* is a technique.

lighter, less bound to the material world. If we had to move to a different location, could we just walk out the door? Would we need a bag? Would we need a truck? Would we need a moving service? Stuff is neither good nor bad. It just depends upon what we want to do. To become unencumbered is not easy; you have to give up some things, to let go, to release them. And so in Aikido training, when you look at your attacker you do not want to attend to useless information like the color of his eye, you have no time to gather such information, so some things you release.

## Randori: Multiple Person Attack

We have discussed how the jo of Aikido helps to bring light or clarity to our practice. Now I want to talk about an open-hand Aikido practice aimed at bringing order out of chaos: this is the practice of randori. When I talk about bringing light, clarity, or order please understand that these are age old symbols for truth. Bringing order out of chaos is not easy but knowing how to do this is useful. Understanding the vagaries of chaos surely leads one to revere order. As drama uses exaggeration to make a point that is easy to miss, I will allude to a famous movie (based on an even more famous play) to help me make the point clear.

And so chaos can be said to symbolize the darkness that covers the truth while order, which allows us to manage reality, symbolizes truth and light.

In Akira Kurosawa's film *Ran*, Lord Hidetora is so blinded by the false flattery of his two older deceitful sons that he banishes his only truthful son, his third and youngest son, because he is saying things the father does not want to hear (like that his brothers are not truthful). The remaining heirs (the two older brothers) driven by power and greed, wage war upon each other. Ultimately a broken man, Hidetora descends into madness, while death and destruction threaten his life and the survival of the kingdom he spent his lifetime building. He made the wrong choice.

In this story a calm, orderly, and aging king attempts to prepare for the future by relinquishing authority to his heirs, only to find himself swallowed in falsehoods and clouds of confusion, and in absolute chaos with the destruction of himself and his kingdom imminent all due to his poor judgment about which heirs are honest. Kurosawa pays homage to Shakespeare's *King Lear,* as he highlights the importance of truth. But disorder and chaos rule in the lives of these kings. By naming his film *Ran*, Kurosawa points to the Japanese kanji for chaos. The etymology of the character for this kanji is one of hands untying tangled threads—putting things into order or bringing things under control from a chaotic mess.

Originally the kanji for *randori* applied to bringing rebellious persons to submission, and thus bringing a disturbance under control. There is a practice in Aikido called *randori*, which is a full-out multiple attack. The point of it is to not get caught, and to not get caught while remaining calm and centered all in a flurry of movement.

Multiple person attacks are common in Aikido; it is a way to practice staying centered while entering (moving forward) through a space fraught with obstacles; often this is called *flowing movement,* or *ki no nagare.* There are several distinct ways to practice defenses from multiple attacks, but randori is the king. Randori involves a full-out attack with at least three attackers. As you might imagine, this is chaotic, as the attackers come striking all at once. This is the hallmark of randori. When attackers take turns attacking you, the practice is called *jiyuwaza,* but in randori they attack at the same time. These attacks may be openhanded, or the attackers may be bearing a jo, bokken, or *tanto* (wooden knife). Because of this randori is chaotic and dangerous. It's another reason why Aikido teachers are so well trained to keep things safe on the Aikido mat. Randori is typically reserved for advanced classes where students are skilled at moving quickly, at timing, and at falling. If you are being attacked in this way, the only way to get through this trial is to stay calm and centered as you enter into the chaos—lest the madness overtake you.

*Fig. 10.3. Susan Perry at the beginning of a seven-person sword attack.*

Randori is a ritual practice but with few rules and constraints. It enables us to check our ability to deal with chaotic and dangerous situations. When we practice dealing with an attack at the dojo, we go very slowly at the beginning. As a student becomes more skilled, the attacks escalate over time from open-hand grabs, to strikes, to slow and orderly multiple-person attacks, and then to randori or something similar. Of course, it may take years for a new student to learn to stay centered in each of these practices. But by staying centered a student learns to keep inner calm, and to deal more effectively with chaos in the world.

### The Rise and Shine Kids

*I caught up with Z just in time; I thought he might kill Bobby. Of course, I'm talking about ten-to-twelve-year-old children who were in my at-risk Aikido class. Holding Z back was not easy; he was straining with every ounce of his power to get to Bobby; he was out of control even though he was smaller and younger than all the other students in my Rise and Shine Aikido class.*

*This class was the result of a special grant awarded to a program I designed specifically for a small group of at-risk kids from a local grade school. The teachers at the school chose the ten to twelve students who were the most troublesome in class. My bank manager had arranged for the local Kiwanis Club to provide bus rides to and from the local grade school to my dojo for classes twice a week. My mission was to see if Aikido training (and aiki-like activities) could help these troubled kids get some control over themselves, so they could perform better in school. These kids had experienced some unimaginable events in their young lives: one student witnessed a boyfriend knife his mother to death, and he jumped from a second story window to summon help for his siblings; a young girl experienced sexual abuse; a young boy who lived in a van with his mother, three siblings, and a lice infestation was pushed to strange heights of self-aggrandizement; another came from a very volatile environment composed of an often-absent mother, gang members in the house, and a father who was feeding him candy for dinner; and a couple of (likely) abused children whose fear made them cry and hide under tables were also in the group. Quite a mixed bag. Sometimes teaching these children seemed like descending into the heart of darkness.*

*Z was at this point blinded by rage, mindless to what might happen, and he just wanted to destroy Bobby—who had a special talent for infuriating others. So as I tried to get some control over Z Bobby continually hurled choice epithets at him. I managed to haul Z into the other room just to separate the boys. This class was starting out poorly. Already I was without my assistants for this day and so, in quiet desperation I asked one of the other students in this class— Michael—to lead the stretches that day. A risky move on my part, to be sure. I rarely asked one of these class members to lead something in my absence, but I had watched Michael and knew that the issues that put him in this class were benign. Michael was quiet and self-demeaning, but he had the ability to listen and follow instructions;*

*he had no self-confidence, but he wanted to please. In the back of my mind I wondered if leading these stretches might even be helpful for him. Thankfully, Michael stepped up without complaint; this enabled me to take a moment or two with Z.*

*Z was crying. His small chest heaved up and down like a restless sea, and his face was drawn and red. In the calm of the unoccupied room, I asked him to sit up. "No!" he cried out. I asked him again. "I can't," he sobbed. I wondered how long this was going to last. But when he expressed how much Bobby had angered him when Bobby called him a loser, I felt we were getting somewhere. I shared with Z that sometimes I felt anger too; I wanted Z to know he was not alone and that his feeling anger was a natural response to undeserved slights from others. He sat up. He looked straight at me, his heaving chest finally quieted, and he waited breathlessly when I said, "Do you want to know a secret?" I explained how I found that going to your center is the only answer to this kind of situation as it helps to control anger, and I instructed him on how to use his breath to get him there. We sat seiza together on the floor in a breath exercise, and I finally heard a weak breath exit from Z, which began to restore him. In a few minutes he was up, straightening his uniform, and wanting to join class. He was called more names, kicked in the shoulder by Raddie "by accident," but Z took all this in stride, and with great emotional balance, he persevered through the class that day. Michael, whom I left with the stretches, did a terrific job of giving me a few minutes with Z. Michael was learning he had leadership abilities, and he beamed when I thanked him in front of the whole class for his good job finishing the stretches that day. I was relieved that I only had one incident to contend with that day (unusual) and that, with the help of a student, it worked out.*

Being attacked creates chaos: a frantic feeling as we search for the proper response as well as for the control to dampen our anger or fear. The attack might seem innocent, like name calling, but it could have the same effect as a punch to the gut. Awareness is the first step to bring order out of chaos, undoubtedly the ultimate aim of Aikido training according to O-Sensei. But O-Sensei thinks big. His goal of "creating one family," or creating world peace can happen only if we restore order to the chaos of fighting and dissent—worldwide. It's clear that O-Sensei thought this was his purpose in life: to bring order out of the chaos by creating an art like Aikido to be spread around the world. Often, I hear that O-Sensei thought he was Susanoo no Mikoto who was sent to quell the discord on earth.

When I was a brown belt and my sensei began to talk about my first black belt test, I learned that he did not teach randori even though it was the finishing demonstration of the test. I had seen black belt tests before, and this last randori demonstration is always the most exciting part. Attackers come fast and furious and you must not get caught, must not back up, must not lose your focus or your center. The attackers are other black belts, usually the most agile black belts step up for this practice. The fact that they are quick on their feet makes the whole ordeal more terrifying. It seemed like there was important stuff there to learn, and I wondered how I would learn it if he wasn't going to teach me.

My teacher thought your first randori experience should happen without preparation for randori; that it must happen "on the fly" to see what you're made of. And so randori was kept as a kind of secret just to test the nerves of us randori newbies. All the more terror would be brought to someone who had never faced such a thing. And indeed I found it terrifying because randori, as he conducted it, involved sitting on your heels in seiza while facing four attackers sitting the same way across from you. At his shout, everyone was to spring up and begin. So from a silent and meditative moment, everything suddenly exploded into mayhem: the four attackers leapt up and into a full-out attack, and your mission was to stand up, and move forward through the attackers without getting caught, and without running away or backing up. So in the face of both the wild action of four attackers and an inner terror at getting caught—I was to calmly enter into the chaos! What drama! Either you transcended your cowardice in that public nightmare and passed, or you didn't! It seemed like a lot of stress to put on someone already stressed out, but Aikido has no competitions or tournaments and so it is through this kind of practice that our fortitude and martial competence is tested.

At the beginning of a randori practice it may be all you can do to keep moving without getting caught. But as the randori proceeds, if you can manage a throw or two, you in effect create more space and time for yourself as a downed attacker takes up space amidst the other quick stepping attackers and it takes time for him to get back up on his feet. In randori practice, you don't wait for the attacker to come to you; you move in to close the distance. This can prevent full recovery for the attacker who is trying to get up on his feet. This entering movement is one of the most advanced practices in Aikido as it takes timing, confidence, and extreme centering skills to pull off. But it interrupts the attackers' timing, which throws them off balance. At this point there are strategies of movement to use to "line up" your attackers so that you can take control of the whole ordeal. At full speed there usually isn't time or space at the beginning of a randori for a throw. But as you enter into the chaos you can break the crowding by interrupting your attackers' timing and by using spins to keep yourself free. (In fact, a useful general tip for self-defense is to turn.) And in this way, it's possible to see some order emerge from the chaos. I came to love the practice. And in my own school, years later, randori would become a popular practice in our black belt classes. I was relieved to learn that if you can survive a randori of four attackers, you can survive a randori with five or six or more attackers. Adding attackers just makes it easier for them to get in each other's way. Tornados and hurricanes demonstrate the power of the center as disparate parts are thrown to the outside of the quietly moving funnel. In this same way, a person spinning is difficult to grab hold of, as the outer part of the person's body is moving faster than the center. If an attacker manages to grab the clothing of the person, a spin could even cause injury to a hand caught in the thick fabric of a uniform; a spin is that powerful.

I think Aristotle would've liked watching a randori practice. He thought the circle was the most perfect shape because a circle is never-ending. It seamlessly comes back upon itself, so there is no beginning or end. Aikido's essential form is a spiral, a circular motion that is expanding or contracting. Circles and spirals are the epitome of motion. Aikido students spend a lot of time learning how to transform energy into a circular movement and into spirals in particular. A spiral coming from a strong, centered person can be explosive.

One might view the movement from Homer's *Iliad* to the *Odyssey* as the bard's deepening understanding of power: from the merely muscular and mechanical that is witnessed in battle action to something deeper, comprehensive, and connected—something with meaning beyond the victory of a single physical fight. In the *Iliad* the physical battles of the Trojan War are painfully documented and described, complete with the personal motivations for one fighter to kill another—as in Achilles's hatred of Hector for the death of his friend Patroclus. But in the *Odyssey,* the story of Odysseus's ten-year return home after the Trojan War—although still a story filled with conflicts, it presents Odysseus's overall singular motivation to complete the journey home, which seems to reach out to him and help him through the many challenges he faced on that journey. It is a story about his perseverance to overcome battle fatigue and the obstacles in his way so that he can once again see his family, and rest comfortably in his kingdom of Ithaca. It is this kind of deepening of physical training that produces the fortitude to continue on to finish a lengthy and demanding task that is uncomfortable or painful, overriding the needs of the body to heal and rest. In these cases the vision of some end pushes a person beyond their normal abilities. I've always thought that taking on larger-than-life tasks, if successful, creates in a person a greater capacity. Like filling a balloon, we—as agents—can expand beyond our normal capacity to create a larger capacity to move through more challenging events and projects.

## *Takemusu Aiki*

*Takemusu aiki* is a principle that at once appeals to the necessity of a harmonious attitude as well as the central purpose of creating protection. The call for spontaneous creativity in providing fitting protection provides a fuller meaning of Aikido's principle of *takemusu aiki*.

Aikido is often completely misunderstood. We say it is an art of peace, an art of harmony with nature, and an art of love. But love, peace, and harmony are active—not passive—properties and so when we refer to "art of peace" it's not a state of being but a life of a certain sort of action we're referring to. There is quite a lot of work that goes into being peaceful or harmonious, work that takes a kind of toughness to perform. This includes both a physical toughness as well as a toughness of spirit. We see this when we reach a barrier or calamity in our life, and often the pain is so much that we think we can't endure, that we can't go on. We hide our eyes and retreat into ourselves in a kind of immobilization—whether it is through self-pity, fear, insecurity, or hopelessness. Some of us remain there, unable to cope; others are able to shake it off eventually and regain perspective. But to be one with nature is not to be stopped at all but to have the strength to accept bad news, and to continue, unflinchingly, in the face of it. It is a kind of steeliness of the soul, our ferocity at work. Like when a mama bear actively protecting her cubs gives an all-out commitment to remove what she sees as a threat; this can unleash an awesome, ferocious power. This is what Aikido training is about.

It's useful to think about warfare here because it illustrates the point so well even though most of us only experience warfare in a poetic or literary manner, or on the news. A samurai in the heat of battle might get cut, maybe badly, but he will surely face death if he folds under the pressure and stops his fight. Of course, to continue fighting against overwhelming odds is expected only of heroes and heroines who display a kind of otherworldly strength and tenacity. Many of those in law enforcement die of the shock of being shot or cut even if the injury is not life threatening; they don't imagine that it would ever happen to them and so, when it does, they go into shock, and often die from shock when it wasn't necessary.

There is a sword practice that ties the sword to cutting through the darkness. To do a proper sword cut takes quite a lot of practice and the sword misogi I discussed on page 168 has its usefulness here. A 1000-cut sword practice will help you learn how to cut from your hips or center rather than your shoulder muscles, as these shoulder muscles will fatigue before you get to 600 cuts. A sword cut uses your hips and not your arms. Your arms must stay free and empty of tension so that the energy coming up through your hips can be used in the cut; if you have tension in your arms, you will block this energy. This idea of clearing anything blocking the avenues of energy is especially important when using the sword, and so here, in the very act of making the sword cut, you can see how unuseful tension must be cut away in order to make way for the energy itself.

Humans may be acting from fear, lack of confidence, or confusion when they turn away from tough problems and accept a lesser life punctuated by self-numbing agents like alcohol or drugs to help them forget that they bailed on themselves. Such people make life more difficult for others by excusing themselves from their responsibilities. But even if someone is a hurtful, arrogant creature, they have the ability to transform into a strong, compassionate being able to help others and serve the community. Of course, this kind of transformation takes time and requires an honest assessment of oneself. To actually face who we are, and to see ourselves is an extremely hard, sometimes terrifying thing to do; we all suffer from illusions of who we are, and what motivates us. In fact, when we come to terms with ourselves and realize that even though left unspoken, every individual has setbacks and challenges and has perhaps endured unfair hardships, we move into a place of more balanced perception, which allows us to accept ourselves and our life's flaws as they are so we can move forward to embrace change. It is the function of the sword to cut through the illusions, to cut through ignorance—it is, then, the sword of truth.

Rituals abound: the very taking off of shoes (the beginning of a transformation of dress), the change of clothes into the Aikido uniform (the keikogi and hakama, the ancient traditional uniform of the samurai), joining the line of students to bow in, the stretching routine. All of these ritual activities share the beginnings of transformation. The techniques of Aikido are part of a practice of purification—misogi—another essential element to Aikido training. Purification is the useful practice of clearing away the clutter to prepare for practice, a training practice that athletes and performers use before performances. This is also ritualistic and helps to keep our observation of the space as sacred. If we come on the mat with our complaints about the last travesty the world has leveled at us and the angry energy of indignation that such a thought causes, we pollute the very space we hope will save us. Sacred space is a necessary concept as much work is done in it. Having physically cleansed and spiritually cleansed, the real work of Aikido can commence.

The reason for all this is to prepare a safe space to deal with our anger, fear, or other forms of emotional turmoil. Aikido is, after all, an art that takes our darkest parts, the places where power resides, where we are raw and forceful, and teaches us to use them in a productive and positive way. It is true transformation.

This is why O-Sensei viewed Aikido as standing on the bridge between heaven and earth. Being of the mud is our organic nature, the part that registers fear, anger, greed, jealousy, egotistical selfishness, and so on. However, our mind can hold the larger picture, a picture that includes informing from the material an attitude of universal love, respect for nature, and unity with all living beings.

The midpoint—the bridge—is what enables us to survive in a healthy and positive way. The mud side is informed by the big picture so that we learn how to move away from base desires and emotions. It's not good to deny emotions; that would be to stop the flow. But truly assessing one's emotional situation and how we deal with it is invaluable. By noticing our own reactions we begin to understand more deeply another person's behavior. The spirit side is also informed by the mud side so that we don't totally neglect our material existence. We learn how to be healthy, and how to conduct ourselves so that we are self-sufficient in our material lives—not begging, deprived, or depraved. We must learn to be strong and stable so that we can be of service to others.

But our mud side is not just the home of base desires and negative emotions; it is the place of power. What makes emotions like fear and anger so bothersome is their sheer force. We all know how the power of anger can move into our everyday thoughts. Sometimes it is difficult to overcome. But rather than repressing our emotions, we need to transform their power into something positive. The Aikido mat, then, is the workplace for this practice. There we can let a little of this raw power out in the safe environment of the sacred Aikido mat, in virtual practice to see how we can manage it, and how we might transform it into something useful; this is the benefit of Aikido training.

ELEVEN

# An Ocean of Energy
## *The World as Vibrations*

*I want considerate people to listen to the voice of Aikido.*
*It is not for correcting others; it is for correcting your own*
*mind. This is Aikido. This is the mission of Aikido and*
*should be your mission.*

O-SENSEI IN KISSHOMARU UESHIBA'S *AIKIDO,* 1978

From what I have laid out in previous chapters, we can clearly see that
O-Sensei viewed this big, wonderful world as full of energy. That O-Sensei
was attracted to nature philosophies is not surprising: even his son mentions Lao Tzu's yin and yang philosophy as something that helps to
explain his father's (see page 101). But we have also seen a lot of Shinto—
another nature philosophy. While some assume Shinto is a religion, it is
not a *religion* in the Western sense of the term, and so I refer to it as a
*philosophy*—although many people resist using the term *philosophy* for reasons I've never understood. In chapter 2, I brought up this issue of religion
with regard to spiritual transmission (see page 33). O-Sensei's teaching,
then, seems very much like Aristotle's in that O-Sensei was searching for a
way of cultivating students to become virtuous agents in the world, people
who would learn Aikido to discover a deep reverence for life, a compassionate outlook, and a spirit of loving protection for all creation.

It's easy to see that O-Sensei's philosophy included the view that energy is all around us. In this chapter, we will consider *vibrations,* and *kototama* as these terms name forms of energy in the world's ocean of energy.

The quotation I began with is a favorite of mine, as it properly seats our attention back toward the cultivation of ourselves, rather than judging others. And I suggest that in reading the material in this chapter, it be done while reflecting back on the reader's own experiences. For those who are not familiar with these topics, get ready for some of the more interesting philosophical views of the Aikido founder.

## The Philosophy of Yin and Yang

The philosophy of yin and yang is part of the *Tao Te Ching* (The Way and its Power) written by Lao Tzu, an older contemporary philosopher of Confucius. As yin and yang (*in'yo, on'yo* in Japanese) constitute an ancient philosophy deeply rooted in many Asian countries, it deserves a mention here as—philosophically speaking—O-Sensei's philosophy is a nature philosophy much like Lao Tzu's. In fact, *tao* is the Chinese word for the same kanji that the Japanese describe as *dou.*

Also, as I said on page 101, O-Sensei's son mentions yin and yang when he explains his father's outlook on life. And since O-Sensei didn't write down a full philosophy, it seems that we can understand his views by looking a little closer at Lao Tzu's. "The subtle essence of the universe is eternal. It is like an unfailing fountain of life which flows forever in a vast and profound valley. . . . The mystical intercourse of yin and yang is the root of universal life. Its creativity and effectiveness are boundless" (Lao Tzu 1989, 61).

Lao Tzu discourages striving for goals; he instead offers a simple philosophy of doing nothing. In other words, his message is to not push against the forces of nature, but to go with them; not to struggle to effect change, but to move spontaneously with nature. He illustrates being humble as like the most powerful river; being below all others.

And he talks about being one with the universe, "[O]ne with a whole mind holds fast to Oneness, and thereby becomes an example to the rest of the world." Lao Tzu's philosophy names a few concepts we see in O-Sensei's lectures and talks: nonresistance, oneness, and invincibility. Where Lao Tzu's philosophy is said to include doing nothing but going with forces of nature, we easily can understand O-Sensei's reference to nonresistance. I explore this very concept in the following story.

## Being Yin

I had become very skilled at controlling things. Like others, I had been encouraged, taught, and rewarded for this skill, which I believe I've put to good use for the benefit of many. I understood how to push to get an interview, how to get a publication ready by deadline, how to "sell" Aikido classes, how to negotiate a more favorable lease, even how to ride the waitress to bring our food to the table in a timelier fashion. But living like this takes a certain personal toll, and so I was ready for something new, something different, and I was ready for a rest. I wanted to just "be."

As I mentioned in chapter 1, I had many conversations with my teacher about conflict and why he thought a certain amount of conflict was necessary. He brought home the point by talking about ego and how ego helps us. In his view our ego is present simply by virtue of having a driver's license as this, and other forms of identification, set us apart from others: They identify us and no one else, and insofar as this is true, our ego contributes to the separation of us from them. These things help us function in the world, and so a certain amount of ego is necessary. (Excessive ego is another matter.) But if we did not assert ourselves, would we need ego? Could we just be?

But how could I just be? How would I explain doing nothing to my staff, my students, my family who were all working so hard? O-Sensei refers to non-fighting and nonresistance in the most admirable way. I didn't feel that I was living like that at all: I was fighting for deadlines, and very resistant to most everything that got in my way. Thinking of myself in this way, it seemed I was far from the Aikido ideal. So I wanted to try not-fighting and not-resisting. I decided to step back, and just be—without pushing, without resisting. In conclusion, I decided I wanted to calmly receive the world without jumping in to control it.

I was very familiar with the concepts of yin and yang, and so I decided upon a lifestyle that focused on the energy yin. Yin and yang are energies of completely different sorts: yin is darkness and calm, while yang is light and active. Their action upon one another explains things energetically. So in my mind, overt control is a yang energy, as it has to do with activity and effort. Yin is its antithesis. Having been a yang person, I now wanted to bring balance by being yin. That would mean that I would receive what the world or another person brought to me. Doesn't sound so bad; actually it has a kind of exalted sense to it, as if I would be receiving like a queen.

### At the Claremont Hotel

*I was able to leave my usual tasks as a publisher, teacher, mother, and puppy trainer for a week's hiatus to go with Ron to an American Philosophical Association (APA) convention in Berkeley. Driving there would give us a good six-to-seven-hour window to enjoy one another's company in comparative quiet. A perfect time for me to try being yin. The APA booked interesting places and this year's convention was to take place at the Claremont Hotel, known as the "grand dame of San Francisco" or the "Elegant Lady," an historic and opulent hotel in the Berkeley hills.*

*As we were still driving in midafternoon with traffic increasing Ron asked me to call ahead to tell the hotel clerk we might arrive late. In my conversation with the hotel clerk I enjoyed a little lighthearted banter at the expense of the philosophers I could hear arguing in the background, I was assured he'd save us a room. And save us a room he did! We skirted the "smoker," which was in full swing, to get settled in our room before anything else. Signing us in, the clerk handed Ron our keys, among which was an elevator key to open the* locked floor. "Locked floor!?" I wanted to ask, but pushing for more information is not "being yin," and so I smiled and followed Ron into the elevator full of noisy philosophers. They quieted when the elevator operator stopped the ascent and asked Ron for our floor key.

The room the clerk reserved for us was a very impressive room, not at all like a regular hotel room: a huge, windowed apartment-suite, it contained a separate conference room, a kitchen, a separate and large dining room, and a well-appointed entertainment center in a huge living room. And down the hallway was a room that looked like a hotel room: bed, bath, telephones, desk. This apartment-suite was situated high up in the tower of the Claremont Hotel, with large picture windows on each side of the tower revealing stunning views of the bay and its bridges. We could see San Francisco across the bay, and in the distance, we could even see the Golden Gate Bridge! The views were absolutely tremendous! Ron reported to me that the whole place was ours to enjoy! I was ready to stay in the "room" forever—certainly for the weekend instead of attending the convention; it was that nice. My brother was so amazed when he saw our room that he asked if his meeting with his book editor could happen in the conference room. So we ordered a pizza and enjoyed the meeting in our opulent accommodation. Being yin felt very queenly indeed.

This happened again on our way home. I had booked us into one of our favorite resorts, which offered cottages, beach condos, and a kind of motel with a large pool. We had stopped there many times in the past on our drives up and down the coast, and so I knew the layout well, so well that I had requested a particular room close to the beach. We took our place at the end of the restless line of fatigued travelers and waited patiently—I didn't mind standing in line and waiting as I was getting comfortable in my new being-yin persona. When it was our turn the clerk handed us the room key, but he pointed away from the beach accommodations. I could feel my being-yin face disappearing, but I bit my tongue and decided instead to accept whatever the universe had in store for us. My old self would not have been comfortable with

*just taking the key without some understanding of what kind of room
we had been given and where on the grounds they had put us. But I
was finding the unsettled nature of these transactions attractive as they
held something unknown to be discovered, a kind of surprise. It made
me feel more awake and interested in life.*

*We followed the clerk's directions and drove to a bungalow:
fireplace, living room, dining room, kitchen, bedroom, bath, deck
tables, and private fenced grounds were ours to enjoy! Whoa! Again,
a nice surprise.*

It wasn't hard being yin during a trip where no expectations were
made of me. But maintaining that quiet and accepting energy got much
more difficult when I returned back to my two demanding businesses
and my puppy. My lesson of accepting what is didn't go unnoticed, however, and I did my best to bring more of a balance to my life because of
these experiences. Instead of striving to make things happen according
to my own view of the world, each time I was pressed to act, I would
take a step back, and with a deep breath shake off the inclination to
control. I became interested in seeing what might happen if things were
to take their natural course instead. It seemed to work fine.

The practice of being yin is about receiving. Yang energy, you may
recall, is the complementary energy to yin energy. I have characterized
them for my purposes as active and receptive energies, respectively. I
use being yin to make a point about receptivity and non-attachment or
nonresistance. But in reality, a person cannot be yin all the time—we
have to eat, move through space, and voice our concerns, all of which
use the active yang energy. And so, as was originally conceived, it is the
combination of yin and yang that makes a whole, that describes reality,
that symbolizes the balance that we seek to emulate.

Here is the symbol of yin and yang energies. The light is yang while
the dark is yin; they exist side by side within a whole circle. Yet there
is always a little yin in the yang, and a little yang in the yin; this is represented by the contrasting dots you see in the fields of light and dark.

*Fig. 11.1. The yin and yang symbol.*

This distinction between yin and yang does wonders for self-cultivation in one's everyday life. But, of course, I include it because it has important ramifications for Aikido practice too. In an abstract way we might view the practice of an Aikido technique between two people as a kind of dialogue of exchanging yin and yang energies. Some think that Aikido is only a passive art. But this is a silly and uninformed view, which probably comes from a student who took an intro class and so thought he was an authority on the matter. In introductory classes, for pedagogical reasons, an instructor may say that the nage (the person being attacked) responds to an attack. So in effect in such a class, the nage is waiting for the attack in order to respond. This does seem passive. But an instructor may choose to present Aikido this way to calm more aggressive tempers that may exist in an introductory class.

When an intro class forms, the instructor does not know much about those who have enrolled in the class. We instructors are unlike O-Sensei in his early years who asked for black belt rank and letters of recommendation from students enrolling in his dojo. And so, for teachers of modern Aikido, it's not clear how students will behave once paired up and yet we must find a way to keep them safe. In an attempt to emphasize the movement you want to show, it's best to discourage all other unnecessary movements that may distract from your point. Many people are anxious to get started and so they find it difficult to stand still for a moment. In detail, two people bow into one another to begin the practice: one is the *uke* (attacker) and delivers a grab or strike to the receiver (*nage*). Already we have the active yang person delivering an attack to the receptive yin person. Once the attack is made, that energy is expended and the yang uke becomes yin while the nage, who now has the active or yang position takes the partner's center and makes a response with the energy that has just been given in the attack. Depending on the technique there may be several exchanges. And so a technique can be seen as a dialogue between the yin and yang roles in the technique until, in the end, the nage (the original yin receiver) throws or pins the uke (the original yang attacker). Full circle.

In Aikido we often refer to the attacks as "gifts" precisely because the attacker is bringing energy to you. Awareness and being centered involve a balance of yin and yang; this is the gateway to self-control. And the Aikido practice of a technique, as I have just described, can be seen as the interplay of energies between the two people involved. For if both partners are yang there is a collision, and if they are both yin there is no energy brought to work with.

Seeing a technique as a dialogue takes time and so, in the beginning, we introduce just two energies: the nage's (who will receive the attack) and the uke's (who will attack.) Everything is simplified for the introductory class. That the nage waits for an attack is another simplification to make things a bit easier to understand. In its fullness, there are ways a nage can elicit an attack from the uke, subtle moves that draw the attack. And so Aikido is not a passive art after all.

## Sacred Space

Many years later, as I became a senior teacher and an older person in the world, I would come to see the dojo as the quiet, calm place that provides for a student's training, and the outside world as a chaotic source of many distractions that test us in many ways. Not an escape from the everyday world, but like a library carrel or a park bench, it is a place where the concerns of everyday life are temporarily lifted so that we can address other issues—in this case, Aikido training—that will better prepare us to live well in the world. I would present it this way to students when I taught them breathing meditation. It takes a new student some time and concentration to get breathing patterns correct; the quiet of the dojo is an important place to practice breath work. Imagine trying to work on our breath pattern at the intersection of two busy streets or at a busy train station! Typically, people will hold their breath in stressful times like this. You might hyperventilate as I once mistakenly did when I tried to calm down with breath work as I drove to my first job interview as I recounted on pages 47–48.

The outside world is a difficult place in which to find your center; too many things are happening at once, and it is noisy, unpredictable, and completely distracting. So the dojo offers a student a quiet place to learn how to become centered and strong. Then, once we develop some understanding and skill, the outside world provides us with a good testing ground for keeping our center under difficult conditions. And it is possible to do this. Moreover, this is the whole point of dojo practice where we can work on ourselves as we train with a partner. Making order out of chaos is a very advanced practice as I discussed on pages 187–89. The first step is to maintain some semblance of internal order, and this is called *keeping your center* or just *being centered*. The next step is to find order in the chaos, which is the practice of maintaining your center in the everyday world waiting for us outside the dojo door.

When we get to the dojo, we are often stressed out by dealing with the obstacles involved in getting there on time, suiting up, and being ready and seated on the mat for the class to begin. We all face obstacles: it might be a meeting that has run late, a demanding partner, child, or friend, traffic, mismanagement of our health by forgetting to eat lunch, unpreparedness as in forgetting our uniform, or even forgetting to gas up our vehicle to get us to the dojo. And depending on what has happened

*Fig. 11.2. Here I am centering before an important demonstration.*
*A large audience brings a lot of nervous energy, which is*
*contagious but not good for demonstration purposes.*

in our day, we may arrive sad, angry, joyful, or nervous. That is to say, we don't necessarily begin with a clean slate—a part of the world follows us in. In my dojo, students left their worldly concerns off the mat as they entered, and they could pick those worldly concerns up on their way out. This was to bring their awareness that they were entering a mat area before class and so did not need all their daily concerns with them in class. In this way, I was training them to treat the matted area in the dojo as a sacred space, to let go of the inessential for a moment.

*Sacred space* is a term that bothers some who think *sacred* is a religious term. This is far from the truth. Of course, in the past *sacred* has been used like the word *holy,* definitely as a religious word. But, like life, language changes. And many dojos I have visited over the years have used this phrase to mean "to treat the mat as a place worthy of respect," or to mean that the mat is "dedicated to Aikido practice." For I find the term *sacred space* useful in focusing students' attention on what they do on the Aikido mat. For example, I have seen students do silly and distracting things on the mat—picking their toenails, arguing with one another, running around the mat instead of sweeping it before class, getting dressed and undressed in front of the shomen wall, even eating on the mat (when it's not part of a dojo function). So, *sacred space* has become a code for me and for students for being respectful of where you are, when you are in the dojo. In my many years teaching Aikido to kids this concept of sacred space helped me a lot. When a child sees the open mat through the doorway, their eyes open wide and they're ready to play. Many adults are like this too. And I understand it completely. But a bunch of people running around increases the probability of injury, which instructors must always guard against. Sacred space, then, is useful to educate people about the purpose of a dojo.

When I lived on Mount Baldy my cabin was in a remote area of the national forest and so I was surrounded by trees. I was not seen. And I was always surprised that people would drive up in crazy ways with music blasting, park their vehicle, and get out and scream and yell. To them I suppose the forest looked empty (except for all the wildlife and residents like me) and a good place to vent. In addition, they would shoot guns, fly drones, and participate in poor hiking practices that would further erode the crumbly Southern California mountain. They were not viewing the forest as a sacred space. I hope this attitude will change.

This kind of training—to respect certain spaces by learning the appropriate way to use them—is also useful to have with regard to our judgments about others. This is a huge problem in the world today where we are encouraged to make judgments about people based on their appearance, religion, gender, where they live, what kind of car they drive, where they went to school, and so forth. And so it's beneficial to begin with a fresh look and leave judgments behind for a while.

So in the sacred space of a dojo, without the distractions of our lives, there is important work to do. We face our fears, deal with our anger, and look idiotic as we try new things on the Aikido mat. When we don't face the chaos and distractions of the everyday world, the deeper issues most of us have may become more visible and may be ready to be acknowledged and addressed. Sometimes a new student, when realizing that important issues come up in Aikido practice, may choose to leave Aikido training for a time until they're ready to work through their personal issues. Of course, many simply use the dojo to work out, and enjoy training, ignoring the deeper lessons that Aikido offers. I always leave it up to the student to decide, so long as they are not disruptive and don't pose a danger on the mat in the meantime.

## Seeing with an Empty Mind

When I was growing up, girls were taught to be non-confrontational, almost passive in relation to men; we weren't to speak up, fight back, complain, or otherwise be assertive. Men had their own lessons involving being kind to and protective of women; a gentleman was just that: gentle. And of course there were girls and boys who didn't learn these lessons well. But the point here is that in partnering up with another new student, especially one who may have received such childhood lessons, a woman may find a man who is disinclined to give her an honest attack. I remember a "grab" one man gave me with his thumb and index finger as if he were holding a grain of rice; he was obviously intimidated by me as a tiny woman. He thought he would break me if he held me too strongly. But I also remember getting a strong grab from a man that left bruises that were difficult to explain to the Philosophy department secretary the next day. And of course I'm sure there are men who had to actually request a focused punch from a woman who had been trained not to hurt anyone.

### Vanessa versus Rex

*As I was riding to lunch with a couple of other Aikido students at the retreat I was attending one day, I overheard a man named Rex, who had the dimensions of Paul Bunyan. Rex is a very gentle man. But he was complaining about Vanessa, another Aikido student at the retreat. Vanessa was a petite woman who was herself an Aikido teacher whom I knew as an acquaintance. Rex was talking to the driver of our car, but I heard the conversation from the back seat. He said, "I don't know what's going on but every time I pair up with Vanessa, she comes at me like a bat outta hell like she's trying to kill me! This time she really hurt me!" Silently I wondered if Vanessa might be intimidated by Rex's size and was over-controlling the technique as a consequence. This is easy to do. Being honest and aware of the actual situation does not always happen. It may be that Vanessa behaved this way whenever she paired up with a sizable man. If so, she needed some insight into how she was treating large men, as I doubt she was aware of this visual trigger she had picked up from somewhere in her past.*

Childhood lessons as well as perceptions from past traumatic experiences run deep; we might think of these lessons as a kind of programming—they are that strong and seemingly fixed. So, it may take more than a request for a solid grab or punch for a person to change. But once a person becomes aware of the issue, work on the solution can begin. This is another example of cutting through the darkness, or finding order in chaos (the person behaving in harmful ways out of ignorance counts here as chaos). And this is the kind of imbalance that we can begin to work through in the safe quiet of the Aikido mat.

## Vibrations, Breath, and Kototama

*Both spirits and material things are kotodama, and the true nature of the Universe is also kotodama. However, common religious leaders cannot understand this truth. Aikido is the wonderful work of kotodama that can make this truth alive. Therefore, aikido is a religion without being a religion.*

O-SENSEI, "TAKEMUSU AIKI," 1976

We can begin by accepting the common and well-known view that energy exists as vibrations all around us. If you think about how we hear things—vibrations coming into our ear to our eardrum to make sound—this point will be readily acceptable. And a quick observation of your breath will assure you that vibrations extend to that source of energy as well.

Kototama refers to sound as something special, and also to a certain study of sound to which O-Sensei was drawn. But let's start by talking about kototama as a useful and essential part of our everyday world. The vibrations of a person's voice carry sound. We know that some voices are grating to our nerves while others are calming. A child whose voice may delight us at one moment is capable in the next of making a sound that could drive most people to instant insanity. It's useful to know the sound of our own voice, as our voice instantly affects those we address. I often practice chanting, and I've been struck by how listening to my own voice tells me of my physical condition that day. If my voice breaks while I chant or takes much more effort on certain days, I view it as a message from my inner self. So, some days when I think I feel fine, but my voice seems very weak, it gives me pause; I become watchful of my energy levels, eat a healthy meal, take a nap, and monitor myself so I don't fall ill. Or we might experience our voice as strong and bold, which can indicate a good day for moving forward on a difficult project.

Or, if we face a dangerous situation, we might hear in another's voice these same things, which may suggest what kind of expectations to hold about their potential actions. More commonly, we might also determine how a child, or a significant other is doing with a difficult situation they are facing by listening to their breath or voice. This is not magic; it is just paying attention to observable behavior. Those of us who enjoy opera can reflect on how sound affects us in that setting. Opera lovers don't just hear "noise"—good singers can put a person into a rapture with their voice. This is kototama again.

As I write this book, I read my words out loud so I can hear how they flow, and how easy it will be for someone else to read them for the first time (even if they aren't reading out loud). And actors may warm up by saying out loud a difficult string of words: "Sally sells seashells by the seashore." When a newborn is expected it is common for family members to sit and suggest names out loud, often putting them into sentences that they expect to use in calling the child for dinner when they're old enough to play outside. These examples point to a different use of kototama that has more to do with the sound of the words or names spoken by looking at their auditory appeal.

It is true that the practice of kototama affects the universe. Chanting and prayers can be attempts to contact other worldly spirits. But chanting is not necessarily a religious act; a chant may just be a good opportunity to exercise your voice and your breath. It can serve as a meditation.

O-Sensei did study kototama through his various spiritual practices. *Kototama* literally means "the jewel of sound," and perhaps it is one of the mysteries of Aikido. Mysteries are hidden and—like the early messages of Christianity or the Eleusinian Mysteries in Ancient Greece—to reveal them takes effort and oftentimes an initiation. And, although I am a curious person interested in learning, I'm not one to engage in religious practices—the dogma of a religion is not something my philosophical nature can accept. But I found that there were many perspectives from which Aikido teachers employed kototama. The origins of their various practices are unclear.

One teacher I studied with used kototama in a spiritually expansive practice involving the triangle as the sound "su," circle as "ah," and square as "ei." He would relate these three basic shapes of the energetic world to the three sounds. The triangle, circle, and square are symbols used in Aikido and some understanding of this will help me explain how the sounds relate to the shapes. The triangle is a figure made by converging lines to a final point. Aikido's entering movements are based on this figure in that the proper position for a sword tip is in front of our center, on our vertical centerline. If we view the tip of the sword as the point of a triangle, then the two converging lines would be the unseen lines from our hips to the tip of the sword. In this way, the triangle is viewed as providing the course of an entry like when the prow of a ship parts the water, or as a knife blade cuts a carrot. The circle is round with no points or handles; it is purely dynamic and so it is used to describe the main circular motion of a technique. The square is immovable like a house sitting on a granite mountain. And so it represents our finishing move, which sometimes is a pin where the nage would be seated in seiza or a throw where the nage would be firmly centered on the mat as he sent someone sailing.

Then regarding the mapping of the sounds onto these forms, let me begin with one and move to the other. In kototama the teacher would guide us in a practice to make the "su" sound: lips close together at the beginning and moving forward as the sound releases and comes to a quick close, the mouth making as much of a point as a mouth can at the end of this sound. This sound is made as I press my fingertips together on my outstretched arms in front of me, making a kind of triangle shape. Moving forward, I enter and close the distance to my attacker. The "su" sound carries with it the energetic dynamics of this shape and its movement. So, making the actual movement to the sound seems very natural. The "ah" sound is made while opening up and turning in a circle and it expresses the circle's expansive nature as the mouth opens wide and lets the sound out on an exhale. The circle is a never-ending shape and because there is no beginning or end, it is the essence of movement, it's dynamic so the circle represents the middle of a technique where the largest movements are found. And the "ei" sound truncates as the mouth widens horizontally and pulls the lips shut. This finishing sound is signified by the square, its abruptness perfect for a throwing motion or pin to end the technique as the person throwing must be grounded at this point. Putting it all together made for a fun practice as he would instruct us how to use it in various techniques. Moving while making those sounds seemed to release a person's inhibitions, and so would make their movements powerful and smooth. My students tell me that this practice forces them to release their breath, which they sometimes hold during practice. Whenever this teacher asked me what I'd like to do in class, I'd call for this kototama practice.

Another teacher who was an authority on kototama would end a workshop with a more formal kototama practice. Using important

Aikido words he would have the entire class stand in a circle and voice them in one breath, sliding the sound by changing our mouth shape: "AaaaaeeeKiiiiiiiiDooooo," (Aikido) "TaaaaKeeeeeiiiiMuuuuuSuuuuuu" (takemusu), or "AaaaeeiiiiKiiiiiiOoooooKaaaaaMiiiiiii" (aiki o kami). To get through all the mouth shapes in a single powerful long breath was exhausting. But it was definitely a nice end to a long day of training. It was a renewal really and the communal nature of it—all of us sounding the same word at the same time—was an uplifting and powerful chant like the chant "om" in yoga.

A sound can be voiced to dive into a deeper state of mind. To go deeper into kototama, it's useful to understand the practices involving different sounds as they are used to create and call different energies. It is the bridge to our communication with other life-forms. I have noticed when I imitate a certain bird call, I invite my bird friends to visit me. But I am very surprised when they come. This is the study of sound, language, and communication. We have a lot to learn about this.

Although mustangs do not speak our language, they are attracted to certain sounds. My Scottish friend Doug noticed a herd of wild

*Fig. 11.3. Herd of wild mustangs on my friend Doug's property.*

*Fig. 11.4. Several mustangs drawn in by the bagpipes Doug played.*

mustangs living on his property in West Virginia when he was surveying the land. And being wild they would not come near him. But when my Scottish friend began to play the bagpipes, some of the wild mustangs came to him, and congregated close by.

Like my own encounter with the wild burros of the San Bernardino mountains, here they were attracted to Doug's bagpipes. We can reflect on how it may be that certain sounds and vibrations summon creatures; they are attracted to the energy of that vibration like the earthworms that emerged and congregated on my feet upon my tapping the jo on the ground. If Doug had been growling and snarling, the behavior of the mustangs probably would have been quite different.

In this brief discussion of kototama we have connected sounds to body shapes or movements. This is practice for creating sensitivity to vibrations as it is much easier to see with sound. But as we know, vibrations exist everywhere and offer information by their existence.

We may notice when someone enters into a busy party even if they are not formally announced. And horror movies know well the language and sound effects to scare the audience when someone enters what they think is an empty house but intuits a presence hiding within.

A scene from another Kurosawa movie—*Seven Samurai*—highlights a relevant point about the importance of being aware all the time of the activity of energy in the space between people.

### Seven Samurai

*Set with the task of finding skillful ronin (disenfranchised samurai) to help a farmer community rid themselves of the bandits who are stealing their grain, the chosen head ronin sets out on his task of building a crew to help him. Going to the nearest village, he sits inside a room with an open doorway to the village center where he can watch the potential hires walk toward the doorway for their interview. The camera shows us this inside view and we can see that posed just inside the doorway there is a swordsman beside the door with an upraised sword ready to strike whomever wanders through it. The swordsman who gets the job is the one who, instead of wandering inside by stepping mindlessly through the doorway, stops himself as if an alarm went off. But there is no alarm, there is only his intuitive sense of the hidden danger, a skill marking a masterful swordsman. This is exactly the skill the head ronin is looking for in a hire, and because the prospective hire survives the test, he is hired as a part of the crew.*

Becoming sensitive and aware of our surroundings is a staple of Aikido. The idea is that nothing is assumed, and everything is respected is the aim. Like the awareness of the prospective hire in *Seven Samurai* a new meaning of being in the here and now emerges. We might call it some kind of intuition to vibrations that exist in what some view as empty space such as the vibrations that we all put out involuntarily with our breath and movement. The samurai movie plays upon the idea that we can detect the presence of those we cannot see yet. Like our friend in the horror movie, I have entered a house I thought was empty and experienced the feeling that someone was inside. Kurosawa was playing on the more subtle side of things. Warriors always seem attracted to esoteric energy.

Not noticing change is never helpful, and not noticing is never mindful. But using sound to change conditions can be meaningful and interesting. We can steer ourselves toward sounds we find pleasant: music of storm sounds or of birdsong. We can listen for our own breath in a quiet moment, go to places of nature and enjoy the sounds there. We can learn how to make sound by playing an instrument, singing, or chanting. We can listen with active appreciation to great music. To attend to sounds from a state of mindfulness is healing to our biological system. We do have the power to heal ourselves, and sound is an important part of that.

In some of the practices of Aikido we learn how powerful the vibrations of sound and breath can be. In advanced practice, a good time to enter into our partner's attack is when they are inhaling, which would be a yin movement (exhales tend to be strong or yang). In Aikido classes students are instructed how to breathe properly, how to breathe from your belly—deep and long. Typically this fuller breath differs from one's normal breath. In our everyday world, stress abounds, and the body's coping mechanism is to close up to hold us safe and tight. But shallow breathing is unhealthy and contributes to poor circulation, sluggish thinking, and pain from the lack of oxygen being accessible to our organs and muscle tissue. So breathing is important to our well-being.

A breathing practice is often used as a meditation—taking a moment and controlling our breath, we relax—and Aikido is all about moving in a relaxed way. In fact, many talk about the strength we find once we relax. This is because when we're tense our movements do not come from our center, but from our muscular tension—which is not our center at all. By accessing the center through relaxation all our movements are made stronger because we're using the whole body. Breath can get us there quickly.

We all make sounds; we may sing, talk, pray, sigh, snore, call to a child, whistle for our dog, and clap at a concert's finish. It is hard not to make sound! Stealthy movement is not soundless. My visits to the famous samurai Nijo Castle* in Kyoto made me value the old squeaky wooden floors of my house in California. At this castle, they proudly call the squeaking of the hallway floors the "chirping" of the "nightingale floors," and I was given a handout about the unique construction it took to produce these chirping floors, which were put in place as a security measure. No one could walk down those hallways without making themselves heard by the "chirping" of the floorboards underneath. I now take great pride in my chirping floors at home.

Voiced sounds are vibrations that ride on the breath. If one's breath is shallow, our sounds will be shallow too. Singers work on strategies for managing air or breath so that they can control the sounds they make in many deep ways: tone, timbre, and volume to name a few. The singer learns how to "load" their body with air in order to unload it with control and create a powerful delivery, and how to hold a note or sing a lengthy and demanding phrase before taking another breath. But breaths, voiced or not, are vibrations in and of themselves. I can hear my pup, Ame, breathing from across the room, and I can tell when she is in distress, or just dreaming deeply about chasing bunnies. As we learn how to incorporate our entire body in our breathing, we can reap the benefits of this simple, natural process of taking a breath. Breaths are vibrations.

It is common to find some students in Aikido classes who have difficulty making sounds. (If only they were the people that visited mountains!) For these students, it's useful to begin with some breathwork and

---

*Nijo Castle was built as the residence of the Tokugawa Shoguns, starting with Ieyasu Tokugawa in 1601.

then ask them to let the voice ride on the breath. Once they try this a few times, their voice takes on wonderful depth and they sound entirely different.

O-Sensei, along with modern scientists, understood that the world is composed of vibrations. The potential hire in Kurosawa's film may have been displaying his detection of vibrations in some way. O-Sensei was said to know when someone arrived at the train station looking for him even though he was a mile away with no cell phone. This kind of sensitivity takes some time to develop. It might be hard to imagine that a human could be capable of this, but many animals are able to detect things very far away with their incredible auditory powers or powers of smell. And we forget how quiet existed in the times of previous generations. When it's quiet outside, I can hear things happening in the near distance, and sometimes several miles away.

Today, a popular way of avoiding the world around us is to walk around with earbuds in our ears. To my mind, this invites danger as we can't hear what is happening around us when we're moving about; you don't want a notoriously quiet Prius to sneak up behind you without you knowing. Of course, I understand the motivation of silencing the chaos by choosing to listen to something calming, something that drowns out unwanted sounds. In fact, too much loud noise is not healthy when it begins to disrupt the inner workings of our body and mind. One experience stands out in this regard.

### Jackhammers

*I was in a hospital suite with my husband who was undergoing chemotherapy in the building's basement. As we settled into the busy suite for his six-hour infusion, I was surprised to hear jackhammers! An older part of the hospital was being demolished that day to make way for something new. So jackhammers and other machines were busy at work while twenty cancer patients faced their day of hell getting infusions. It didn't seem like a good idea, and I was disappointed at this new level of ignorance on the part of institutes of health. Although*

*I dutifully sat with my husband for the six hours as his advocate while he slept through the chemotherapy, that day I felt completely annoyed.*

*I mentioned to our chemo nurse that the hospital should schedule the demolition crew for Saturday—a day when the hospital chemo suite was closed. She laughed at me, and looked at me as though I was an idiot. I explained that the stress of chaotic and loud noise is not good for healing and restoring especially for very ill patients, and that the sounds from the jackhammers were producing a stressful environment for these twenty people (and for me) who must sit in place for six hours and endure it. Stress and healing most often work against each other; even if the stress comes with wanted sensations (as at a party or amusement park), still good stress can work against healing as the body needs rest and relaxation in order to rebuild and restore. In my mind, Kaiser Hospital should have voluntarily paid more to ensure the chemo suite was quiet for their patients as they had much more to gain by featuring people who managed to get healthy there. After all, their motto is "thrive!" But I knew the world was not yet the place I hoped it would be.*

*When the hospital director involved with the demolition project walked into the room, our nurse led him over to me, and said by way of introduction, "This is the guy to talk to!" Without much hope that my insights would change anything, I persevered: I explained why the noise from the jackhammer demolition was working against these patients, creating a chaotic environment that they were helpless to change. I asked if the jackhammers and the demolition in general could be rescheduled for Saturday when the chemo suite was closed. I was prepared to be laughed at again, and for my request to fall on deaf ears. But he said, "Well, I'll take care of that right away," and he walked out of the room purposefully.*

*I did not expect this hopeful response: he didn't shut me down, but I didn't know if he was being sarcastic or authentic. Then about ten minutes later the jackhammers stopped. I'm sure my mouth dropped open . . . could it be true? Then all the other machines of destruction stopped too! In confirmation, the floor nurse walked over to me and told me the demolition had been rescheduled for Saturday. And that afternoon in the basement of Kaiser Hospital, the chemo suite was quiet and orderly, and one woman's estimation of Kaiser went up a notch. Although our nurse thought I was nuts as she said she didn't notice any difference, I did hear a patient audibly sigh and say, "What a relief!" as her body noticeably unwound on an exhale; settling into the chair she soon fell asleep.*

*I learned an important lesson that day: not to give up on yourself. After the initial reception I received from our nurse, I was going to give up; not because it wasn't a worthy battle, but because I felt I was outnumbered. But step by step our nurse actually helped me move forward, and she brought me someone who listened and was persuaded. Life is so unpredictable that giving up is just the laziness of a coward. And we mustn't forget the lesson of Fudomyo: to be steadfast and true to yourself like an immovable rock.*

In classes at my dojo students were instructed in a number of different ways to slow and deepen their breath. This frees up the ki so that we can relax and move more easily. But these lessons in breathwork help us to hear ourselves too. And in hearing ourselves, we can begin to work on our extension and control over the vibrations we put out. Learning how to modulate our voices gives us more control over how we affect others. A soft voice assures, and maybe attracts those listening, while a shrill voice sends people running. Sometimes people speak so softly they make themselves inaudible to others. When I lived in the mountains, I particularly enjoyed the blue Steller's jays of the mountains. In fact, I would put seeds out for them when I sat on the deck, and I'd call them— "blueblueblueblue"—and it wasn't long before one arrived, big and full bellied, always wanting more. Every time I called "blue," he'd often come with four blue Steller's jay friends. When I'm not in the mountains, I see blue looking into my motion-sensor Ring camera. I wonder. . . .

A strong breath is required for a ki ai—the aiki shout, which is strong and sharp so as to create openings. And, of course, as we learn how to incorporate our body in our breath, we reap the benefits of connecting to our center—the true place of power and relaxation—by being able to give a piercing shout. Again, for the most penetrating shout it must come from your center and on an exhalation; otherwise, you'll tear up your throat like most fans do at concerts or at football games. Most students couldn't handle an entire class on breath and sound; it requires the strength and flexibility of the intercostals, diaphragm, lungs, and abs. But it is in this practice that the power of Aikido technique is developed. And, in the final analysis, creating a strong center is essential to discovering health and power.

Some people are embarrassed to make a sound. They have never experienced the power of their own voice. The sword class was a perfect time to instruct students how to ki ai, and once they got past the embarrassment of voicing a shout, they loved it. So kototama is a subtle practice in swordwork; the same can be said about brushwork.

Breath and sound are resources that O-Sensei put to good use. We are not very skilled in the West with these resources, and so it is much easier to wave them off as the religious ramblings of the founder. But before we make rash judgments, we might discover something meaningful and true in these esoteric practices. That is really the premise of this book: to bring into the light the sources of our modern practices for a deeper understanding of the art.

# TWELVE

# Symbolic Jewels

## *The Hidden Aspects of*
## *Inner Cultivation*

*Aiki is not about fighting or breaking an opponent. Aiki is the path to make everyone (humanity) one family in harmony with the world.*

O-Sensei, "Takemusu Aiki," 1976

Throughout this book, we have understood that cultivating our center, in the broadest sense, leads to developing self-control, honesty, and compassion: powerful virtues that help us cut through the darkness. As our cultivation deepens along this path, we will be able to address the states that O-Sensei advocates: nonresistance, being one with the universe, being invincible, and being compassionate toward all living things. In short, if we realize one of these states, we will feel the joy of being in the moment. I heard an Aikido teacher say that Aikido is the world's best-kept secret: if people knew how good a person feels after an Aikido class, there'd be a line at the door to get in!

Being nonresistant refers to the calm disposition of being in the moment, allowing us to see what we would normally miss when distracted by other things. When we slow down enough to actually see, we access more directly our sensory perceptions so that cracks might appear in our everyday map of reality. When we relax, we slow down, and time slows with us. It reminds me of being a child waiting for the first snow—even if it was predicted to come that day, it still seemed to take forever; time could move so slowly. But when I'm busy writing a chapter of this book, time flies; a day seems to go by in fifteen minutes. Our experience of the passage of time changes depending upon our energetic state. It's similar with space: A famous Eastern saying is "the journey of 1000 miles begins with a single step." If I think of 1000 miles, I may give up the journey before I begin, but if I focus on a single step the action seems easy and immediate and then I can take another. Our perspective affects our actions.

From chapter 8, we have come to understand that O-Sensei viewed budo as about protection and stopping the fight. Biographers say that his brilliance is found in his statement, "Budo is Love." We need only consider the ferocity that a mama bear brings in protecting her cubs for this to make sense. Of course, it's not the fight the mama bear brings to which I refer, but rather the unconditional loyalty and sacrifice she's willing to make for her young that motivates her to bring the fight in the first place. This example of the mama bear is often the paradigm for a mother's love. Looking outward at a broader application, then, perhaps we can say a samurai's feelings for his community could be understood to be along these same lines: loyalty and sacrifice.

If Aikido is budo, and budo is love, it follows that Aikido is love— but we don't need logic to tell us this, because O-Sensei says it many times. He even took enjoyment in wordplay using these two homophone characters pronounced "ai" as in "fitting" or "appropriate" (such as the "ai" in *Aikido*) and "ai" as in *ai,* meaning "love." Like most Japanese, O-Sensei enjoyed puns and punning. What a playful way to open the minds of his students!

The character *ai* in Aikido means fitting like a key fits a lock (in fact, this character is used on locksmith's signs in Japan to mean just that), but a more popular use is "in union with," "in harmony with,"

*Fig. 12.1. Ai: the kanji for love.*

or "coming together". But there is another Japanese character that is its homophone, and it is the character *ai* meaning "love." O-Sensei used these characters interchangeably many times in his calligraphy work and probably in his lectures.

I would visit my teacher for a week every year outside of the many seminars and camps I would attend as it would give me some quiet time to focus on my training. He lived in Washington, D.C. Often I would stay at the family home so I could take class as well as spend some private time with him—often interviewing him for my magazine, we had many projects and plans we would discuss during these visits. Although I did not take formal calligraphy lessons from him, he was a very powerful calligrapher, and I admired his calligraphy. Every so often he would show me a few things about brushwork. One day we took the Metro to Chinatown for lunch, and I was surprised when he led me into a shop and bought a small stone for a seal (chop). It was not yet carved. But that night as we sat on his living room floor after dinner, he gave me my brush name—Su zan—by carving it into this stone. "Su" is a seed sound that means the beginning of creation, often viewed as the sun, and "san" is mountain, so Sun over Mountain. It doesn't get much better than that. I use that seal on all my artwork with great pride.

In the last chapter, I presented a symbol for yin and yang that displayed just two *tamas* ("jewels," or "souls") in a visible circle. And I must admit I am most familiar with that symbol and its usefulness in explaining human tendencies. But there is another similar symbol with three tamas (really four, but one is hidden) and because Aikido dojos use it frequently, I'd like to touch on it here. The Japanese call it *mitsu domoe* (three jewels). Just as the kami from the *Kojiki* are now manga (Japanese comic) characters, you may have seen this symbol on t-shirts, drums, corporate logos, or school insignias: it is one of the common Japanese symbols used everywhere. Even on the internet, there seems to be a cartoon game using this symbol as well as the names for the four energetic powers it symbolizes. But I doubt many of the cartoon game users know of its true meaning as it comes from Shinto esoterica. Having said that, it is difficult to find a clear written account of this symbol that elaborates on the four aspects of the soul represented here: *ara mitama, nigi mitama, sachi mitama,* and *kushi mitama.* Like most Shinto scholarship, there are many disagreements, and O-Sensei's explanations are not completely clear. But my understanding of the meaning of these tamas is as follows:

1. Ara mitama refers to the raw, rough, and wild aspects of a being. Young children best display these tendencies, as well as older adults who are not cultivated: it is the rough, rude, and violent tendencies we sometimes see. Perhaps such propensities can be cultivated into the virtue of courage.
2. Nigi mitama is a functional and socialized aspect of human behavior that supports qualities of empathy, trust, and respect.
3. Sachi mitama is the source of love and happiness, and the unseen and hidden.
4. Kushi mitama is the wise and wondrous aspect of our soul.

Mitsu domoe is a symbol of four aspects of our soul or self that, like the yin and yang energies, exist at the same time. Ara mitama

*Fig. 12.2. Symbol for
mitsu domoe.*

and nigi mitama seem to be at odds as ara mitama consists of raw
and wild energy while nigi mitama signifies gentle energy, and so
is the preferred state. So it is important to quiet the ara mitama,
so it doesn't completely overtake or block the cultivation of nigi
mitama.

The point of all this is that in order to become the best that we
can be, cultivation or the proper balancing of these aspects is necessary.
This has echoes in the West: Aristotle, too, thinks cultivation from
wild, uncontrollable emotions and desires is the key to the training of a
good, wise, and virtuous human being.

A prominent and popular Aikido sensei from the United States,
Mary Heiny, gives an account of O-Sensei's view of how Aikido nurtures and develops human life.* She says:

O'Sensei used to talk about . . . KI-IKU, CHI-IKU, TAI-IKU,
TOKU-IKU, JOSHIKI. He said these were the five areas Aikido

---
*See the Mary Heiny website for more.

practice developed. O'Sensei thought that Aikido nurtured each person in the areas [mentioned above] of understanding KI, increasing our knowledge and wisdom through study and experience, strengthening and purifying our bodies, increasing our understanding of ethical behavior and social sensibilities.

Although we are all different, we are not born as balanced creatures; there is some cultivation that will smooth out the rough edges as human beings, make us better, polish up our souls or ourselves (polishing the mirror and pounding the steel—both images used to illustrate misogi practice—are allusions to cultivating ourselves). Our parents, teachers, and coaches help us along the way somewhat. But people rarely reach a true balance without focused effort to bring it all together.

You probably know of someone who is a yang person, active and forceful sometimes to a fault, or a yin person, calm and quiet to a fault. The yin–yang symbol shows a contrasting dot in the field of black or white; this dot indicates that there is no purely yang or yin state. Like the image in chapter 11, the aim is to balance the two sides so a yang person develops their yin side, and a yin person develops their yang side. Both sides being in balance at every moment is necessary to self-realize, self-cultivate, to become complete, to become a person with the health, power, and wisdom to do amazing things.

In talking about mitsu domoe we find out that despite the name—*mitsu* refers to three—there are really four tamas, as one is hidden.

The hidden tama stands for something overriding the other three as a wise and wondrous aspect. Could it be that this hidden tama IS the hidden power of Aikido? I'll leave that for experts of Japanese mysticism to decide. There are many pitfalls awaiting one who attempts to interpret such things. But mitsu domoe offers a nice illustration of what the ancient Japanese thought on the matter of human cultivation. It is not so far from what we're used to here in the West.

Clearly, it is that which Aristotle aims to cultivate in a person to make them virtuous and happy. And similarly, when O-Sensei talks of having a loving heart or extending loving protection toward all living things, he is speaking of a disposition, a tendency to act in a certain way. When we speak of the "power" of Aikido we are talking about something active, something energetic. My book has attempted to color in what this energy is all about and why it's so distinctive to Aikido.

Having begun with O-Sensei and Aristotle, it'd be nice to finish our inquiry with a simple look at their common ground: the concept of benevolence works nicely. *Benevolence* is an old term from Latin that means "goodwill," or "the wish to do good," or even "the disposition to be good." *Virtue* (Arete) itself is often translated as excellence, and so the virtues are various ways of doing good. Clearly, in O-Sensei's view, such an understanding would comfortably cover the attitude of loving kindness he promotes.

---

### Taking in the Isle of Crete

*We did not share a language, but we communicated just fine. It was my first trip to the island of Crete in Greece, and I was traveling alone. As I stepped off the boat that had taken me across the Aegean Sea from the island of Santorini, I stopped at my little hotel a few blocks away from the waterfront. Excited to see something of this new place before I retired for the evening, I asked the concierge to rent me a car, and to suggest where I might go before dinner.*

*She directed me to a little village in the mountains just outside of the big city of Heraklion where I would be spending the week. This village, Anogeia, had a past famous for the hardships encountered during war. An unforgiving place populated mostly by shepherds and goatherds as the land was virtually unfarmable, Anogeia was razed to the ground in 1882 when fighting the Turks, and again during World War II when the Germans left Anogeia without any men and burned down most of the houses so not even a brick stood upon another. A tough and resilient people, Anogeia was rebuilt, and the women took to sewing and weaving beautiful textiles to sell. The concierge said that if I went there, the women would invite me in to look at their handiwork if they saw me walking along the street. I followed her instructions, and sure enough the women there invited me in to see their lovely handiwork. I did end up buying many small pieces of beautiful textiles and embroidery for friends and family back home.*

*As the day became dusk, I got back into the car, and started down the street to return to Heraklion. I was in heaven and my little jaunt had gone with no difficulty, so now I was hungry and heading back into the big city. Suddenly a large, middle-aged woman stepped out in front of my car. I stopped and the next thing I knew she opened the passenger door and sat down beside me. I was not alarmed; something drew me to her. She was clean cut even though her smile revealed a few missing teeth. She had a cloth bag with her, which she set between her feet. She smiled and looked at me and said "Heraklion?" I nodded and said, "Nai," (yes) and so an agreement was made. I had no problem with this woman in my car. She was friendly, and even though I was not fluent in modern Greek, her voice was calming. We took off for Heraklion. With my Attic Greek language skills, I managed a few things like "beautiful moon" as we drove the Mt. Psiloritis pass toward an amazing moon that appeared in a purplish glow. She smiled and agreed. We even chuckled at the strange camaraderie we had.*

*On the outskirts of Heraklion she called my attention to a wooden sign hanging down in front of a vine-covered doorway on the right side of the road. Knowing the Greek alphabet, I read the word for* music *on the sign. Through a kind of sign language, I asked if she wanted me to let her out there. She indicated no and pointed me straight ahead, down the road. With her gestures directing me we wove through streets and then into a parking lot by an apartment building. I stopped. She got out and leaned her head in and said "perimeno" and then turned and took off with her cloth bag in hand. I was trying to remember what* perimeno *meant. I thought it meant "wait" but I rarely trust my first inclinations without checking a source. But, without my lexicon, there was only one way to tell. I waited. Sure*

*Fig. 12.3. Moon over Mount Psiloritis (Painting by Susan Perry)*

*enough, she returned, and once again got in the car. Then she said the word for* music, *and I knew exactly where she wanted to go.*

*Once there, she indicated I should come with her inside. As we passed through the vine-covered doorway, I saw a magical sight: strings of lights in the open-air venue, many tables, and a stage. It was a beautiful outside taverna—empty—as Greeks eat around 8 p.m. She led me to a table toward the back near the kitchen door where several men were sitting. They knew her and welcomed both of us. She signaled to me to sit down, and the men at the table made room for me. It is astounding how many people can sit around a small table in Greece; no one seems to mind this charming practice. And the start to the most amazing evening was underway. The table filled up with food of all kinds: meat, veggies, watermelon, beer, wine, grapes, and many other dishes. This evening was payback for the ride that I gave her down the mountain. Her husband was Psarantonis,\* the Bob Dylan of Crete, and this was "his" taverna. When the restaurant filled up, there appeared a tall lean figure with wild hair flowing all around his face, and he began to play his lyra. Everyone danced those wonderful Greek dances that move in a circle, and as the music picked up to a dizzying speed the dancing followed. I only fell off the stage once! I was learning about those powerful spirals already. Back at the table I made a friend. He was one of the men at the table who welcomed me when I arrived; he could speak English well and was the librarian at the local university, which I found strange as my Greek colleague back at California State University, Fullerton was encouraging me to look up his friends at that university. I had their names written down in my purse, but I had decided against looking them up; I was on vacation. And so we began a conversation. He told me about the woman that got into my car: She was a nurse and the wife of Psarantonis who, I learned many years later, comes from Anogeia!*

*I found it odd that, having decided against collegiate companionship*

---

\*His real name is Antonios Xylouris.

*of any kind, I ended up quite by accident talking to this man who turned out to be the librarian of the university. And even curiouser that Psarantonis was born in Anogeia! So from the time I set foot in Crete and was directed to Anogeia by my hotel concierge, some interesting coincidences arose.*

*Before the night was over the librarian had invited me to accompany him on a tour of some archaeological sites the next day on the southern side of Crete. A thrilling night of surprises turned into several days of intense wonderment as I was driven to many Minoan ruins I probably otherwise would never have seen. And I made a good friend; I kept up a correspondence with him until I returned to Crete again.*

In this story, something quite extraordinary happened, and it happened because of an open willingness to engage. Psarantonis's wife stopped my car in the middle of a small Greek village as the sun was going down at the end of the day. I didn't know her. I had never been to the village before but there was nothing in the situation that alarmed me. In fact, there was a palpable feeling of love and safety. Was it nurse energy? Perhaps. But looking back, even my more logical mind says that it was extremely unlikely that a native Greek, like the concierge at my hotel, would tell me to go to this small village where I'd be invited into people's homes if there had been any problems occurring there with tourists. Moreover, I had "spoken" to village women as I was looking at the different textiles. Not once did I feel any subterfuge, deception, or danger. And so this story stands in great contrast to the other stories of deception and threat. This kind of encounter led to nothing short of an amazing adventure with a blissful outcome that I have never forgotten. The difference here is the honesty, the sincerity that the actors brought to one another.

On my trip to Anogeia, even walking the streets of the village, I felt accepted and welcomed. And so when a stranger stopped my car and opened the door to get in, I wasn't afraid . . . maybe intrigued or surprised, but not afraid. Honesty was everywhere: She didn't prop her action up with a sob story, she didn't offer me money, she simply asked for a ride to the place I was already going. There was no suspicion I might decline; she just gave me a nice smile and that was enough. I felt no need to resist. It felt good to have her in my car. One human getting a ride from another: two great hearts at peace.

I began this book by comparing O-Sensei to another of my favorite philosophers, Aristotle, which is the greatest compliment I can pay to either thinker. I did this for two reasons: First, I want readers to understand that Aikido is not a religion, but a practice with a strong philosophical element that needs to be included in training—not by lectures, but by informed practice. Because O-Sensei relied heavily on stories from the *Kojiki,* and because the *Kojiki* is regarded by some as a religious book, too many people see O-Sensei's views as religious ramblings that can be ignored. From my own philosophical cynicism, I have become convinced that we can appreciate O-Sensei, not as someone who is proselytizing his religion, but as someone who had the insight to use the *Kojiki* stories—filled as they are with the strangest of characters—already familiar to his students as illustrative of deep points he wanted to make about Aikido. I'm hoping you'll join me in looking at them in this way to better appreciate what O-Sensei saw in them.

And second, O-Sensei has shown himself to be serious and profound in the aims he's picked out for Aikido. Aristotle and O-Sensei both are concerned with what constitutes the highest form of a human being, and they are unique thinkers in that they see the process of self-cultivation as one of embodying important principles. In O-Sensei's case, he even has provided an art to do just that. So by beefing up our training on the mat we can continue the process of self-cultivation by embodiment, which will bring us closer to developing a warrior spirit, and closer to world peace and happiness.

It takes some time to develop a warrior spirit, but it surely is needed in the world in order to, as O-Sensei would say, quell the discord. And as you can tell from my stories, movement forward is made along the way in the most unforeseen and amusing experiences. Embodying O-Sensei's principles enriches our training experience, and makes us more effective in our daily activities, as well as better workout partners in the dojo.

For those unsure about how Aikido functions in the world outside the dojo, I have presented in this book many stories of my own to suggest how the embodiment of the art's principles might show up in a person's life. Of course, my stories are largely about my moments of discovery in success and in failure. It's not always easy to understand how to move forward in a certain moment, but this is how it goes: step by step, moment by moment. Learning from our failures is a good thing, as there is a promise that next time it can be different. Like remembering a professor's marks on a class paper were not about me personally, but about the paper, I have come to laugh at my mistakes, as they serve as learning opportunities, and sometimes my choices are just as funny as they are revealing.

I've described the mat room as a sacred space just because the mat provides a calm and supportive place to work on difficult personal issues should they come up. And I've described the busy everyday world as the chaotic hell that exists outside the dojo doors because once you step outside there is precious little time for the kind of introspective work that the mat affords. In the last chapter, I imagined a person trying to do some breathwork on a sidewalk by a busy intersection; not the best place for work of this kind because there are too many distractions. But we are grateful to have both places to give us different experiences to guide our progress. And trying breathwork in such a busy and distracting environment can indicate how much focus we are capable of, making it a test of a kind once we get our bearings. During the holiday seasons when I was just a few years into my Aikido practice, I would walk in busy shopping malls just to test out my center and see if I could make it to the end of a walkway without getting bumped off balance by distracted and anxious shoppers with many bags.

Many have chastised me over the years for my beliefs about extending Aikido off the mat, but I believe that this is where a certain number of O-Sensei's teachings happened. To penetrate his philosophy is no easy matter partly because he did not write it down. But we can look at his life's actions through the many excellent biographies of him to see what kind of person he was. In fact, I believe he emulated his philosophy in action as if he were providing for the rest of us a real-life illustration of what his art is about. For instance, I believe O-Sensei did want humans to take an active role in stewarding the future, and he exemplified this in his Hokkaido project, and in his work protesting the government's attempt to take forest and shrine land in their consolidation program. Although he quietly protested the government build-up to World War II, his stance against the war was easy to read by those around him. Years later, we see him transporting to Tokyo food that he grew at his Iwama farm to bring to hungry neighbors in need after the war. He also followed his son's lead in overcoming the obstacles to teaching Aikido in a postwar world. I have a picture of him constantly participating in classes, in demonstrations, and traveling to his students' dojos to teach there. In short, he put himself out there.

It is up to us to recognize the embodiment of these lessons to become genuine students of O-Sensei. I am not the most learned voice, but I have tried to contribute to the great body of books and teachings of my Aikido colleagues an illustrative explanation of some of O-Sensei's more elusive statements. I have been inspired by the intellectual history of the ancient traditions of Japan; and knowing a little bit more about this has actually made me take Aikido more seriously. In this book, I have given a reading in chapter 5 to a *Kojiki* story that helps to explain one of Aikido's principles: *masakatsu agatsu katsuhayabi* (true victory is self-victory).

When we read O-Sensei's words, he is constantly urging us to cut through the darkness, to be nonresistant, to be sincere, to be centered, to purify ourselves, and to extend loving kindness to all living creatures. "I am the universe" is a declaration made by someone who believes they are completely reflecting what is. And you cannot be a complete reflection if there is one iota of doubt involved. At some point, the doubts of a skeptic can be put to rest if one does the work of investigating and discovering the truth. This is what it is to find certainty about something. And, of course, certainty can be a fleeting state, if the truth we think we've discovered is not the real deal: some clouds of deception may continue to float around, but by working to make a discovery, we get closer and closer to the unbridled truth, the rock we can stand upon in conviction. As a budding philosophy student I once would explain myself to others by saying that I just expect the worst to happen and if it does, I'm not surprised—and if it does not, I have a moment for celebration. I thought I was clever in developing this win–win attitude. But Aikido made me realize that this attitude was one of discouragement and excuse-making: I was hedging my bets, I was choosing to participate only after the outcome was known. It was the attitude of a coward who demands safety before acting. But Aikido is a warrior art, and being a warrior takes courage and commitment. It takes the energy of Fudomyo standing on the rock being true to himself, having quelled the demons of ignorance by his sword of truth.

Both Aristotle and O-Sensei have a view of what a human can become, and the cultivation necessary for that realization. Aristotle calls it the development of a virtuous person, and O-Sensei views it as the development of a loving heart. (O-Sensei talks of a kami heart, but as you will see below there is good reason to use "loving heart," which clarifies it for Western readers.)

I see similarities between them: In developing a virtuous disposition, Aristotle calls for a person to see the truth, to have awareness of what they're doing, to make the proper choices in terms of doing the right thing, at the right time, for the right reason, in the right place, and for their choices to spring from a firm disposition to act in that way.

O-Sensei thought that by ridding yourself of impurities, which you can do through misogi practice, you make a loving heart (a divine heart). This is a kind of Eastern view of cultivation; often the allusion is pounding out the impurities in the process of making a gleaming samurai sword (one of the sharpest swords made), or of polishing the mirror. Regarding the cultivation of a virtuous person, O-Sensei says, "First, we make our heart like the kami (loving) heart." He describes a kami heart as being surrounded by love "present all around, past and present." It is important to O-Sensei that you have no opponents at all. He continues, "Whoever is an opponent has a fighting heart, already does not have a kami (loving) heart" from *Takemusu Aiki.*

So his statements suggest that if you have a loving heart then you do not fight, and not fighting with anything is the way to be in harmony with the universe and thus invincible. At any rate, we can surmise from O-Sensei's seeing Aikido as a misogi practice that Aikido is a training ground for developing a person with a loving heart. O-Sensei goes one step further than Aristotle, who tells us what a virtuous person is; again, O-Sensei not only tells us but gives us an art to help produce that person! Such a person who is in harmony with the universe and is invincible is about as virtuous as you can get.

Aristotle does not call his virtuous person a person with a loving heart, but he did think that one of the necessary conditions for becoming virtuous is that a person's choices spring from a firm and fixed disposition. Of course, one of the Aristotelian virtues is magnanimity (greatness of soul), which is not exactly the same thing as a person with a loving heart but close. Whether Aristotle would point to the heart as the place where these dispositions reside is doubtful; he would probably point to the head, as most Westerners do when referring to themselves. And this is a well-recognized difference in custom from West to East, as in the West we tend to locate our identity in our head, while in the East it's the heart. (And *kokoro* is the single term used for both heart and mind.) Still, it is true that Aristotle saw the cultivation of a virtuous person as a change to something intrinsic and deep enough to alter the disposition of the person for the better.

O-Sensei calls for a loving heart, which he says is a heart that does not fight, does not have enemies, and that is in harmony with the universe. He sees love as an energy that connects us to the world. He talks about true budo being the cultivation of attraction that can draw a person to you. And of course he talks about the importance of being nonresistant.

If love is boundlessly created in our hearts, then no one can take it away, and it is ours to give freely. Sharing love with those around you creates a thread that can lead to a deeper bond. Giving love enriches us by connecting us to the world. With these conditions a strong picture is painted of embrace, of open arms willing to receive. And who isn't drawn to open, loving arms in an embrace, especially when that embrace will not resist or reject you. To my mind this is the attraction of a person with a loving heart. "Inhale your partner" finally makes sense. There is a beauty to Aikido movements and when done masterfully, all the principles are there rolled into one: harmony, love, nonresistance, invincibility, openness, and acceptance.

The universe is one very large, but connected, thing. Consider a still pool of water into which a rock is thrown; the explosive entry of the rock immediately changes the calm nature of the pool, and the many ripples that emanate from this meeting of rock and water cause an alteration of the entire pool. We can use this imagery to help us imagine, in the meeting of two strangers, how the vibrations of life interrupt the stillness of the status quo to communicate through the space between them. Often this happens without either person being cognizant of anything happening as the world is a very active place, and it takes awareness to detect this kind of thing: it might be the widening or narrowing of the eyes, or the opening or closing of the body so that even without speech a person can get a sense of whether to go forward or not. We can see in the meeting of dogs how they receive one another by watching their shapes change the energy of the meeting: ears, tail, posture, and fur going upward or downward can demonstrate, alternatively, dominating aggression or calm submission (yang or yin). I've talked about bears and dogs in this book, but it's not so different with humans: a squaring of shoulders with the jaw coming forward makes us seem larger and more imposing. Warriors once wore headdresses and epaulets to increase their visual size to their opponent. Of course, in studying a martial art, becoming sensitive to this kind of sensory information is key to protection, as knowing where and when an attack may come is essential. Those who become sensitive to this view of the world pick up on danger signals before they get too close to the source.

Back to the thrown rock: not only the water in the pond but everything in it—the fish and plants below the surface—are affected by the rock's disruption. In the same way, if we make ourselves aware of the many changes in the world, we could have a virtual encyclopedia of information at our disposal—if we can overcome some of our conceptual limitations.

With the help of Aikido we can become aware that, like the pool, we are a unified energy field that registers incoming energies and vibrations as a whole. Like the clay in the story about Yankee Hill Brickyard, these energies coalesce more tightly in some places, looser and more free flowing in others. When anything happens there is an alteration of the entire field, but perhaps not the exact same alteration everywhere. A tight part will move in one way, and a loose part may move differently.

We are becoming accustomed to this big picture, especially with climate change: a smokestack in one corner of the world affects the pollution level in another corner of the world; we are not as separate as we thought, and as the world becomes smaller in our minds, it's important that it also become friendlier. O-Sensei did not promulgate a divisive way of thinking: he included all nationalities and genders as worthy recipients of his art. World peace cannot happen in a vacuum but must bring all life together. I am, like O-Sensei, convinced that with a more cultivated populace, world peace would be possible. And I do believe humankind is changing and learning to embrace change. This is critical. Can we aspire to rid ourselves of a fighting mind? It would bring great changes to be sure. But even though we cannot wave a magic wand and change the world, we can work on ourselves. I will continue to work on myself, and to steer others, as best I can, to the pleasures of reaching for that feeling that Aikido can bring.

We all came into this world with a cry to announce ourselves and take our place in the world; this is our initial inhale, and we will leave on an exhale. What will we do with the breaths in between? I hope for good things, but mostly I hope we all learn to experience boundless joy.

> *Always keep your mind as high as the highest mountain,*
> *as deep as the deepest ocean, and as vast as the biggest sky,*
> *empty of all thoughts.*
>
> MOTTO OF AIKO INSTITUTE

# Glossary

**aiki**   fitting or harmonious energy. Literally, "confluence of life-energy." To perform a technique with *aiki* is to blend physically and mentally with one's attacker.

**Aikido**   "the Way of harmonious energy," sometimes more loosely translated as "the Art of Peace." A modern Japanese martial art, which—though useful in self-defense—emphasizes harmony, cooperation, and nonresistance. Aikido's founder, Morihei Ueshiba, realized that the essence of budo (martial Way) is love, and he urged his students and followers to act in "the spirit of loving protection for all of Nature's creation." Aikido is a budo, a Way of personal transformation and cultivation.

**Amaterasu Omikami**   the Sun goddess in Japanese mythology. One of the major figures in Shinto she is portrayed in Japan's earliest philosophy of the universe, the *Kojiki*. She stands for compassion as she brings light to everyone. A more abstract representation of acceptance of what is stems from her non-judgmental character.

**Anogeia**   a Cretan village located in Rethymnon on the slopes of Mount Psiloritis at 2,300 ft. It is the birthplace of Antonios Xylouris, a.k.a. Psarantonis, the famous lyra player of Crete, Greece. Legend has it that this village was founded by villagers from Axos where the Minoan city Oaxos was located. Its history throughout wartime is heartbreaking, but it seems to have dusted itself off since my visit and today is a tourist site.

**ara mitama**   wild, rough, and untamed aspect of our soul/self like yang energy. Often represents aggression and forcefulness, which, when tamed, can lead to courage and valor.

**Aristotle**    ancient Greek philosopher (384–322 BCE). Student of Plato's academy in Athens during the classical period (347 BCE) for over fifteen years. After Plato's death, he was tutor to Philip II of Macedon's son, Alexander (to be Alexander the Great). He founded the peripatetic school of philosophy in Athen's Lyceum. His writings cover a broad range of subjects and are known to have laid the groundwork for the development of modern science and moral thought.

**Ayabe**    a city located in Kyoto Prefecture, Japan, and situated in the mountains of Northern Kyoto alongside the Yura River. Ayabe is the town where Omoto kyo's compound was located; O-Sensei visited Onisaburo Deguchi there on his way home from Hokkaido; it is the location of his first dojo. O-Sensei and his family moved and lived in Ayabe for a time.

**bokken**    a wooden sword approximating the size and shape of a samurai sword and used in Aikido and the martial art of kenjutsu.

**Buddhism**    an Indian spiritual practice based on the teachings of the Buddha (Siddhartha Gautama) who taught that people can avoid suffering. He taught that freeing oneself from attachments—largely through meditation—would ease their sufferings. From India it spread throughout much of Asia and is now the world's fourth largest spiritual system.

**budo**    commonly (and mistakenly) translated as a "martial art," budo is more precisely the "Way of protection," as seen by Aikido founder Morihei Ueshiba.

**chado**    primarily influenced by Buddhist monks (Eisai/Ikkyu), chado is the ceremonial preparation and presentation of matcha, a powdered green tea, which supports a perspective of awareness described in the famous saying, "one moment, one meeting."

**daito ryu aiki jujutsu**    a system of atemiwaza (joint-locking techniques and nerve-striking movements) used by Takeda's ancestor Yoshimitsu Minamoto. Daito ryu jujutsu became known in the early twentieth century under Sokaku Takeda whom O-Sensei studied with during his years in Hokkaido.

**do**    means the Way. It is often seen as the last syllable in the name of Japanese arts such as Aikido, Judo, Chado, and so forth. The addition of this character bears great meaning however as it signifies that the study is philosophical and deep.

**dojo** literally, "place of the Way," in Aikido it designates a school of Japanese arts.

**doshu** the leader of the Way; hereditary head of world Aikido. The second Doshu of Aikido was the founder's son (Kisshomaru Ueshiba Sensei), and the third and current doshu is the founder's grandson (Moriteru Ueshiba Sensei).

**Emperor Hirohito** the 124th longest reigning emperor of Japan (1926–89). Hirohito was revered as a god. In the 1930s and 1940s the imperial expansion wars were waged in his name with the participation in World War II as a member of the Axis Powers with Germany and Italy. Hirohito surrendered on August 15, 1945, and on January 1, 1946, Hirohito, pressured by the Allies, renounced his divinity. Posthumously he was known as Emperor Showa, the name of his reign of power.

**Fudomyo** a venerable wisdom king, remover of obstacles and destroyer of evil as a wrathful manifestation of the buddha Dainichi Nyorai. He is a wrathful spiritual being in Mikkyo and East Asian Buddhism.

**guji** the chief priest of a Shinto shrine.

**hakama** baggy, divided trousers often worn as a part of the traditional Aikido uniform.

**hara** the place of our vital energy, the source of life and the gate of the spirit. In Japan, the hara is also a spiritual center, and in the West, it is often understood as our "center." Hara refers to our lower abdomen and figures prominently in Eastern medicine as it is interrelated to the dimensions of the physical, psychological, and spiritual elements.

**Heraklion** founded in 824 by the Arabs, and occupied by many foreign powers, it has a port that has existed from the early Minoan period (3500–2100 BCE) and today Heraklion is now the largest city and capital of Crete; home to the Minoan Palace of Knossos (also known as the palace of Minos), the city is enjoying the fastest growing tourism trend of late.

**hiragana** literally, "flowing" or "simple" kana. One of two syllabary systems that, along with kanji, make up the Japanese language.

**Hokkaido** Japan's northernmost and second largest island. Long considered an outback to Japan's more southern islands, Hokkaido was inhabited by the Indigenous Ainu people.

**iaido**   the Way of drawing the sword. Also called *iai,* this training involves developing awareness and quick draws of the sword.

**irimi**   an Aikido entering movement difficult to perform as, rather than using a turn to deal with an attack, the entry is straight, which requires impeccable timing to accomplish. The advantage to an irimi entry is the close proximity accomplished in a single move.

**jo**   the wooden staff used in Aikido training. It is approximately fifty inches long and made of a hardwood.

**judo**   a Japanese martial art developed from jujutsu's unarmed fighting techniques. Judo is often practiced as a competitive sport. It is a well-known Japanese grappling art founded by Jigoro Kano sensei, a Japanese educator.

**kami**   a divine energy or being venerated in Shinto.

**kanji**   literally, "Chinese characters." Borrowed from Chinese language script (Chinese languages being approximately 6,000 years old). Kanji function as concepts, a linguistic element broader than the Western word.

**Kano, Jigoro**   founder of Judo. Japanese educator, he served as director of primary education for the Ministry of Education from 1989 to 1901. Also the first to become an official Asian member of the International Olympic Committee (IOC) (1909–38).

**kendo**   literally, "the Way of the sword or blade." A Japanese martial art, sometimes practiced as a sport, in which *shinai* (split bamboo sticks) are used to simulate samurai swords.

**ki**   universal energy or life force. Also, Qi, ch'i, or chi in other Eastern languages.

**Kobukan**   the name of O-Sensei's original Tokyo dojo.

*Kojiki*   Japan's oldest book of cosmogony. One of the sacred books of Shinto, Japan's indigenous nature philosophy, the *Kojiki* contains an account of the creation of the world. It was an oral tradition that was written down around 682–712 CE. O-Sensei enjoyed its fascinating stories and because they were widely known, used them in his teachings to illustrate certain deep philosophical principles like *masakatsu agatsu katsuhayabi.*

**kokoro**   literally, "heart." It is the ideogram heart, its etymology showing the heart's chambers. Because in the Japanese conceptual system it refers to both the heart and the mind, Westerners often translate it as "heart-mind."

**kokyu**   literally, "inhale/exhale," the cycle of breath.

**kokyu nage**   "breath throw." Breath is what ki (energy) rides on. Some of Aikido's throwing techniques are called kokyu nage because of their timing and feel.

**koshi nage**   judo hip throw.

**kototama**   literally, "word spirit," a spiritual practice centered around words or voiced sounds. We can see kototama as string theory in quantum physics where the universe is maintained by vibrating strands of energy that resonate and in various ways tie everything together.

**Kumano Mountains**   located in the Kii Peninsula of the Wakayama Prefecture in south-central Japan, the Kumano Mountain area—often called *land of the gods*—is known for the tallest waterfall in Japan and its high, rugged mountains. It is famous for its natural beauty in ancient forests and inspiring ocean views. It is where many pilgrimages, often mystical, begin, such as pilgrimages to Mount Koya, birthplace of Shingon Buddhism (the esoteric form of Buddhism, which O-Sensei studied as a young man) and Mount Omine, birthplace of Shugendo (a Buddhist mountain religion of ascetic practices that incorporates elements from shamanism and Daoist magic from the earliest of times). But perhaps especially the pilgrimage activity on Nakahechi—the oldest route to the three principal shrines known as the Kumano Sanzan: Kumano Hongu Taisha, Kumano Nachi Taisha, Kumano Hayatama Taisha. It is an area rich in UNESCO World Heritage sites for individual shrines and temples as well as for the routes connecting them.

**ki ai**   in Japanese martial arts, a ki ai is a short shout expressed when making an attack.

**Kumano Hongu Taisha**   an important Shinto shrine in the Kumano mountains on the Wakayama Peninsula, Japan. Today it is a World Heritage site.

**Kumano Juku Dojo**   dojo in Shingu, Wakayama Prefecture where Michio Hikitsuchi—one of O-Sensei's oldest students—taught for 50 years.

**Kumano Kodo** in the Muromachi period (1333–1573), Kumano pilgrimages were popular, and samurai and aristocrats frequented the area. These pilgrimages were so frequent and continuous they were called "pilgrimage of ants." One of many ancient forest paths for pilgrimages on the Kii Peninsula.

**kushi mitama** one of the four souls involved in mitsu domoe. Kushi mitama is the hidden soul: wise, wonderous, and experienced aspect of our soul/self.

**maai** the space or time interval between two opponents in martial arts. In a more cosmic application, maai applies to both space and time as it is found in the world around us.

**makoto** a Japanese name for heartfelt truthfulness, and sincerity.

***masakatsu agatsu katsuhayabi*** "true victory is self-victory." The main principle of Aikido calling for the clearing of the fighting spirit in one's heart.

**Meiji Shrine** a Shinto shrine in Shibuya, Tokyo.

**Minakata, Kumagusu** a widely traveled environmentalist who ultimately inspired O-Sensei to take a community to settle Japan's northernmost island, Hokkaido.

**misogi** an ancient Shinto purification practice, a cleansing of the mind and body with water, breathwork, or rigorous training to "burn off" the impurities that collect in us every day. O-Sensei said Aikido was a *misogi*. In Aikido, there is also the practice of *misogi no ken* (with a sword) and *misogi no jo* (with a staff).

**mitsu domoe** a Shinto symbol picturing three curved jewels and representing the four aspects of our spirit: ara mitama, nigi mitama, sachi mitama, and kushi mitama. Kushi mitama is the hidden fourth aspect, its wondrous nature is not visible so in the symbol only three of the four are displayed.

**Mount Baldy** Mount San Antonio is the proper name for this Southern California mountain. It is the highest peak (10,061) in the San Gabriel Mountain range that runs east and west just north of Los Angeles.

**Mount Kuruma** a mountain to the north of the Japanese city of Kyoto. It is said to be home to Sojobo, King of the tengu.

**mudra** a symbolic or ritual gesture or pose from India.

**Nachi Falls** found in Nachikatsuura, Wakayama Prefecture in Japan, it is one of Japan's longest waterfalls in Japan.

*Nicomachean Ethics* one of Aristotle's best-known works on ethics: the good life or that which is the goal at which all our actions aim.

**nigi mitama** typically seen in contrast to wild ara mitama, nigi mitama is the refined, educated, and tranquil soul that helps to cultivate a person's soul/ self. It is the functional and socialized aspect of soul/self like yin energy.

**norito** a Shinto prayer.

**Omoto kyo** originating from Shinto tradition, Omoto kyo is a spiritual organization founded by Nao and Onisaburo Deguchi in 1892. While Aikido's founder may not have formally been a member of Omoto kyo, he was certainly inspired by Omoto kyo's spiritual leader, Onisaburo Deguchi (1871–1947).

**onami** literally, "great wave."

**ran** "chaos;" also the name of a famous Kurosawa film.

**randori** multiple-person attack practice.

**rokudan** sixth-degree black belt.

**sachi mitama** the happy and loving aspect of our soul/self. The soul of blessing and prosperity.

**samurai** a member of the warrior class of feudal Japan.

**sankyo** the name for the third wrist/arm lock in Aikido.

**Sarutahiko Okami** viewed as a patron of Aikido and father to martial arts. He is enshrined in Tsubaki Grand Shrine as well as in O-Sensei's Aiki Shrine in Iwama. A huge earthly kami, the memorable stories of him take place on the bridge between the earthly and heavenly plains. You might say he is the protector of the bridge as the stories about him depict him helping kami make the passage from the heavenly plain to the earthly plain. He is a towering figure with a jeweled spear; he shares the tengu features of a long nose and ruddy complexion as well as being connected to martial arts. He is a symbol of strength and misogi.

**seiza** a Japanese sitting position with shins on the floor, sitting on your heels.

**sensei** literally, "one born before." A term of respect for a teacher or elder.

**Shingu** Japanese town just north of Tanabe; home of the Kumano Hayatama Taisha and the Kumano Juku Dojo.

**Shinto** literally, "Way of the gods," the beliefs and traditions of the Japanese people. Japanese folk beliefs, rites and ceremonies, nature worship.

**shrine**    a place of Shinto practices.

**shodan**    the first degree of the ten-degree black belt ranking system.

**shodo**    literally, "the Way of the brush," The art of Japanese calligraphy.

**shomen**    the shomen is the head wall in a dojo. It is usually the place for a tokonoma displaying a photograph of the founder of the art.

**Sojobo**    mythical figure, King of tengu.

**State Shinto**    a sect of Shinto observed by the Japanese emperor through World War II.

**Susanoo no Mikoto**    a god of the earthly realm.

**Takeda clan**    a samurai clan.

**Takeda, Sokaku**    Daito Ryu Aiki Jujutsu teacher.

*takemusu aiki*    spontaneous creation of protective life spirit; the principle of spontaneous and creative spirit of unlimited transformation in harmonic protection.

**Tanabe**    city of O-Sensei's birthplace and childhood home.

**tanto**    a wooden knife used in Aikido practice.

**tengu**    Shinto forms of protective (or disruptive, in early Buddhism) creatures that had bird-like as well as human characteristics. A tengu appears in a variety of shapes, but they were sought after by young warriors wanting to learn swordwork, strategy, and magic. Tengu live in the mountains: Sarutahiko Okami and Sojobo are two famous tengu.

**tokonoma**    an altar-like structure usually indented into a wall often in an aristocratic home, business, or an aikido dojo. In Aikido dojos, it typically bears a photograph of the Founder, a calligraphy that says "Aikido." Often there is a shelf for a bell or flower as well.

**Tsubaki Grand Shrine**    Shinto shrine in Japan's Mie Prefecture where Sarutahiko Okami landed and was buried. It was founded by the order of Princess Yamato in 3 BCE where Sarutahiko Okami, the ancient earthly kami, landed and was later buried. O-Sensei knew Yukiteru Yamamoto Guji, priest of Tsubaki Grand Shrine. And so when O-Sensei visited the shrine, he would pay his respects to the shrine as well as to Yamamoto Guji. It is said that O-Sensei also would practice water misogi in the sacred waterfall there—Kinryu Myojin no Taki.

**Ueshiba, Kisshomaru**   O-Sensei's son and second Doshu (hereditary head of world Aikido).

**Ueshiba, Morihei**   founder of Aikido; O-Sensei.

**Ueshiba, Moriteru**   O-Sensei's grandson and current Doshu, he presides over Aikido World Headquarters in Tokyo, Japan. He continues to teach worldwide, as well as maintaining a teaching schedule at Aikikai Hombu Dojo. He is the author of several technical books on Aikido.

**Ushi tora no Konjin**   spirit of the Northeast, the Shinto spirit that used Nao Deguchi as a medium to tranmit what later became Omoto kyo.

**Yamamoto, Yukitaka**   the ninety-sixth chief priest of the Tsubaki Grand Shrine in Mie Prefecture, Japan. As a boy, he came to know O-Sensei as O-Sensei came to the shrine to visit with his father, Yukiteru Yamamoto.

**Yamamoto, Yukiteru**   the ninety-fifth priest of Tsubaki Grand Shrine, father of Yamamoto, Yukitaka.

**yin and yang**   an ancient Chinese philosophical system of interconnected opposites; yin refers to receptive and calm energy, while yang refers to active energy.

**yudansha**   people with a black belt.

**Zen**   a Japanese school of Buddhism emphasizing meditation directed toward enlightenment.

# Bibliography

Aristotle. 1934. *Nichomachean Ethics*. Cambridge: Harvard University Press.

Brousse, Michel, and David Matsumoto. 2005. *Judo in the U.S.* Berkeley, Calif.: North Atlantic Books.

Diamond Jonny, 2022. "The Old Man and the Tree." *Smithsonian Magazine,* (January).

Drews, Annette. 2020. "Washing the Heart: Core Elements in the Practice of Shinto and Aikido." Zittau/Gorlitz University of Applied Sciences (website).

Hall, Edward. 1966. *The Hidden Dimension*. New York: Doubleday.

Heiny, Mary. "Five Ways Aikido Nurtures Human Life." Mary Heiny (website).

Herbert, Jean. 1967. *Shinto, At the Fountainhead of Japan*. Crows Nest, Australia: George Allen & Unwin Ltd.

*Kojiki*. 2016. Translated by Donald Philippi. Princeton University Press.

Miller, Jessica. 2006. *Reiki's Birthplace*. Sedona, Ariz.: Infinite Light Healing Studies Center.

National Park Service. "Not just a great valley." Accessed October 1, 2018. Facebook (website).

*Nihongi: Chronicles of Japan from the Earliest Times to AD 697.* 1993. Translated by W. G. Aston. Clarendon, Vt.: Tuttle.

Perry, Susan. 2001. *Remembering O-Sensei*. Boulder, Colo.: Shambhala.

Pulvers, Roger. 2008. "Japan's Wild Scientific Genius: Minakata Kumagusu." *Asian Pacific Journal* 6, no. 1 (January).

Stevens, John. 2010. *The Heart of Aikido*. Tokyo: Kodansha.

———. 1997. *Invincible Warrior*. Boulder, Colo.: Shambhala.

———. 2001. *The Philosophy of Aikido*. Tokyo: Kodansha.

———. 1995. *The Secrets of Aikido*. Shambhala.

Tanahashi, Kazuaki. 1995/1996. "Years Before Pearl Harbor," *Aikido Today Magazine,* no. 43 (December/January): 45.

Tzu, Lao. 1989. *The Complete Works of Lao Tzu: Tao Te Ching and Hua Hu Ching*. Translated by Hua-Ching Ni. College of Tao and Traditional Chinese Healing.

Ueshiba, Kisshomaru. 2008. *A Life in Aikido*. Tokyo: Kodansha.

———. 1978. *Aikido*. Tokyo: Hozansha Publishing.

———. 1984. *The Spirit of Aikido*. Tokyo: Kodansha.

Ueshiba, Morihei. 1992. *The Art of Peace*. Translated by John Stevens. Boulder, Colo.: Shambhala.

———. 2007. *The Secret Teachings of Aikido*. Translated by John Stevens. Tokyo: Kodansha.

———. 1976. "Takemusu Aiki." Edited by Hideo Takahashi. Shizuoka, Japan: Byakko Shinko Kai Publishing Division.

Wohlleben, Peter. 2016. *The Hidden Life of Trees*. Greystone Books, David Suzuki Institute.

———. 2019. *The Secret Network of Nature*. New York: Penguin Random House.

Zhang, Jianfeng. 2020. "Evaluation of Air Negative Ion Effect in Rural Human Settlement Forests." In *Study of Ecological Engineering of Human Settlements*, 303–312 Singapore: Springer.

# Index

# Books of Related Interest

**The Art of Mastery**
Principles of Effective Interaction
*by Peter Ralston*

**Aikido and Words of Power**
The Sacred Sounds of Kototama
*by William Gleason*

**Embodying the Mystery**
Somatic Wisdom for Emotional, Energetic, and Spiritual Awakening
*by Richard Strozzi-Heckler*

**The Writer Who Inhabits Your Body**
Somatic Practices to Enhance Creativity and Inspiration
*by Renée Gregorio*

**Qigong Teachings of a Taoist Immortal**
The Eight Essential Exercises of Master Li Ching-yun
*by Stuart Alve Olson*

**Shaolin Qi Gong**
Energy in Motion
*by Shi Xinggui*

**The Inner Structure of Tai Chi**
Mastering the Classic Forms of Tai Chi Chi Kung
*by Mantak Chia and Juan Li*

**The Spiritual Practices of the Ninja**
Mastering the Four Gates to Freedom
*by Ross Heaven*

INNER TRADITIONS • BEAR & COMPANY
P.O. Box 388
Rochester, VT  05767
1-800-246-8648
www.InnerTraditions.com
Or contact your local bookseller